I love this book and wish I'd written it! The authors describe Bronfenbrenner's theory in its most up-to-date version, and do so in very accessible language. They clearly explain the theory's relevance for early childhood scholars and educators, and do so using a wealth of examples drawn from their own observations in classrooms and from research. Children's typically occurring activities and interactions with peers and teachers feature throughout, and the authors show how the children's own characteristics and the environment (including the classroom setup, the children's home background, and the broader sociocultural context) influence those activities and interactions. The authors also invite their readers to reflect on their own experiences in light of the relevant theoretical concepts, and at the end of all but the first and last chapters appear carefully considered "implications" and "key concepts" for practice.

**Jonathan Tudge**, *Department of Human Development and Family Studies, University of North Carolina–Greensboro, USA*

Although Bronfenbrenner was one of our great public intellectuals, his legacy has been understood in terms of a static systems model which explains, rather than challenges, inequality and disadvantage. In this new book, this legacy is revealed instead as a complex and dynamic account of relationships and interactions. The authors explore how Bronfenbrenner developed his description of the network of influences which shape children's lives, emphasising the processes, rather than the contexts, within which development takes place. In unravelling this interplay between people and places they show how transformative processes can be set in motion by early childhood practitioners in their daily work with young children and their families.

**Liz Brooker**, *Emeritus Reader, University College London Institute of Education, UK*

In a necessarily short endorsement it is hard to capture the wealth of thinking in this highly readable book. Far from static, Bronfenbrenner's work is presented as dynamic, evolving and rich. Powerful concepts which the authors present accessibly but accompanied by provocative and reflective questions for early years practitioners will be a call to make linkages to practice. In promoting the applications of a bioecological approach to early years, the authors are encouraging a form of practitioner-activism, which sees small children as active in their own learning and development in collaboration with others around them and together in the environments in which they spend their lives. A great contribution to the early years field.

**Professor Aline-Wendy Dunlop**, *University of Strathclyde, UK*

# INTRODUCING BRONFENBRENNER

The influence of Urie Bronfenbrenner's model of development has been extensive in different areas of developmental science and education, and it continues to inform contemporary research and practice in many fields, including early childhood education. This book presents a comprehensive introduction to Bronfenbrenner's model of development in reference to early childhood education. It draws on practice-based research to identify and animate key elements of the model impacting early educational pedagogy and practice.

This new and revised second edition identifies and explores the key elements of Bronfenbrenner's model by referring to contemporary understandings of how children learn. It also includes a new chapter which considers repositioning early childhood education settings as interactive, relational spaces and provides a broader focus on the concept of transitional experiences in children's daily lives. Along with new content on leadership and associated roles and practices in early childhood education, this book illustrates how Bronfenbrenner's model can help bring quality to early learning environments and show how it can be incorporated into daily work with young children through vignettes, case studies and examples of good practice.

*Introducing Bronfenbrenner* serves as an ideal read for professionals around the world working with children in early childhood settings, and students training to become early childhood professionals at degree level on undergraduate programmes, as part of vocational training or as part of continuous professional development.

**Nóirín Hayes** is Visiting Academic at the School of Education, Trinity College Dublin and Professor Emerita, Technological University Dublin, Ireland.

**Leah O'Toole** is Lecturer/Assistant Professor in Early Childhood Education in the Froebel Department of Primary and Early Childhood Education, Maynooth University, Ireland.

**Ann Marie Halpenny** is Lecturer in Psychology and Child Development in the School of Languages, Law and Social Sciences at the Technological University Dublin, Ireland.

**Introducing Early Years Thinkers**

Series editor: Sandra Smidt, writer and consultant in early years education.

Sandra Smidt's insightful series focuses on the seminal work of early childhood writers who have heavily influenced thinking and practice in this field. The titles are guides for both practitioners and students in early years education and care and are written in everyday language to make complex ideas accessible. The authors helpfully draw on a range of illustrative and relevant case studies and maintain a global rather than a local or national perspective, with examples of thinking and practice from around the world.

**Introducing Piaget**
A Guide for Practitioners and Students in Early Years Education
*Ann Marie Halpenny and Jan Pettersen*

**Introducing Freire**
A Guide for Practitioners and Students in Early Years Education
*Sandra Smith*

**Introducing Bronfenbrenner**
A Guide for Practitioners and Students in Early Years Education
*Nóirín Hayes, Leah O'Toole and Ann Marie Halpenny*

**Introducing Trevarthen**
A Guide for Practitioners and Students in Early Years Education
*Sandra Smidt*

**Introducing Bronfenbrenner, Second Edition**
A Guide for Practitioners and Students in Early Years Education
*Nóirín Hayes, Leah O'Toole and Ann Marie Halpenny*

For more information about this series please visit: https://www.routledge.com/
Introducing-Early-Years-Thinkers/book-series/IEYT

# INTRODUCING BRONFENBRENNER

A Guide for Practitioners and Students in Early Years Education

Second Edition

Nóirín Hayes, Leah O'Toole and
Ann Marie Halpenny

LONDON AND NEW YORK

Cover image: Saidbhín Lou O'Toole

Second edition published 2023
by Routledge
4 Park Square, Milton Park, Abingdon, Oxon, OX14 4RN

and by Routledge
605 Third Avenue, New York, NY 10158

*Routledge is an imprint of the Taylor & Francis Group, an informa business*

© 2023 Nóirín Hayes, Leah O'Toole and Ann Marie Halpenny

The right of Nóirín Hayes, Leah O'Toole and Ann Marie Halpenny to be identified as authors of this work has been asserted in accordance with sections 77 and 78 of the Copyright, Designs and Patents Act 1988.

All rights reserved. No part of this book may be reprinted or reproduced or utilised in any form or by any electronic, mechanical, or other means, now known or hereafter invented, including photocopying and recording, or in any information storage or retrieval system, without permission in writing from the publishers.

*Trademark notice*: Product or corporate names may be trademarks or registered trademarks, and are used only for identification and explanation without intent to infringe.

First edition published by Routledge 2017

*British Library Cataloguing-in-Publication Data*
A catalogue record for this book is available from the British Library

ISBN: 978-1-032-16260-7 (hbk)
ISBN: 978-1-032-16259-1 (pbk)
ISBN: 978-1-003-24776-0 (ebk)

DOI: 10.4324/9781003247760

Typeset in Bembo
by SPi Technologies India Pvt Ltd (Straive)

# CONTENTS

| | |
|---|---|
| *Preface* | *ix* |
| 1  Introducing Bronfenbrenner | 1 |
| 2  The bioecological model of human development | 12 |
| 3  Proximal processes and relationships | 28 |
| 4  Understanding development in context | 46 |
| 5  A bioecological perspective on transitions | 59 |
| 6  Locating the child at the centre of practice | 77 |
| 7  Creating rich learning environments | 91 |
| 8  Early education as a dynamic process | 111 |
| 9  Nurturing children's learning and development | 127 |
| 10  Relational spaces linking people, places and resources: Positioning early childhood settings | 144 |
| 11  Reflecting the bioecological in early years practice | 159 |

**viii** Contents

| | |
|---|---|
| *Glossary* | *171* |
| *Abbreviations* | *174* |
| *References* | *175* |
| *Index* | *193* |

# PREFACE

Since the publication of the first edition of *Introducing Bronfenbrenner* in 2017 a great deal has changed in the world and in early childhood education. In particular, the impact of the COVID-19 pandemic has had a profound effect on early childhood services, highlighting the central role of early childhood education and care in the lives of young children and their families. The experience has also made visible the crucial role of early childhood professionals and their flexibility and adaptability to changing contexts. With these changes have come new challenges and new opportunities presenting us with an opportunity to revisit and review our book, update references, make changes to some chapters and add one full new chapter. This edition provides those working in early childhood with a comprehensive introduction to the work of Bronfenbrenner and its relevance to contemporary early educational practice. It illustrates how the model acts as a responsive framework within which the quality of early educational pedagogy can be understood and enhanced. The chapters are presented in two sections. The first section, Chapters 1 through 5, introduces the bioecological model and discusses different theoretical aspects of the model. The second section, Chapters 6 through 11, focuses more on the practical application of the model in early years settings. The reader should note that male and female pronouns are used in alternate chapters in order to facilitate a gender-balanced approach.

Chapter 1 remains largely unchanged and provides an overview of Bronfenbrenner's life, highlighting key biographical details of relevance to his work and drawing attention to his many achievements within the field of developmental psychology, early education and in the wider social context.

In exploring the development of the bioecological model Chapter 2 discusses Bronfenbrenner's well-known concepts of microsystem, mesosystem, exosystem, macrosystem and chronosystem, as well as elaborating on the more up-to-date version of the model which emphasises the interaction of 'process', 'person', 'context'

**x** Preface

and 'time'. In this edition, the section on 'person' has been expanded to take account of our current fluid understandings of gender and the value and importance of providing children with opportunities for learning about non-traditional gender roles.

Chapter 3 focuses on process through exploring the nature and power of the concept of the proximal processes. In this new edition an extended discussion of the dynamic, reciprocal nature of proximal processes has been presented. In addition, more examples from practice have been included with a stronger focus on supporting educators to understand and respond to their own role in the dynamic 'dance' of relationships in Early Childhood Education and Care (ECEC). It illustrates that relationships are vital for children's development emotionally, socially and cognitively and goes on to explain why building good relationships matters in early childhood practice.

Chapter 4 remains largely unchanged. It explores the idea that children's development through relationships must be understood in context and further emphasises the importance of understanding individual and cultural differences, showing how the 'person' and 'context' factors interact.

Chapter 5 has been significantly revised. It acknowledges the range of transitional experiences in the lives of babies, toddlers and young children, taking a bio-ecological lens to vertical or major transitions (bigger more visible events involving transitions between educational settings, e.g. transition from preschool to primary), horizontal or minor transitions (happening in the daily or weekly routine of the child, e.g. home to day care each morning) and mini transitions (smaller less visible transitions within settings throughout the day, e.g. transitioning from naptime to active play).

In Chapter 6 the concept of children as active, interested and influential agents shaping their own learning in early childhood settings is explored. The arguments around agency in childhood have been more fully elaborated and the shortcomings of understanding agency as an innate characteristic have been set against a fuller understanding of the constellation of factors that can influence the development of agency. Drawing on key principles within Bronfenbrenner's theory, the importance of building a pedagogy that promotes and respects children and child-initiated practice in early childhood is reinforced. The chapter emphasises further how adults more generally, and adult–child relationships in particular, are central to the development of children's agency.

In Chapter 7, we consider how best to provide a rich and stimulating learning environment that contributes to children's positive development and wellbeing. The chapter discusses features of good-quality early learning environments and the potential impact of both indoor and outdoor environments and materials. In this revised edition a section on rich outdoor learning environments and the importance of safe risk-taking has been included. There is more emphasis and detail on the value of natural outdoor environments and the richer learning experiences associated with such an environment. The potential for children engaging in rich learning environments beyond the early childhood education (ECE) setting is also briefly highlighted.

In Chapter 8, Bronfenbrenner's emphasis on development as a dynamic process is explored and the important role that early childhood settings play in connecting with, learning from and enhancing the home learning environment is identified. The importance of engaged and respectful interactions with even the very youngest children is explored with reference to contemporary neuroscience research.

Chapter 9 explores how best to develop the skills of observation and reflection, both of which are central to a nurturing pedagogy, which emphasises the importance of relationships. These skills enhance practice and planning, are manifest in well-managed and yet reasonably flexible practice and assist in the provision of a learning environment that includes children and supports and extends children's learning. This chapter elaborates on the importance of play to quality practice and considers mechanisms and approaches to sustaining quality through an expanded discussion on the importance of pedagogical leadership.

Chapter 10 is a new chapter in which we consider the important role of the mesosystem and the wider learning ecology in which young children develop and learn. We explore the possibilities for children (and their families) to connect to the community through engagement with ECE settings. We investigate the central role of the early childhood setting as a communication hub within society and the need for settings to develop their potential to become more versatile, inclusive and diverse. We link this to the notion of *interactive relational space*. The expansion of the learning environment through the widespread presence of technology in our lives is also examined as are the implications for the bioecological model in contemporary practice.

The final chapter presents an opportunity to review the theory and practice sections of the book, reflect on the key aspects contributing to good-quality early childhood practice and consider how best to utilise this knowledge in enhancing children's experiences and learning in early childhood settings.

We hope you enjoy this new edition.

**Nóirín Hayes,**
**Leah O'Toole,**
**Ann Marie Halpenny**
Dublin, September 2022

# 1

# INTRODUCING BRONFENBRENNER

Children grow and develop in the midst of society; the people, places, objects and ideas they encounter form the basis of their learning and development. The role of early childhood experiences and the importance of those who work in early childhood settings are now well established and understood. Much of this understanding is due to the work of Urie Bronfenbrenner (1917–2005). Although his name may not be as familiar as that of Vygotsky or Piaget, he has had a profound effect on the way we think about child development and our approaches to working with young children and their families.

Urie Bronfenbrenner was born on 29 April 1917 in Moscow to a Jewish family of professionals. However, to escape persecution, in 1923, he moved with his mother to the United States, where his father, a pathologist, had found work at a hospital in Pennsylvania. Urie settled into his new country and was one of many immigrant children attending his local primary school. He and his father both learned to speak fluent English, but his mother continued to speak Russian and taught Urie to appreciate the language and literature of his place of birth. Later, the family moved to Upstate New York, where his father was appointed to head a laboratory studying the characteristics and causes of what was then referred to as 'feeble-mindedness'. As he grew, Urie assisted his father in the laboratory, "running experiments and nurturing his incipient interest in psychology" (Panken, 2005, p. 10).

Following his schooling, Uri Bronfenbrenner studied psychology at Cornell University, graduating in 1938. After completing his master's in developmental psychology at Harvard University, he then studied at the University of Michigan, where he received his PhD. The focus of his doctoral research was the development of children within their peer group, setting him on course to invest the rest of his long life researching child development. During World War II, he was a

DOI: 10.4324/9781003247760-1

**2** Introducing Bronfenbrenner

field psychologist at various military hospitals, and in 1948, he returned to Cornell University as a professor of psychology and human development.

Bronfenbrenner was a prolific author and scholar-activist who believed that it is the responsibility of academic scholars to engage directly with policymakers and professionals and use academic work to ameliorate the problems of society. He wrote many non-theoretical papers reporting research on the lives of children and their families (Rosa & Tudge, 2013), and using these research studies and his understanding of the dynamic nature of development, he sought to persuade policymakers of the importance of family support and early childhood education. His particular ambition was to develop an understanding of the complexity of human development and build this understanding into policy, practice and research. He did not shy away from addressing wider societal issues and their impacts on children and families and became involved in public policy, frequently acting as an expert witness on child development and testifying before committees and the US Congress. In his commentaries on social issues, he drew attention to the changing nature of family life in the United States and his concerns about the developmental impacts of increased urbanisation and of children spending extended periods in the care of others. Referencing the emerging research evidence from fields of psychology, sociology, education and health, he noted that the support and involvement of the entire society is necessary to raise children successfully. In particular, he recognised and valued the important role that state-supported early childhood education and care could play in achieving this objective. While this is a view that few would dispute now, it was radical in the United States of the 1960s, where independence and self-reliance were highly valued and the state saw little or no role for itself in providing family support services.

Bronfenbrenner's views on early child development and education were out of line with many other academics commenting at the time. For instance, in 1970, he participated in a forum at the White House on the subject of children and parents. When the final report was submitted, he added a minority report in disagreement with it. He later wrote that the report failed "to convey the urgency and severity of the problem confronting the nation's families and their children" and did not "alert the reader to the critical role played by business and industry – both private and public – in determining the lifestyle of the American family" (Bronfenbrenner, 1970a/2005, p. 211). These concerns about the wider influence of society on children's development and the position of children in society provided the foundations on which his later work was based.

Many of the views articulated by Bronfenbrenner in his early policy presentations and articles are echoed in our current theorising and understanding of the importance of early child development and education (Siraj & Mayo, 2014). He played a critical role in advancing the public's recognition of the importance of early childhood education both for the sake of the child and to add value to the family and society at large.

Introducing Bronfenbrenner **3**

Although rarely presented as a key theorist in early childhood education, his work has underpinned much progress internationally in early education, and his model of development is one that has informed research, curriculum design and professional education. For instance, deriving from research in the United Kingdom by the Effective Provision of Pre-school and Primary Education (EPPE) project (Melhuish, Phan, Sylva, Sammons, & Siraj-Blatchford, 2008; Sylva, Melhuish, Sammon, Siraj-Blatchford, & Taggart, 2004), we now recognise the importance of early learning environments, both the home and early childhood settings, to children's early development. This echoes Bronfenbrenner's views as far back as 1967 when he wrote that research points to the home background as "the most important element in determining how well the child did in school" (1967/2005, p. 203).

His work looked beyond individual development to take account of wider influencing factors and the context, or ecology, of development. He drew support for his integrated ecological perspective on development not only from his own academic work but also from the experiences he gathered through his academic exchange visits to the Union of Socialist Soviet Republics (USSR). Although Bronfenbrenner did not consider himself to be Russian, he spoke the language fluently and was interested in the Soviet Union; he spent almost two decades of his career researching and writing about the country of his birth. It was in the USSR that Vygotsky was born and had worked. It is interesting to note that Vygotsky (1896–1934), who, although born in what is now Belarus, spent his working life in Moscow, also recognised the importance of context to learning and development, emphasising the role of culture in driving human development. His attention to the critical role of the social context to individual learning and development can be seen as a precursor to Bronfenbrenner's later ecological model of development (Parrish, 2014). While Vygotsky's views differed from Bronfenbrenner's, which highlighted the vital role of interactions as driving development, it does not put the two theorists in opposition but, rather, highlights their different points of emphasis.

Post–World War II relations between the United States and the USSR were strained in what was termed the Cold War. Many political efforts were made to bridge the divide between the democratic, capitalist US and the communist USSR. Given Bronfenbrenner's fluency in the Russian language, he was able to avail himself of a number of scholar exchange opportunities so that he could investigate and write on the differences between childrearing and family practices across both countries. Bronfenbrenner left a vast collection of unpublished reports, field notes, letters and commentaries, and a review of these by Panken (2005) sheds light on both the man and the Cold War as the context for US/USSR relations.

The culmination of his work in the USSR was the publication in 1970 of his book *Two Worlds of Childhood: US and USSR*. This book drew out the differences between children's experiences in the USSR and in the United States, highlighting

**4** Introducing Bronfenbrenner

the impact of different cultural experiences. Bronfenbrenner was impressed by the good behaviour of children in the USSR: "They are well-mannered, attentive, and industrious … they reveal a strong motivation to learn, a readiness to serve society" (1970b, p. 227). He concluded that, generally speaking, the children of the USSR conform to "a more homogeneous set of standards" (1970b, p. 229) than their counterparts in the United States. One explanation he provided for this was the collective upbringing of young children in the USSR where there was harmony between the values of the family and society. This, he believed, eased children's transition into and adjustment to society. He noted that, by contrast, US society "emerges as one that gives decreasing prominence to the family as a socialising agent" (1970b, p. 230). He voiced concern that since World War II, *de facto* responsibility for the upbringing of children had shifted to other settings, such as schools, which may not see this as their role. While he made it clear that this was no reflection of the affection or concern parents have for their children, he argued that it does decrease the "power of the family in the lives of children" (1970b, pp. 229–230).

Deriving from this cross-cultural study, Bronfenbrenner argued that American parents were spending less time raising their children as they had to work to survive. The result, he argued, was that many children were growing up without enough contact with adults and were, therefore, separated from society. This interrupted the socialisation process so that children learned from each other rather than from responsible adults. To rebalance the situation, he proposed increased government investment in social programmes offering support to families, such as providing childcare, and saw this as an investment in the future.

Lyndon B. Johnson declared a 'war on poverty' when he became president of the United States in 1963 following the assassination of President J. F. Kennedy. He established the preschool intervention Head Start with the aim of counteracting many of the educational problems faced by poor children by giving them a short educational input before they started primary school. The idea of intervening early in the educational lives of poorer children led President Johnson to establish the Office of Economic Opportunity. This office put together a committee of experts to plan a project that would help communities meet the needs of preschool children. Two early childhood experts were appointed to this design committee: Edward Zigler (who has written a history of the development of Head Start; Zigler & Muenchow, 1992) and Urie Bronfenbrenner (Neugebauer, 2010). The establishment of Head Start was announced in 1965. In its original design, it was an eight-week summer preschool programme, staffed by volunteers, for over five hundred thousand low-income children who were due to enter primary school in September of 1965. It was later offered as a year-long preschool programme. Gradually, the name Head Start came to refer to a wide range of early interventions meeting the needs of disadvantaged young children and their families. In reflecting on Head Start, Bronfenbrenner noted that "the principal purpose of the programs is not remedial education but giving children and their families, from all levels of society, a sense of dignity, purpose and meaningful activities" (1967/2005, p. 208). Head Start has been researched and expanded and has grown extensively over the years in both the length of the intervention and the age at which children are targeted. It remains the standard early intervention programme in the United States (https://www.nhsa.org).

Throughout his career, Bronfenbrenner exhibited an intense interest in the family, family support and the social policy context in the United States (Rosa & Tudge, 2013). He wrote many papers and articles linking his theoretical position on human development to implications for policy and for practice. He also considered that there was an absence of sound 'real-world' research to inform policy and practice. He developed his model of development as a framework within which to locate research, particularly emphasising all the elements affecting individual development in context.

## Bronfenbrenner's ecological model of human development

Early and influential psychological studies developed their knowledge through researching the individual in isolation and paid relatively little attention to the dynamic impact of the context within which development occurred. Criticising this approach, Bronfenbrenner wrote that "much of developmental psychology is the science of the strange behaviour of children in strange situations with strange adults for the briefest possible period of time" (1977, p. 513). This laboratory-based approach to studying child development changed with the growth of interest in the ecological approach, which took account of the actual environments and systems within which human beings live, the relationships between individuals and these systems and the relationships between the systems themselves.

Reflecting this shift, more recent research in psychology, sociology and education has moved away from the traditional approach to studying children in isolation. Increasingly, attention is given to understanding childhood in a wider sociocultural context where children are seen as active participants. Bronfenbrenner's work has been central to this shift (Bronfenbrenner, 1979, 1995; Bronfenbrenner & Morris, 1998, 2006[1]). Writing in the foreword of *Making Human Beings Human: Bioecological Perspectives on Human Development*, Richard Lerner observes that the growth and acceptance of dynamic, integrated and holistic approaches to considering human development in context "owe their origin, persuasive articulation, and refinement to the singularly creative, theoretically elegant, empirically rigorous, and humane and democratic scholarly contributions of Urie Bronfenbrenner" (in Bronfenbrenner, 2005, pp. ix–x).

Given the improved understanding of the integrated and dynamic nature of learning and development and the value of considering many theoretical positions when studying development, Bronfenbrenner saw the need for a developmental framework within which to consider psychological theories of learning and theories of educational practice. This required a level of complexity to accommodate the variety of factors influencing learning while, at the same time, providing a framework within which these factors can be considered, reconciled and responded to in pedagogical practice, policy and planning. Bronfenbrenner's ecological model of human development presents such a framework. Although the model was detailed in his 1979 book, its roots can be found as far back as his doctoral thesis, submitted in 1942 (Bronfenbrenner, 1942/2005, p. 22).

In the 1970s, Bronfenbrenner (1967/2005, 1977, 1979) began to refine his ideas as he recognised that good practice in understanding child development, including early educational practice, required a deep understanding of the developing child in context, which, he argued, required a complex 'ecological' theory of development. He used the word *ecological* to capture the embedded and holistic nature of human development. His most influential book, *The Ecology of Human Development: Experiments by Nature and Design* (Bronfenbrenner, 1979), described such a model. The ecological approach to understanding development recognises that individuals are embedded in and affected by different levels of context: both macro (the large scale, at a distance) and micro (small/local, close by). In considering studies on human development, Bronfenbrenner (1977) criticised researchers who studied development out of context. For him, development was a function of the interplay between the individual and their environment. Therefore, he insisted on locating development within environmental systems. He defined the 'ecology of human development' as involving

> the scientific study of the progressive, mutual accommodation between an active, growing human being and the changing properties of the immediate settings in which the developing person lives, as this process is affected by relations between these settings, and by the larger contexts in which the settings are embedded.
>
> *(Bronfenbrenner, 1979, p. 21)*

From the very beginning and through its various iterations, his model has addressed both the structural or biological aspects of development alongside the process or sociocultural dimensions (Bronfenbrenner, 1979, 1989a; Bronfenbrenner & Ceci, 1994; Bronfenbrenner & Morris, 1998, 2006). An additional feature of the model is its emphasis on the dynamic, bidirectional relationships between people and context. Siraj and Mayo recognise Bronfenbrenner's model as having value across disciplines as it "bridges the social and psychological aspects of human development" (Siraj & Mayo, 2014, p. 16). In his original model, Bronfenbrenner located the developing child within a series of four systems, which he called the 'microsystem', the 'mesosystem', the 'exosystem' and the 'macrosystem'. These systems, or levels, are organised from those closest, or proximal, to the child to those whose influence is indirect or distal (Greene & Moane, 2000). Reflecting his Russian background, Bronfenbrenner referred to these systems as 'nested' each within the next like a set of Russian dolls (the matryoshka dolls). Later, recognising the importance and influence of time (and history) in development, he included a fifth system, which he called the 'chronosystem'. Studying individual development through the lens of this model allows early childhood educators to contextualise child development and take account of the overlapping and interacting nature of the different levels. The model has been influential in both early educational practice and curriculum development, most notably in its use by the New Zealand Ministry of Education in the development and implementation of their early year's curriculum *Te Whāriki* (Ministry of Education, New Zealand, 1996).

The child's closest and most familiar microsystem is the family, but there are other microsystems, including settings close to the child such as day care, preschool and school. The mesosystem refers to communication and interactions between the various elements of the individual's microsystems. In early education, this would include the relationship between family members and early childhood educators. The third level in the ecological system model, the exosystem, refers to more distant influences, factors external to the children and adults but impacting them nonetheless, such as educational policy or curriculum design. The macrosystem represents the influence of even more distant factors, such as societal values and the cultural view of the child. Finally, the chronosystem refers to the influence of time on development. This takes account of time from the individual's perspective but also takes into account historical time; it is of relevance to early childhood educators when, for instance, considering issues of transitions.

The ecological model of human development was appealing and very quickly became accepted as a useful framework within which to study development, being taken up by psychologists, sociologists and teachers. It began to feature in textbooks, and the idea of nested systems seems to have provided a very useful visual guide in accounting for the myriad factors that affect development. In fact, Bronfenbrenner wrote of "an instance of what might be called 'the failure of success'" (Bronfenbrenner, 1992/2005, p. 107). Having argued over the years that research in developmental psychology had failed to take sufficient account of the context within which development occurred, he now found it to be in danger of losing sight of the developing child, with "a surfeit of studies on 'context without development'" (Bronfenbrenner, 1992/2005, p. 108).

Over time, the model went through periods of change. Rosa and Tudge (2013) identify three specific phases of development from the original *Ecological Model of Human Development* in 1979 to the final iteration as the *Bioecological Model of Human Development* in 1998/2006. Reflecting on the relatively limited attention that is given to the later, more powerful version of the model of development in research and practice, Rosa and Tudge (2013) argue that this may actually be a result of the success of the earlier version. It may be that the first presentation of the model, introducing the concepts of different levels or systems of context, had such a powerful impact across disciplines – notwithstanding its limitations, recognised most thoroughly by Bronfenbrenner himself – that his later work suffered. Rosa and Tudge write that

> [t]here is really no reason for continuing to treat Bronfenbrenner's theory as one of contextual influences on development, or ignoring the focus, during the third and final phase, on proximal processes and the use of the PPCT [Process–Person–Context–Time] model as a guide for research using the bioecological theory.
> (Rosa & Tudge, 2013, p. 256)

## The bioecological model of human development

Due to over-attention to the specific systems of development at the expense of the position and influence of the developing individual, Bronfenbrenner reconsidered the title of his model in order to foreground the individual. In his article "Ecological systems theory", his definition of the ecology of development includes the addition of the text in italics:

> The ecology of human development is the study of the progressive, mutual accommodation, *throughout the life course*, between an active, growing human being and the changing properties of the immediate settings in which the developing person lives, as this process is affected by the relations between these settings, and by the larger contexts in which the settings are embedded.
> (Bronfenbrenner, 1992/2005, p. 107; emphasis in the original)

The emphasis is added by Bronfenbrenner to highlight the importance of the individual over time. The new title for the model, the 'bioecological model' of human development, was proposed in 1994 by Bronfenbrenner and Ceci. In all the iterations of his model of development from the initial presentation of his ecological model in 1979 to its most recent configuration as the bioecological model (Bronfenbrenner & Morris, 1998, 2006), Bronfenbrenner has identified the need for researchers and educators to pay close attention to the individual developing in a complexity of interacting systems. The bioecological model, which in its title highlights the importance of the developing individual,

> represents a marked shift in the centre of gravity of the model, in which features of the earlier version are first called into question, but then recombined, along with new elements, into a more complex and more dynamic structure…the model presented, while still evolving, is now called the bioecological model.
> (Bronfenbrenner & Morris, 1998, pp. 993–994)

A driving force behind the development of the bioecological model was the challenge to developmental psychologists posed by the American psychologist Anne

Anastasi as far back as 1958. In a paper titled "Heredity, environment, and the question 'how?'" she identified the need for developmental psychology to uncover the mechanisms through which the genetic code of an individual (the genotype) is transformed into observable characteristics and behaviour (the phenotype). While not attempting to definitively answer this very complex challenge, Bronfenbrenner, with his colleague Stephen Ceci, wrote a paper in which they addressed some of Anastasi's questions and proposed the first draft of the bioecological model of development (Bronfenbrenner & Ceci, 1993). They made a critical distinction between 'environment' and 'process', with the latter occupying a central, driving position in development and having a meaning that is quite specific to the model. In fact, process is at the core of the revised model. The construct of process (P) encompasses particular forms of interaction between organism and environment, often termed nature and nurture, respectively. They called these processes the 'proximal processes' to emphasise the fact that they are located within the microsystems of development and operate over time; they are posited as the primary mechanisms producing human development. The power of these processes to influence development varies based on characteristics of the person (P), of immediate and remote environmental contexts (C) and the time periods (T) in which they take place. To capture the integrated nature of the various elements, the model is characterised as the PPCT model, and it is through proximal processes that an individual's genetic potential is made visible in their behaviours and actions. They suggest that the investigation of proximal processes, and their developmental consequences under different environmental conditions, provides developmental psychologists with an indirect strategy for testing the role of both genetics and environment in contributing to individual differences in psychological growth.

Elaborating on the role of process in development, Bronfenbrenner and Morris (1998, 2006) argue that human development, especially in the early years, takes place through processes of progressively more complex reciprocal interactions between an active and evolving biopsychological human organism (the child) and the persons, objects and symbols in the immediate external environment. To be effective, these interactions must be of high quality and occur on a fairly regular basis over extended periods. Examples of enduring patterns of the proximal process can be seen in early years settings, including feeding or comforting a baby, playing with a young child, child–child activities, group or solitary play, engaging in conversation and dialogue, reading, learning new skills, athletic activities, problem-solving, caring for others in distress, making plans, performing complex tasks and acquiring new knowledge and know-how (Bronfenbrenner & Morris, 1998, p. 996).

## The bioecological model and early education

In identifying proximal processes as key to development, Bronfenbrenner and Morris (1998, 2006) provide us with a clear focus for early years practice, and more recent research supports their view by illustrating the importance of interaction and relationships to healthy child development. Positive, high–quality, interactive early

**10** Introducing Bronfenbrenner

learning experiences facilitate the development of generative or positive dispositions as opposed to disruptive or negative ones. Bronfenbrenner and Morris note
that the model introduces

> [c]oncepts and criteria … that differentiate between those features of the
> environment that foster versus interfere with the development of proximal
> processes. Particularly significant in the latter sphere is the growing hectic-
> ness, instability and chaos in the principal settings in which human com-
> petence and character are shaped – in the family, child-care arrangements,
> school, peer groups and neighbourhoods.
>
> *(Bronfenbrenner & Morris, 1998, p. 995)*

The concept of proximal processes has important implications for early education,
highlighting the power of interactions and the important role of the adult. Through
reflective observation of the child, adults can come to understand the characteristics
of the child and the environment, which will facilitate positive development and
learning. Drawing on many different studies of child development with children
of different ages, Bronfenbrenner and Morris (1998, 2006) describe the positive,
generative dispositions valued by Western culture. One example of generative disposition given is the extent to which the child tends to engage and persist in progressively more complex activities. For example, given a facilitating environment,
children will elaborate, restructure and create new features in an environment,
not only physical and social but also symbolic. Another class of developmentally
generative disposition they describe reflects the increased capacity and active pro-
pensity of children, as they grow older, to conceptualise their experiences. This,
Bronfenbrenner and Morris argue, contributes to the development of "directive
belief systems" (Bronfenbrenner & Morris, 2006, p. 811) about oneself as an active
agent both in relation to the self and to the environment. This is particularly important and relevant to early years practice as these personal belief systems, emerging
in early childhood, are the foundations for self-directed learning, attention and
problem-solving. The manner in which adults respond to, guide and support children's development can profoundly impact the adult the child becomes.

Different theories of development shed light on different aspects of development,
with varying suggestions and challenges for educational principles and practices.
The value of a model such as the bioecological one is that it provides a framework,
allowing us to visualise complex dynamics in different contexts and reflect on the
various different factors impacting the development of children. However, system
models, such as that proposed by Bronfenbrenner, have been criticised as being too
preoccupied with individualism and ignoring the power of interactions and discourse between parents, teachers and children in early education (Dahlberg, Moss,
& Pence, 1999; Downes, 2014; Penn, 1997). These criticisms seem particularly
misplaced in relation to the bioecological model of development, which actively
stresses the importance of good-quality interactions, relationships and communication, through locating the construct of proximal processes as the central factor

driving development. The quality of these proximal processes is mediated by social interactions, and this provides a link between the structural (biological) factors influencing development and the processes which support it.

Bronfenbrenner's model presents a valuable framework of development within which to link psychological and educational theory to early educational curriculum and practice from both a research and pedagogical point of view. It is a model with sufficient detail to allow attention to all the complex systems of early educational experience whilst, at the same time, highlighting the reality, dynamism and complexity of everyday life.

## Note

1 We use these two articles interchangeably. The work was originally published in 1998 and the slightly revised version was published posthumously in 2006.

# 2
# THE BIOECOLOGICAL MODEL OF HUMAN DEVELOPMENT

## Introduction

Bronfenbrenner identified some interesting concepts regarding the multifaceted systems of influence on children's lives. This chapter highlights the significant ways in which he continued to develop and update his theory up to the time of his death in 2005. While much emphasis has been placed on Bronfenbrenner's systems of contextual influences, developed in his earlier theorising, less attention has been paid to the important role the individual plays in her own development and the central importance of proximal processes – reciprocal interactions between the child and her environment:

> Especially in its early phases, but also throughout the life course, human development takes place through processes of progressively more complex reciprocal interaction between an active, evolving biopsychological human organism and the persons, objects, and symbols in its immediate external environment. To be effective, the interaction must occur on a fairly regular basis over extended periods of time. Such enduring forms of interaction in the immediate environment are referred to as proximal processes.
> *—Bronfenbrenner and Morris (2006, p. 797)*

The aim of this chapter is to unpack the implications of Bronfenbrenner's model of human development for understanding early childhood. The chapter tracks some of the new directions that he brought to his model over time. We also consider some current reflections on Bronfenbrenner's theory and its implications for early years practice.

Before outlining the theory, let's consider an interpretation of the term 'ecological' as it is used in the theory. According to Bronfenbrenner, "[e]cology implies

DOI: 10.4324/9781003247760-2

an adjustment between organism and environment" (1975, p. 439). Later, he wrote a more complete definition:

> The ecology of human development involves the scientific study of the progressive, mutual accommodation between an active, growing human being and the changing properties of the immediate settings in which the developing person lives, as this process is affected by relations between these settings, and by the larger contexts within which the settings are embedded.
>
> (Bronfenbrenner, 1979, p. 21)

Bronfenbrenner was interested in "how environments change, and the implications of this change for the human beings who live and grow in these environments" (1975, p. 439). Using an ecological approach, he explored the interrelations between the developing person and the changing micro and macro contexts in which development is embedded. In early years learning, this implies that development is influenced by changing micro contexts, like family, friends and communities surrounding the child, and by changes within the macro contexts – the broader social and cultural context in which they are growing. This approach also foregrounds ongoing change and adjustment in development and the importance of recognising the progressive and dynamic nature of development, reflected in a later emphasis on proximal processes.

The development of Bronfenbrenner's work can be characterised in three phases, moving from his initial emphasis on the role of context in development to recognising the active role of the child to the final phase where he captured the dynamic nature of development in his Process–Person–Context–Time (PPCT) model of development, drawing attention to proximal processes and demonstrating how they are influenced by the context in which they occur (Navarro, Doucet, & Tudge, 2020). Importantly, Bronfenbrenner gave much greater prominence to the characteristics of the developing child in his later work. The model is represented in Figure 2.1.

## Nested systems of influence: development in context

The first 'version' of an ecological model of human development conceived of thedevelopment of the individual within the environment characterised as four systems: microsystem, mesosystem, exosystem and macrosystem. The most direct influences, closest to the child (e.g. family, friends), are envisaged as being embedded or nested within those located more remotely from the individual (e.g. political systems, cultural contexts). Significantly, the child is located at the centre of the model. Microsystems include aspects of the environment impacting the daily life of the child. Parents, siblings, extended family members, early years educators and settings and other children within day-care settings comprise the microsystems that exert primary and direct influence on children's lives.

In early years practice, the child as learner and the learning environment are closely connected. The child develops language abilities in settings where adults talk to children and to each other; the child learns to explore in settings where exploration is valued and the curriculum reflects these values.

# 14  The bioecological model of human development

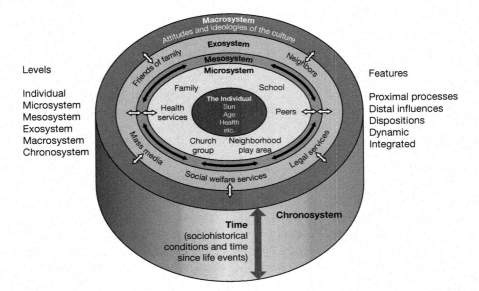

FIGURE 2.1  Bioecological model of development
Source: Adapted from Santrock (2007)

---

**REFLECTION**

Think about the microsystems of the children you work with. Can you identify some of them? Who are the main actors within them? How do these microsystems affect the quality of children's experiences?

---

Bronfenbrenner called the second level of influence the mesosystem. This describes the level of context that takes account of interconnections between two or more settings (such as school, peer group and family) and acknowledges their impact on the child. In short, the mesosystem is a system of two or more microsystems. This is a very powerful concept, showing how behaviour in any one setting is influenced by experiences not just within that setting, but in the full range of settings experienced by the child. "[A]n individual's relationships in every setting are impacted by relationships in other settings in that individual's life. There is … a chain of activity that individuals drag with them across microsystems" (Slesnick, Prestopnik, Meyers, & Glassman, 2007, p. 1238).

Partnership with parents in the early years context provides a good illustration of two microsystems (home and early years setting) interacting with each other. Links between home and early years setting are important. The environment, routines and people within a home provide opportunities for spontaneous learning that should be a feature of all early years contexts (Dale Tunnicliffe & Gkouskou, 2019;

The bioecological model of human development **15**

Mitchell, Wylie, & Carr, 2008). A mesosystem could include a meeting between a parent (from the child's family microsystem) and an educator (from the microsystem of the early years setting). Connections like those between practitioners and parents may facilitate a greater understanding of the child's exosystem and macrosystem, especially regarding parents' occupations, family culture and other important details in their lives (Neal & Neal, 2013).

---

## REFLECTION

To what extent do you facilitate partnership with parents in your setting? Can you identify other important mesosystem communications that can contribute to best practice in early childhood education?

---

In the exosystem, Bronfenbrenner highlighted less visible and more distant influences on the child's life, such as decisions made by the manager of a setting, the quality of the parents' workplace, social media and informal social networks. The exosystem also encompasses conditions influencing the wellbeing of the adults in children's lives. Exosystems include settings that influence the child but in which the child does not directly participate. For example, a child's parent may be experiencing stress within their workplace and this may influence the quality of their interactions with the child. A further example of an exosystem is the education policymaking community; an individual child generally does not play a role, yet educational policies nonetheless influence the child's educational experiences. For example, the increasing international pattern of providing a universal free preschool year may allow greater access for young children to preschool education and thus influence the microsystems in which they interact.

---

## REFLECTION

What role does the family context of the child play in helping you understand her learning and development? Does the local neighbourhood influence how children develop? Does the community within which your setting is located influence how you respond to children?

---

Finally, macrosystems encompass those influences that take place at a cultural level; for example, sociocultural beliefs about the value of early childhood care and education and about the rights and responsibilities of children (National Council for Curriculum Assessment [NCCA], 2009). Although children are not in direct contact with macrosystems, the decisions generated at this level significantly influence their lives. Additionally, each cultural community that children belong to will influence the specific demands which may arise (Capobianco, Bush, & Best, 2019).

## 16 The bioecological model of human development

> **REFLECTION**
>
> How does cultural context influence the design of the setting, the pedagogical principles underpinning practice and the routines that evolve from these principles? How does the cultural context in which you grew up influence your practice with young children? Is your practice inclusive and reflective of the diversity of children's backgrounds?

In addition to the four core systems, Bronfenbrenner (1986a, 1986b) later introduced the chronosystem, reflecting change or continuity across time and influencing each of the other systems (Navarro et al., 2020; Neal & Neal, 2013). Transitions like the move from preschool to primary school are part of the chronosystem while also being part of the mesosystem. The historical time in which a child develops also influences the nature and quality of her experiences. Children growing up in the 1950s and 1960s had a very different experience of technology than children born in this century. The chronosystem also has relevance regarding the particular values and attitudes to childhood evident at a particular historical time. Childhood is shaped by the circumstances in which children grow, and the beliefs and attitudes of that historical time influence the roles that children are allowed to take. Typically, in the early part of the twentieth century, children were not afforded an active role in their learning and development. In the late twentieth century and the early twenty-first century, the role children play in their learning and development has evolved from a peripheral, passive one to being more central and active. We elaborate on the chronosystem later in this chapter, detailing some of the subsystems associated with this level of context – macrotime, mesotime and microtime.

> **REFLECTION**
>
> How does the historical time in which you are working influence the nature and content of your practice? To what extent does information and communication technology play a role in children's learning and development in your setting?

## Context without development? Focus on the active role of the developing child

In a second phase, broadly between 1980 and 1994, Bronfenbrenner renamed his model a 'bioecological model' of human development to better reflect the active role the child plays in shaping her development and to provide greater emphasis on biological influences (Tudge, Mokrova, Hatfield, & Karnik, 2009). Avoiding the implication that context impacts solely *on* the child, Bronfenbrenner moved his theory on to reflect a more dynamic process whereby the context or environment impacts *with* and *through* the child's participation.

In this phase, Bronfenbrenner expanded on his descriptions of the different levels of the ecological environment. He noted the fact that humans are not only the product of but also the producer of their own development. While highlighting development as being *nested* within contexts, Bronfenbrenner now placed greater emphasis on the processes that translate these contextual experiences into development. These processes include "not only the objective behaviours occurring in any given interaction but also the relevant subjective psychological states, such as beliefs and opinions of the interacting individuals" (Rosa & Tudge, 2013, p. 249). Bronfenbrenner's increasing interest in the complex processes enabling development evoked the sense of a network of influences that was dynamic by nature. Such a 'networked' model of development views ecological systems as "an overlapping arrangement of structures, each directly or indirectly connected to the others by the direct and indirect social interactions of their participants" (Neal & Neal, 2013, p. 722).

This further elaboration of the model addressed the concern that little explicit attention was paid to the role of the individual in Bronfenbrenner's earlier writings. Making the child more visible at the centre of her development sits well with the notion of 'agency', involving children's capacity to understand and act upon their world and foregrounding children's competence (Greene & Nixon, 2020; James, Jenks, & Prout, 1998). This approach seeks to understand the meanings children give to their own lives. Bronfenbrenner's revised perspective sees the child as actively participating in her own childhood, and this is in accordance with Malaguzzi's concept of the 'rich child' – the child who is "rich in potential, strong, powerful and competent" (Bronfenbrenner, 1993, p. 10). This acknowledges that in addition to expressing their desires and wishes, children as agents can negotiate within their environment; critically, these interactions ultimately result in changing their environment.

Thus, Bronfenbrenner's bioecological theory goes beyond simply highlighting the active role that the child plays in her own development. It emphasises the fluid and relational nature of development through a focus on personal characteristics influencing present and future development. Bronfenbrenner criticised some of the shortcomings in his previous theorising:

> Existing developmental studies subscribing to an ecological model have provided far more knowledge about the nature of developmentally relevant environments, near and far, than about the characteristics of developing individuals, then and now.
>
> *(1989a, p. 188)*

Bronfenbrenner emphasised three kinds of characteristics of the developing child: (1) active behavioural characteristics/dispositions, (2) resource characteristics and (3) demand characteristics.

**18** The bioecological model of human development

### *Active behavioural dispositions*

The term *active behavioural dispositions* refers to variations in the child's motivation, persistence and temperament. Even when children have equivalent access to resources, their developmental courses may differ as a function of an individual's personal characteristics.

---

Lauren is 18 months old and sitting on the floor in her crèche. She is interested in the soft teddy sitting beyond her reach on the sofa. She crawls near the sofa and tries to pull herself up, hanging on to the sofa in order to try to reach the teddy. After several attempts, she falls back into a sitting position on the floor. Having looked around the room to see if anyone can come to her aid, she finally begins to tug cautiously on a rug hanging down from the sofa. As she pulls the rug, slowly teddy, which is sitting on the rug, moves forward. Lauren stops and looks around again, not sure about what she should do next. Eventually she pulls on the rug, and this time teddy comes tumbling down into her arms.

*Source: author observation in an early years setting*

---

Lauren is demonstrating evidence of positive active behavioural dispositions such as the motivation to gain access to teddy and the perseverance to patiently experiment in different ways until she finally succeeds in achieving this. While her success in reaching teddy may not be a significant achievement regarding her developmental pathway, at the same time, the positive dispositions she has shown are likely to be reinforced by the success of her attempts. Bronfenbrenner provides a rationale for how environments influence personal characteristics. However, a significant feature highlighted in this phase of his work was the potential for personal characteristics to change environments. The interaction between humans and their environments is one of reciprocity – the context in which a child is developing impacts on her development and, in turn, the child may shape her environment through these interactions. The particular characteristics of children, their ability to focus, show interest in things, become excited about events, contributes to shaping our responses to these children. In turn, we are affected by and through our interactions with the different children in our care.

Active behavioural dispositions may be positive or negative in impact. 'Generative' (positive) dispositions are characteristics likely to enhance interactions and elicit responses from the environment. These are associated with the ability to initiate or maintain reciprocal interactions with parents or other caregivers (Bronfenbrenner, 1993) and include curiosity, attentiveness and the ability to defer gratification. Let's imagine how these might play out in the context of early years practice.

The bioecological model of human development **19**

> Markus is curious about dinosaurs and uses every opportunity to learn more about them. When the early years educator working in his day-care setting invites him to read with her, he responds enthusiastically by selecting one of his favourite books, which provides a comprehensive and colourful overview of the history and evolution of dinosaurs. Miniature figures of different types of dinosaurs are included with the book, and Markus actively demonstrates some interesting facts about dinosaurs. This in turn elicits a positive and interested response from the educator working alongside him.
>
> *Source: author observation in an early years setting*

'Disruptive' (negative) dispositions are those characteristics which prevent or disrupt responses from the environment, including distractibility, aggressive tendencies, inability to defer gratification and tendency to withdraw from activity.

> Lena wants to play at the sandbox. Julie, the educator, has explained that at the moment there are too many children playing at the sandbox. She encourages Lena to wait a short while until there is more space for her to play safely there. Julie invites Lena to join a different activity, and Lena insists on joining the other children at the sandbox. As there is not enough space for all children to play at once, some of the other children who were already playing with the sand become annoyed and refuse to allow Lena to play with them.
>
> *Source: author observation in an early years setting*

## Resource characteristics

Resource characteristics are not as immediately recognisable as dispositions. These include mental and emotional resources, such as past experiences, intelligence and skills, as well as material resources like access to housing, education and a responsive caregiver. According to Bronfenbrenner and Morris, these characteristics involve no selective disposition to action but, rather, are described as "biopsychological liabilities and assets" influencing the capacity of the child to initiate and sustain interactions (2006, p. 812). Developmental assets can take the form of ability, knowledge, skill and experience, which as they develop and evolve, expand the range of options and sources of growth available to the child.

> Jack loves music and enjoys the "music and movement" sessions that take place in his early years setting weekly. During these sessions, the children are introduced to musical instruments and invited to experiment with them. He particularly loves the percussion instruments, and his enthusiasm when playing with them motivates the children and adults in his room to explore further and enjoy these possibilities.
>
> *Source: author observation in an early years setting*

**20 The bioecological model of human development**

Other resource characteristics may operate to limit or disrupt the extent to which a child can thrive or even their ability to become involved in available interactions and activities. These characteristics include genetic inheritances like low birthweight, physical disability and severe or persistent illness. Bronfenbrenner shows how the impact of these characteristics depends on a variety of factors. In the context of a 'social model' of disability (Berghs, Atkin, Hatton, & Thomas, 2019; Brewster, 2004; Oliver, 1983), the physical, social and attitudinal environment can disable a child far more than any impairment (Lund & Seekins, 2014). Consider how a supportive early years setting limits the impact of a potentially disruptive resource characteristic in the following example.

> Elena is a bright, outgoing three-year-old, and today is her first day in preschool. Elena's mother has been anxious about her starting preschool because she has cerebral palsy and uses a wheelchair; her mother is worried about the ability of the staff to meet Elena's needs. However, since the family and the preschool have spent time planning together, this morning Elena is met at the door by the preschool teacher, Sarah, who wheels her chair up the ramp, through the doors and into the preschool where she introduces Elena to another three-year-old, Hanna. "Hanna is feeling a bit shy this morning, Elena. I know that you really like chatting and playing, so can you spend a bit of time with Hanna and help her feel less worried?" As the girls play, Sarah shows Elena's mother the accessible bathrooms and the raised flower beds in the garden where Elena will take part in the planned gardening with the other children.
>
> *Source: composite of author experiences working*
> *with children with disabilities*

In Elena's case, her cerebral palsy could have represented a disruptive resource characteristic limiting her ability to benefit from early education. In some settings, she might not have been able to enter the building due to lack of wheelchair access, or it may be that staff fears would have left them unwilling to engage with Elena as a child with strengths as well as challenges. Here, the accessible environment and Sarah's recognition of Elena's social skills frame the latter's experiences and the perception of her resources very differently, to the benefit of Elena, her mother and Hanna, the little girl who may now have a supportive friend to help her through the transition from home to preschool.

## *Demand characteristics*

Demand characteristics are those qualities of the developing person that can invite or discourage reactions from the social environment, influencing the way in which

The bioecological model of human development **21**

proximal processes are established. Demand characteristics include an agitated or calm temperament, attractive versus unattractive appearance, hyperactivity and passivity. Other characteristics that are more externally accessible, like age, gender and skin colour may also affect the establishment of effective interactions. The bioecological model of human development emphasises the importance of interaction between person and context; the personal characteristics and dispositions of the child elicit responses from the environment, and these responses influence the personal characteristics of the child and elicit further responses from the child. Thus, demand characteristics, as well as active behavioural dispositions and resource characteristics, are influences on development and, at the same time, a developmental outcome, or a result of development (Bronfenbrenner & Morris, 2006). This process of interaction and influence can be understood as a spiral dynamic in which the personal characteristics of the child interact with and influence the people and the environment around them in an ongoing cycle of transformation. In understanding these influences, early childhood educators gain insight into children's behaviour, recognising the variety of factors that may influence behaviour. This allows early childhood educators to respond more sensitively to individual children.

## Process–Person–Context–Time: networked systems of influence

In the last phase of Bronfenbrenner's bioecological model, four key interacting elements of development are highlighted. This phase explored how individual characteristics of the child alongside features of their context, both spatial and temporal, influence proximal processes. Bronfenbrenner's model is often characterised as the individual developing within the nested systems. Although widely embraced, the model is not without its critics. For example, Downes (2014) argues that to contain the individual within the nested systems is to limit the impact of the systems on the individual and the individual on the systems. This can lead to a perception of static systems that are very difficult to change. Others argue on the contrary that the networked version of the model provides the possibility of considering the individual as an active agent within a dynamic context of interacting systems (Neal & Neal, 2013; O'Toole, Hayes, & Mhic Mhathúna, 2014). To reflect the dynamic nature of the PPCT model, Tudge (2008) has adapted the original model as shown in Figure 2.2.

Through a focus on this final phase of the evolution of the bioecological model of human development, we consider the four components of the PPCT model and look at how these can inform our interactions with children in early years practice. It is worth noting that while we have outlined details of these four constructs separately – proximal processes, person, context, and time – Bronfenbrenner at all times emphasised the reciprocal and dynamic nature of these constructs, with each influencing and impacting others (Xia, Li, & Tudge, 2020).

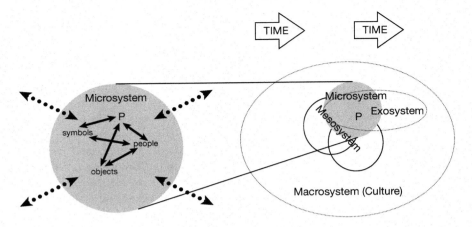

**FIGURE 2.2** Urie Bronfenbrenner's PPCT (Process, Person, Context, and Time) model. The active *person* (P) engaging in *proximal processes* with people, symbols and objects within a microsystem, in interaction with other *contexts*, involving both continuity and change over *time*

Source: Tudge (2008, p. 69)

## *Process*

The distinguishing feature of Bronfenbrenner's later writings is his emphasis on processes in human development. Although he referred previously to proximal processes, it was only in the 1990s that they were defined as the "engines of development" (Bronfenbrenner & Ceci, 1994, p. 584; Bronfenbrenner & Morris, 1998, p. 996). Traditionally, the behaviour of others towards the developing person had been treated under the more inclusive category of the environment. However, in the bioecological model, a distinction is made between the concepts of environment and process, with the latter occupying a central position. Proximal processes relevant to early years practice include interactions like feeding or comforting a baby, playing with a younger child, activities between children of the same age, group or solitary play, reading and learning new skills.

Bronfenbrenner suggests that proximal processes are the primary mechanisms in development as it is through engaging in these activities and interactions that children make sense of their world (Merçon-Vargas, Lima, Rosa, & Tudge, 2020). To be effective, interactions must occur on a regular basis and last for extended periods. The value of the adult role in respecting, supporting and extending children's learning is foregrounded in this conceptualisation. The nature and effect of proximal processes vary according to the characteristics of the individual, the features of the environment and the historical time in which development takes place. Proximal processes are generally characterised as having a positive impact on development. However, they may, under certain circumstance have a negative impact. To recognise this Merçon-Vargas et al. (2020) have introduced the term 'inverse proximal

The bioecological model of human development **23**

processes' pointing out that they can, 'in higher levels produce dysfunction and reduce competency' (p. 321).

> The form, power, content, and direction of the proximal processes effecting development vary systematically as a joint function of the characteristics of the developing person; of the environment – both immediate and more remote – in which the processes are taking place; the nature of the developmental outcomes under consideration and the social continuities and changes occurring over time through the life course and the historical period during which the person has lived.
>
> *(Bronfenbrenner & Morris, 1998, p. 996)*

## *Person*

Earlier we reflected on the different personal characteristics that Bronfenbrenner identified – active behavioural dispositions (generative or disruptive), resource characteristics and demand characteristics – and how these operate to enhance or inhibit growth and development. We saw that although children may have equal access to resource characteristics such as intelligence and competence in a particular area, their developmental trajectories will be quite distinct depending on how these personal characteristics operate to interact with the environment.

Bronfenbrenner went on to provide a clearer view of children's active role in changing their context. Sometimes change is brought about in a relatively passive way. For example, a child's presence in an early years setting generates a change in the environment simply on the basis of how people respond to demand characteristics such as age, gender and skin colour. Let's focus on an important demand characteristic – gender – and how it might impact the quality of child–educator relationships. Early childhood educators are sensitive to children's behaviours, and the quality of their relationships with children is likely to be influenced by their perceptions of the children's behaviours. However, early childhood educators' perceptions of a child's behaviour may be as much about what behaviours are *expected* as they are about the behaviours themselves, and gender stereotypes may be one source of these expectations. Educators may accept certain behaviours in boys but hold girls to account for the same behaviours. A recent longitudinal study explored the extent to which children's gender influences the quality of the adult–child relationship in the early years (Runions, 2014). Findings suggest that educators' relationships with children are, in many cases, influenced by their perceptions of children's behavioural tendencies; however, in some cases, gender moderates the quality of these relationships. Specifically, boys who show greater emotional problems during the prekindergarten year and the kindergarten year were at risk for higher levels of conflict with adults than were girls who had emotional problems. The authors suggest this is possibly due to gender stereotyping, such as the expectation that boys do not cry or get upset. An interesting finding emerging in the follow-up study two years later was that emotional problems among girls tended to more negatively impact the establishment of close relationships with the teacher in primary school. The negative impact that emotional problems had on teacher relationships with boys is in line with the risk evident in the previous two years. The authors suggest that the change in educators' responses to girls showing emotional problems may be explained by the fact that the environment is more structured and that there is more pressure on educators to facilitate academic achievement. These findings support Bronfenbrenner's thesis that demand characteristics like gender can enhance or inhibit interactions and, subsequently, child growth and development. These findings also support the notion that educators' relationships with learners are differentially influenced by gender expectations, which inform and even direct their interpretation of children's behaviours (Runions, 2014).

It is important to highlight that current understandings of gender and sex identities are much broader than those that have traditionally been outlined. While traditionally we refer only to gender terms such as *girls*, *boys*, *females* and *males*, we acknowledge the complexity of gender and sex identities which have emerged and become established in recent years. Moreover, an increasing number of transgender children – those who express a gender identity that is "opposite" to their natal sex – are socially transitioning or presenting as their gender identity in everyday life (Fast & Olsen, 2018). Given the central importance of gender in terms of how children begin to categorise the social world, the value of providing children with opportunities for learning about non-traditional gender roles is emphasised.

---

**REFLECTION**

Identify the practical ways boys and girls are treated differently in your setting, either consciously or unconsciously. In light of increased attention to gender issues, what might the implications be for your practice?

How can you encourage and support children who wish to behave outside of traditional gender roles?

To what extent do you support and promote flexible thinking about gender?

---

The child's resource characteristics, like the ability to communicate or skill in using technology, operate in a more active way to change the environment within the setting. A child who is a confident and competent communicator can motivate other children and adults to interact with greater ease. Educators can also provide an environment that motivates children to interact with each other and with the objects in the setting. The importance of providing appropriate materials that can facilitate children's positive interactions with their environment is foregrounded in Bronfenbrenner's focus on children's resource characteristics. A child who is curious about and skilled in information technologies will further develop these skills when provided with opportunities to engage and interact with such technologies.

However, where no such opportunities are provided, the chances for developing these characteristics further will be restricted.

## Context

Context is the component that is often most readily associated with Bronfenbrenner's theory. As we saw earlier in this chapter, Bronfenbrenner drew attention to the many contextual influences on children's lives, both proximal influences which are those immediate influences such as family, school and neighbourhood contexts and more distal influences such as sociocultural beliefs and values and the policies that are informed by these beliefs. Children's learning environments extend beyond the immediacy of the early years setting. While the child and her immediate environment are at the centre – the first level of influence – other levels, too, have a powerful influence on the child's wellbeing and capacity to learn. The microsystem contains the major settings experienced by the child: her home, the service or setting beyond her home, her friends and neighbours. The mesosystem refers to influences arising from the relationship between these environments, as for example the interactions between her parent and staff within the early childhood setting. A further level of influence, which also impacts the quality of children's experiences, is called the exosystem and encompasses the world of work, the neighbourhood, social media and informal social networks. This level includes the conditions that influence the wellbeing and support of the adults in children's lives: the demands, the stresses and the opportunities for development experienced by significant adults in each child's life. A more distal level of influence is the macrosystem which refers to the cultural and societal influences on a child's learning and development. A particular cultural group may share a set of values, but for any particular value system to have an influence on a developing person, it has to be experienced within one or more of the microsystems in which that person is situated.

## Time

The final component of the PPCT model is time, represented by the chronosystem. Bronfenbrenner identified three ways in which time could impact proximal processes in children's development: 'microtime' – what is happening during the course of a particular interaction or activity; 'mesotime' – the extent to which activities and interactions occur with some consistency in the developing child's environment; and 'macrotime' – the historical context for a child's development and the timing of certain events in a child's life (Greene et al., 2010). For early childhood educators, being aware of and tuned into the concept of microtime allows them to support children to engage with their environment in a meaningful way and without interruption, enhancing opportunities to participate in proximal processes (Tudge, Navarro, Merçon-Vargas, & Payir, 2021). One illustration of the significance of microtime and mesotime for children's development is in free play. The time made available to children to engage in free experimental play, both the

**26** The bioecological model of human development

duration of periods of interaction and their frequency of occurrence over weeks and months, are relevant to the concepts of microtime and mesotime. The frequent availability of opportunities for free play facilitates play becoming more varied and complex over time (Santer, Griffiths, & Goodall, 2007; White, Thibodeau-Nielsen, Palermo, & Mikulski, 2021b). An example of this is highlighted by Siraj-Blatchford, Sylva, Muttock, Gilden, and Bell (2002) who note that in experimental play, children begin to categorise objects, an activity which comes before the development of more complex knowledge and understanding in mathematics and science. Bronfenbrenner suggests that developmental processes are also likely to vary according to the specific historical events that occur as the developing child reaches a particular age (macrotime). If we think of the children of refugee families in Europe, we understand that events closely linked to the historical time in which they are developing impact substantially on their development. Similarly, how these events may impact a toddler is likely to be different from how they impact an adolescent. Tudge et al. (2021) draw attention to the fact that Bronfenbrenner's PPCT model and its subcomponents were not merely abstract ideas but also emphasised throughout his practice-oriented advocacy and publications. We further explore the application of these concepts to practice within early childhood education settings across the chapters in this book.

## Implications for practice

In this chapter, we have explored how Bronfenbrenner's bioecological model of human development provided a focus on nested layers of influence that impact a child's learning and development, including both proximal and distal contexts. We also outlined how the model evolved over time to provide a greater emphasis on proximal processes, interactions that take place on a regular basis and over extended periods. Looking at a late phase of the evolution of Bronfenbrenner's theory, we reflected on the PPCT structure and the implications of process–person–context–time factors for early years learning and development.

## Key concepts for early years practice

1   *Children's development and learning are influenced by the changing contexts* surrounding the child, such as family, friends and communities, and by changes within the broader social and cultural context in which she is growing.
2   *The child as learner and the learning environment are closely connected.* A child develops language abilities in a setting where adults talk to children and to each other. Similarly, a child learns to explore in a setting where exploration is valued and possible and where the curriculum adopted reflects these values.
3   *Children's personal characteristics and dispositions interact with the personal characteristics and dispositions of other children and adults* in the early years setting.

The bioecological model of human development **27**

4    *This process of interaction and influence can be understood as a spiral dynamic* wherein the personal characteristics of the child interact with and influence the people and the environment around her in an ongoing cycle of transformation.

5    *The child has a central role in how her development plays out.* As well as expressing their desires and wishes, children as agents can negotiate and interact within their environment, and these interactions ultimately result in changing their environment.

# 3

# PROXIMAL PROCESSES AND RELATIONSHIPS

## Introduction

One strength of the bioecological model, perhaps not fully developed during Bronfenbrenner's lifetime, lies in its potential to help us make sense of other theories within psychology, sociology and education. These disciplines are often experienced by those studying them for the first time as a collection of disparate theories with little obvious relation to each other or to real-world situations. Bronfenbrenner's focus on a network of development allows for many factors to be considered and enables us to bring together many theories. Real children with real families in real early childhood settings do not exist in compartmentalised worlds for ease of study, and this is recognised by the bioecological approach. Bronfenbrenner's theory offers a powerful framework for understanding how different theories fit together.

In engaging with psychology, sociology and education, students often begin with a search for 'truth', or real solutions that apply in most, if not all, settings. They expect solid answers to their questions that are definitively 'right' or 'wrong'. This mirrors the development of the disciplines themselves over time. For example, we see in psychology the behaviourist emphasis on objective measurement of behaviour and developmental stage approaches, like those of Piaget, Kohlberg and Freud, which attempted to describe the development of all children regardless of circumstances. However, students quickly discover that the social sciences provide little in the way of 'hard facts', and many well-established theories may even contradict each other. This leads students, following in the footsteps of the disciplines themselves, to wonder if it is all relative and whether the only answer that social science can give to questions on human experience is 'it depends…'. This can sometimes bring students to an experience like that described by Gergen (1997, p. 4) as a "crisis in social psychology" – the questioning of whether psychology has anything to offer at all if there is no agreement on anything! However, the student that persists

DOI: 10.4324/9781003247760-3

Proximal processes and relationships **29**

will notice commonalities across theories that may, when explored further, offer glimpses of a more coherent whole.

This chapter identifies one such recurring theme, the importance of interactions and relationships for child development. It aims to enhance understanding of the concept of 'process', drawing on other theories you may already have heard of: attachment theory, updated by reference to the work of Tony Ryle and others on 'reciprocal roles'; Baumrind's 'authoritative' parenting; Rogers' ideas on 'the relationship'; insights from sociocultural theory; and finally the cognitive theories of Jean Piaget.

## Proximal processes

Bronfenbrenner considered interactions and relationships to be the main mode through which children develop, "the engines of development" (Bronfenbrenner & Morris, 1998, p. 999).

In Chapter 2 we introduced the concept of proximal processes:

> Especially in its early phases, but also throughout the life course, human development takes place through processes of progressively more complex reciprocal interactions between an active, evolving biopsychological human organism and the persons, objects, and symbols in its immediate external environment. To be effective, the interaction must occur on a fairly regular basis over extended periods of time. Such enduring forms of interaction in the immediate environment are referred to as proximal processes.
>
> *(Bronfenbrenner & Morris, 2006, p. 797)*

Earlier, Bronfenbrenner (1973) wrote about the importance of these interactions occurring "with persons with whom [the child] has established a mutual and enduring emotional attachment" (p. 119), and he reinforced this in 1985, writing about "strong and enduring mutual emotional attachment" (p. 175). He also famously stated that, when it comes to supporting positive outcomes for children, "[i]n short, somebody has to be crazy about that kid" (Bronfenbrenner, 1988/2005, p. 262). Thus, while there may be some distinction between the concept of 'proximal processes' and the idea of a more general 'process' (Merçon-Vargas, Lima, Rosa, & Tudge, 2020), looking across the body of Bronfenbrenner's work, we can see the importance of both specific interactions in the immediate environment and the ongoing and enduring relationships that are built on these interactions over time. The powerful role attributed to 'process' is the defining component of the later bioecological model (Navarro, Doucet, & Tudge, 2020; Rosa & Tudge, 2013).

The bioecological model shows that lives are lived interdependently through a network of shared relationships, or 'linked lives'. According to Bronfenbrenner, the effect of process is more powerful than that of the context in which it occurs (Bronfenbrenner & Morris, 2006). More simply, strong, positive interactions and relationships may have the power to overcome the impacts of the most damaging environments, and even very positive environments may not be good enough without warm, loving relationships and stimulating interactions. In this way, proximal processes are seen as buffers for children (Merçon-Vargas et al., 2020). Regarding early education, this means that we must support the development of positive interactions and relationships between adults, between adults and children, and between children and their peers. For example, Page (2018) characterises the principles of 'professional love' in ECEC, and it is becoming increasingly common for early childhood practice to consciously centre relationships, even to the point of using the word 'love'. When we think about 'quality', we should focus just as much on the interactions and relationships that happen in early years settings as on environmental factors (O'Toole, Regan & Nowak-Lojewska, 2019) since education that is characterised by stimulating and supportive interactions and relationships is most effective for children (O'Toole & Hayes, 2020).

---

**REFLECTION**

Think about the systems that measure the quality of service where you work. Do they measure quality of relationships between adults and children? Do they focus more on structural factors like cleanliness or availability of materials? Which aspects of quality do you think are most important for a good early years service?

---

In early education in recent years, attention has increasingly moved away from 'instruction' towards understanding the power of the interpersonal and the role of relationships in learning. However, Bronfenbrenner's concept of process goes beyond the interpersonal to incorporate "progressively more complex reciprocal interaction with objects and symbols" (Bronfenbrenner & Morris, 2006, p. 814), so in spite of the emphasis on interpersonal relationships, we cannot disregard the quality of the learning opportunities provided for children in early learning environments. It may be that good-quality early years services think about the quality of their contexts *and* the relationships within them.

## Relationships in psychological theory

A number of key psychological theories may be incorporated within the framework provided by Bronfenbrenner's concept of process. One that was explicitly acknowledged by Bronfenbrenner as relevant to proximal processes was attachment theory (Ainsworth, Blehar, Waters, & Wall, 1978; Bowlby, 1973, 1988), which offers one of the most well-known explanations of how babies and young children develop security within relationships.

### Proximal processes and attachment theory

The central argument of attachment theory is that the attachment formed by an infant with the primary caregiver forms the basis of future relationships and psychological well-being. According to Bowlby (1988), the growing child needs to develop a sense of trust and, later, a growing independence; these are facilitated through affection, caring and the reasonably prompt satisfaction of infants' needs. When babies are hungry, in pain, fatigued or anxious, they cry. Bowlby thought that parents' responses in these circumstances form the basis of attachment between infant and parent. If parents respond consistently and warmly, the baby learns to trust that his parent will always be there when he is in need, and a secure attachment is formed. If parents fail to respond to the infant's needs, in situations such as abuse or neglect, the baby learns that adults are, at best, unreliable and, at worst, scary and develops an insecure attachment to the parent.

It is often said that attachment provides 'a secure base from which to explore the world' – securely attached children can confidently explore the world because they know that their parent will be there for them when they return, but this only develops over time. Of particular interest to early childhood educators is the occurrence of 'separation anxiety' in babies when separated from their primary caregivers. Think about what happens when a parent first begins to drop a baby off to a crèche. Very often he cries when the parent is leaving, although sometimes, as he gets to know the educator, the separations in the morning become less painful over time. Ainsworth would say this is because the baby has a secure attachment to his parent – he wants to be with the parent all the time because he feels safe when they are together (Ainsworth et al., 1978). However, as the baby starts to develop a 'secondary attachment' (Bowlby, 2007) to his early childhood educator, it becomes easier to say goodbye to his parent because he still feels safe in the relationship in the crèche. This is explored in more detail in Chapter 5, which takes a bioecological perspective on transitions, and it shows the importance of strong relationships in early years settings, as predicted by Bronfenbrenner.

As children grow, their attachment becomes less reliant on being physically near their parent and more dependent on abstract qualities like affection and trust. The quality of attachment becomes 'internalised' as the child grows – a baby needs to be physically beside his parent to feel secure, but as he grows within loving relationships, he develops the understanding that he is loved and safe regardless of whether his parent is physically beside him. In attachment theory, this is known as the 'internal working model' (IWM) of the relationship with the attachment figure. Therefore, separation anxiety tends to lessen in older and securely attached children. However, separation anxiety may be sparked in children when they are under stress, even when they are older or securely attached – have you noticed how a child who falls while playing often runs back to his parent for comfort before going back to play? Bowlby would explain this by saying that a stressful situation (the fall) caused the child to seek his 'secure base' (the parent) for comfort and that once that comfort has been achieved, he can go and 'explore the world' again. Separation anxiety can also be provoked during transitions (O'Connor, 2013), and this is also explored in Chapter 5.

Importantly, the internal working model forms the basis of the child's concept of 'self' ('I am loved and lovable' or 'I am unloved and unlovable') and provides

**32** Proximal processes and relationships

direction for future relationships, including those formed with adults and children in early years settings. When a child expects the world to be comforting and supportive, he approaches new relationships with this expectation; thus, securely attached children tend to invite future supportive relationships. Equally, when a child expects the world to be dangerous and unsupportive, he approaches new relationships with this expectation; through defensiveness and fear, he may show difficult behaviour and reduce the chances of forming positive relationships in the future (Bowlby, 1973). This reflects Bronfenbrenner's description of the impact of demand characteristics on the response of others, with implications for future development.

This process of interaction between the child's traits and his experiences is known as 'internalisation' – personal characteristics both shape and are shaped by experiences in context. The concept of internalisation is important because it shows the power of relationships to influence the direction of future development. In the terminology of the bioecological model, early proximal processes produce proximal processes throughout development. In this way, proximal processes are the method by which internalisation happens. Indeed, Bronfenbrenner's statement that "through progressively more complex interaction with their parents, children increasingly become agents of their own development" (Bronfenbrenner & Morris, 2006, p. 797) could have been written by an attachment theorist.

Some aspects of attachment theory are contested, and Duschinsky, Van Ijzendoorn, Foster, Reijman, and Lionetti (2018) have highlighted some outdated perceptions, identifying how the theory has evolved over time. First, they note that when early theorists like Bowlby and Ainsworth were writing about attachment, the phrase 'primary caregiver' usually referred only to the child's mother, but nowadays we recognise that this is inappropriate. Ideas of mother–infant attachment are sometimes misused for political reasons to argue against women's right to work outside the home, and families take many different forms, not always including one mother as the primary caregiver. Nowadays, the phrase 'primary caregiver' usually means the person who takes care of the child the most, and we also know that babies and children can form attachments with a number of important adults. Second, Duschinsky et al. (2018) problemitise the original assumption that security of attachment was 'set in stone' by three years of age and could not be changed after that. We now understand that while early experiences are highly influential, 'neuroplasticity' means experience shapes the brain even in older children and adults (Maconochie, 2019). Third, early attachment theorists thought that daycare damaged children, but Duschinsky et al. argue that attachment-informed day care limits difficulties and high-quality day care can, in fact, benefit children.

These may be particularly important considerations for early childhood educators in centre-based services as the requirement to respond to the needs of many children at the same time can be challenging. Nonetheless, Ahnert, Pinquart, and Lamb (2006) found that once caregivers had attended to the needs of the group, it was then still possible for secure attachments to be formed in centre-based settings. For the individual child, the essential feature here is the extent to which the adult

Proximal processes and relationships **33**

is engaged with either the group or the child himself. Cárcamo, Vermeer, van der Veer, and van IJzendoorn (2016) also found positive changes in attachment security in children who attended daycare centres, and McDermott (2016) notes the effectiveness of key-worker systems in supporting positive secondary attachments.

---

### REFLECTION

What can you do to help reduce 'separation anxiety' for babies and small children and help them build a secure secondary attachment to you? How can you help them begin to trust that they are safe in the early childhood setting? What systems in crèches, preschools and other early years settings might inadvertently contribute to separation anxiety or insecure secondary attachment?

---

Many central ideas surrounding attachment theory are supported by research in neuroscience. Studies of the brains of infants have shown that when the stress hormone cortisol is released too often due to distressing experiences, it can change the structure of a baby's brain so that his future behaviour may be affected on the basis of those experiences (O'Toole & Hayes, 2020). Equally, when the anti-stress hormones opioids and oxytocin are released during loving experiences, this can also change the structure of a baby's brain and so have an impact on his future behaviour (O'Connor, 2013). In early childhood, love matters because affection actually shapes a baby's brain (Gerhardt, 2004). The Center on the Developing Child at Harvard provide multiple resources explaining how babies' brains are shaped by their interactions and relationships in a process they call 'serve and return' (https://developingchild.harvard.edu/resources/).

Children who are securely attached in infancy have been shown to be more curious and to have better problem-solving skills at age two, to have more social confidence at age three and to have more empathy and independence at age five, and they are less likely to have behaviour problems at age six (O'Toole & Hayes, 2020). Therefore, the security of attachment may predict the kinds of behaviours seen in crèches, preschools and primary school classrooms in the early years. Insecure attachment can lead to withdrawn behaviour when insecurity is directed inwards (psychologists call this 'internalising') or aggressive, violent behaviour when insecurity is directed outwards (psychologists call this 'externalising'). A neglectful or abusive parent may inhibit curiosity in the child – he is afraid to go and explore the world because he does not trust that the parent will still be there when he gets back – perhaps leading to withdrawn behaviour in the early years setting. Alternatively, these negative early experiences may provoke feelings of 'hypervigilance' (always being on alert for danger, even when it does not really exist), leading to aggression, defensiveness and challenging behaviour in the early years setting (see O'Toole & Hayes, 2020, Chapter 4 for an attachment-informed

**34** Proximal processes and relationships

understanding of children's behaviour in early years settings). A calm atmosphere in which practitioners are engaged and attuned to young children may mitigate the difficulties that could arise. This fits both with attachment theory and the bioecological model, whereby early experiences become incorporated into the person characteristics of the individual and, in turn, influence future experiences and processes.

Thus, future relationships may reflect the original attachment relationship that a baby forms with the primary caregiver, and Bronfenbrenner specifically identified teachers and early childhood educators as potential partners with children in the development of relationships whose prototype lies in the parent–child relationship. The person characteristics of important adults in the child's life such as early childhood educators are, in bioecological theory, incorporated into the microsystem of the child, and the model predicts that person elements of those adults will impact proximal processes just as much as the personal characteristics of the child (Bowlby, 2007). Put simply, the relationship between an adult and a child depends on the personal characteristics of both adult and child. This is supported by research on attachment between teachers and children: teachers' own attachment style impacts the relationships he forms with the children in his class (Riley, 2011).

Think about and discuss how Bronfenbrenner's concept of proximal processes and theories about attachment would explain what is happening in the vignettes involving Luka and Jamie.

---

Luka is usually an independent boy who likes to engage in self-directed play in his early years setting. However, today he has a cold and is not feeling well. He has spent the morning following his early childhood educator around the room and cries when the educator leaves to go to the bathroom.

*Source: author observation in an early childhood setting*

Jamie has recently been taken into care because his father was behaving violently at home. In school today, the class are learning a dance to go with the rhyme 'head, shoulders, knees and toes'. When his teacher takes his hands to show him how to place them on his head, Jamie kicks her and runs to hide under the table.

*Source: author observation in a primary school reception class*

---

Bronfenbrenner emphasised that proximal processes are reciprocal, influenced by the characteristics of both the child and the person with whom he is interacting (Merçon-Vargas et al., 2020). Relationships between adults and children in educational settings may, like all human relationships, be based on what Ryle (1998, p. 307) calls the reciprocal 'dance'. The temperament, previous experience of relationships, culture and expectations of both parties can influence the outcomes of interactions. For example, a child with a controlling or aggressive parent may interpret an educator's offer of help as trying to control him and so react badly, leading to the educator, who after all was only trying to help, to in turn react badly, and so on. Alternatively, if it is the educator who grew up with a controlling or aggressive parent, he might interpret a child's independence as criticism or rejection, again leading to a negative cycle of interaction. It is easy to see how such incidents of transference can escalate into incidents of negative behaviour (from both child and adult) unless an educator is theoretically informed.

The work of Ryle and Kerr (2002) on Cognitive Analytic Therapy (CAT) further develops the idea of an internal working model into a more nuanced conceptualisation known as Reciprocal Roles. Rather than broad categories of secure or insecure attachment, the concept of reciprocal roles acknowledges that we inhabit many different roles in many different circumstances, and these are dynamic and responsive to the behaviour of others we encounter. According to the Association of Cognitive Analytic Therapy (ACAT; n.d.), the idea of reciprocal roles highlights the fundamental importance of how we relate to each other, showing that we tend to treat people the way we anticipate they will treat us and that we learn how to relate to ourselves from the way others relate to us. CAT proposes that we replay relational patterns established early in life. Early relationships are viewed as dynamic two-way processes in which the child is an active participant; these early relationships provide the child with an internal working model of relationships (reciprocal roles), which then influence how he is in future relationships (with others and himself) and how he anticipates other people will be with him (Nowak-Łojewska, O'Toole, Regan, & Ferreira, 2019). This emphasis on reciprocity of relationships leading, over time, to developmental outcomes clearly mirrors Bronfenbrenner's ideas on proximal processes.

The concepts and tools of CAT have recently been applied to early childhood education for the first time (Nowak-Łojewska et al., 2019; Regan, 2019), proposing a radically relational understanding of ECEC Early Childhood Education and Care (ECEC). The THRIECE (Teaching for Holistic Relational and Inclusive Early Child-hood Education) project was the first to apply the learning and tools of CAT to the educational sphere, also bringing a bioecological lens to the understanding of relationships in context given by the concept of proximal processes. It aimed to support educators to reflect on the dynamic nature of the ongoing relationship with a child, a parent or the system and on their role in this relational dynamic. One interesting outcome has been to support the development of approaches to supporting positive behaviour through a radically relational lens (O'Toole & Hayes, 2020; Regan, 2019). Consider the reflections of some of the educators participating in the THRIECE project on how a relational understanding has supported them to work with children's behaviour, particularly in terms of the concept of a reciprocal role and their own part in the behavioural dynamic.

## 36 Proximal processes and relationships

> "We have taken on some of the key words, we would think about relationships more... The reciprocal roles...I have started to think a lot more about that... why is this impacting on me and where is it coming from? I don't think I would have ever thought as deeply about that before... had the language or thought about the relationships and how they were causing it to happen or how they were making me think it out...Identifying the feeling in yourself first...."
>
> "It's helped me with the way I think before I react to his [child's] actions... [reflecting relationally] it's like you "hover" over it and I've had time then to think about things before something happens in class with him because he would do the same things on a weekly basis".
>
> *Source: O'Toole & Hayes, 2020, p. 53*

### Proximal processes and parenting styles

The concept of proximal processes also allows for the incorporation of the ideas of Diana Baumrind. Bronfenbrenner indicates that a child's world must be stable, consistent and predictable. If his routine is chaotic, with no established rules, children find it hard to cope. However, if rules are too rigid with no room for flexibility, this is not beneficial either. This links with Baumrind's work showing that the parenting style of an individual parent or carer can strongly influence the quality of proximal processes between parent and child. Incorporating the work of others who have extended her original findings, Baumrind identified features that consistently differentiate effective parenting styles from those that are less effective, including acceptance, involvement and emotional support, appropriate control to guide behaviour, and support for independence and autonomy, promoting self-reliance.

Baumrind (1978, 1996, 2005) identified three main parenting styles: authoritarian, permissive and authoritative. Authoritarian parents are low in acceptance, high in control and do not allow independence. They are often rejecting and expect the child to accept their judgment unquestioningly. Authoritarian parents suppress children's self-expression and independence, and they often criticise children and withdraw parental love when they are dissatisfied. Such psychological control can leave children unable to make decisions for themselves, leading to both withdrawn behaviours and defiant behaviours. Such parenting styles have been linked with anxiety disorders, low self-esteem, increased self-monitoring for errors, ineffective coping strategies, perfectionism and fear of punishment and these impacts can last into adulthood (Banica, Sandre, & Weinberg, 2019). Noser et al. (2018) even linked authoritarian parenting with poorer glycaemic control in children with new-onset type 1 diabetes. This is consistent with the prediction of the bioecological model that extreme rigidity of experience may have negative effects on children (Bronfenbrenner & Morris, 2006).

The other extreme identified by Baumrind is permissive parents. These parents exercise little control over children and allow them to make decisions for themselves even when they are not yet ready. In some cases, parents genuinely believe that this is the right way to raise children. They are warm, accepting and overindulgent, and they are permissive because they believe that children should be allowed to decide for themselves. Alternatively, some parents lack confidence in their ability to control their child and may not try to. Sometimes they are emotionally detached, and this is often linked to parental depression where parents are so overwhelmed by life stresses that they have little energy for interacting with their children. At its extreme, this style of parenting is child neglect, and this latter category is often treated as a fourth parenting style. Again, as predicted by the bioecological model, such extremes of disorganisation and lack of predictability within parent–child relationships have been linked with poor outcomes for children (O'Toole & Hayes, 2020).

The most successful parenting style identified by Baumrind is the 'authoritative' style. This involves high acceptance and appropriate control while also allowing some freedom. Such parents are warm, attentive and emotionally fulfilling while maintaining firm and reasonable control (Noser et al., 2018). They focus on encouraging self-regulation but also on emotional expressiveness, communication and, where possible, joint decision-making, reminiscent of Bronfenbrenner's ideas on environments that are neither too fluid nor too rigid. A bioecological perspective indicates that these concepts only have value when viewed through the lens of cultural diversity. When we reduce 'good parenting' to checklists and simplistic formulas, we miss the point that there are many ways to be a good parent (Brooker, 2015). For example, the extent of 'autonomy granting' deemed appropriate varies across contexts and cultures. Equally, Belsky (1984) presents a model of parenting that shows the multiple determinants of parental functioning, illustrating that the behaviour of individual parents depends on many factors, such as the contextual supports and stress they experience. Viewing the work of Baumrind through a bioecological lens also highlights the importance of considering the multitude of influences on parenting styles.

Baumrind's work is sometimes simplified into two aspects of authoritative parenting that seem to contribute to its effectiveness (Gregory et al., 2010): 'support' (parental warmth, acceptance and involvement) and 'structure' (strictness and close supervision as reflected in parental monitoring and limit-setting). This conceptualisation is useful when thinking about parenting across contexts – it indicates that children need to know that they are loved (as shown in ways that are culturally and individually specific) and what the (culturally specific) rules and boundaries are. Discipline and support for emotional expression are not seen as opposing each other but, rather, as coexisting, equally important aspects of good parenting, and authoritative parenting has been shown to have positive cognitive and socio-emotional outcomes across cultures (Kim et al., 2018).

The idea of 'styles' of interacting with children also makes sense within early years settings, helping us understand 'process' between children and adults. An authoritarian early childhood educator would focus on strict discipline that may be perceived as unfair by children. He would use punishment and 'zero-tolerance' sanctions for even minor violations of rules, giving little consideration to the

## 38 Proximal processes and relationships

circumstances of behaviour or the child's intentions. Alternatively, a permissive educator would tolerate a wide range of behaviour, often with a level of disorder that inhibits children's learning. Like parents, permissive educators may be indulgent or neglectful. Authoritative early childhood educators aim for a 'middle ground'. This allows for consistency, fairness and predictable routine, while also ensuring that children can express their creativity and direct the course of their own learning, where their emotional needs are met and where attuned educators can respond to children's cues when a change of routine is beneficial (Early Childhood Ireland, 2016). In the early years, children require both structure and support.

---

**REFLECTION**

What style do you display in your interactions with children? Do you need to develop more structure and predictability for children, having had perhaps too 'permissive' a style of interaction to date? Do you need to be more emotionally supportive to children? Are your expectations unreasonable, perhaps leading to too 'authoritarian' a style of interaction? Think about specific examples of interactions with children that did not go as you might have liked – what would an 'authoritative' adult have done in those circumstances?

---

Within a bioecological framework, we see that neither parenting nor early education happens in a vacuum. Baumrind shows how adults influence children, but Bronfenbrenner shows us that children also influence adults. The characteristics of children are also an element of Belsky's (1984) model of parenting. For example, if the parent is firm but warm, the child tends to comply with what they say, and when the child complies, the parent is likely to be firm but warm in the future. However, when parents discipline with harshness and impatience, children tend to rebel and resist; this is stressful for parents and they become harsher and more impatient, increasing their use of punishment. There are bidirectional influences between adults and children, each influencing the other – a key principle of the bioecological model. Equally, there are broader influences on family and school dynamics, such as socio-economic class and poverty, so parenting and teaching style may vary with context. Nevertheless, many psychologists believe that with appropriate support, most adults have the capacity to create positive contexts for children's learning and development. This idea is key to the work of other influential thinkers such as Carl Rogers.

### Proximal processes and Rogers' humanism

Carl Rogers was a psychologist who originally worked as a therapist. Unlike other therapists who analysed people and told them what they should do, he relied on the capacity of the client to elaborate the issue. He focused on the ability of the

Proximal processes and relationships **39**

person to direct the course of his own life, consistent with Bronfenbrenner's view of human beings as active agents in their development. Rogers believed that people are fundamentally good and would figure out the right course of action and behave well as long as they were given a supportive relationship within which to do so (Joseph, Murphy, & Holford, 2020; Murphy & Joseph, 2018). This conscious rejection of a 'deficit model'[1] of human functioning in favour of a focus on growth has much in common with Bronfenbrenner. Rogers, like Bronfenbrenner, believed that people develop through the relationships they experience.

Rogers' techniques in therapy involved listening to the person and reflecting back to him what he said in an accepting and understanding way. For Rogers, this respect for self-direction (or, in Bronfenbrenner's terms, 'agency') applies even when the person seems to choose goals that do not make sense to the therapist; the function of therapy is to provide a supportive relationship within which the person can make decisions for himself. Rogers' concept of the relationship echoes Bronfenbrenner's concept of proximal processes in that both are impacted by the person characteristics of those involved. Unlike other therapeutic approaches that demand objectivity and separateness from the therapist, a Rogerian therapist makes up an important part of the human equation – "what he does, the attitude he holds, his basic concept of his role, all influence therapy to a marked degree" (Rogers, 1995, p. 19). Rogers required therapists to exhibit three central characteristics that are also relevant to education: congruence (genuineness), unconditional positive regard (acceptance, trust) and empathy (understanding from the client's viewpoint – or their 'internal frame of reference') (Swan, Chen, & Bockmier-Sommers, 2020).

Considering this approach in an educational setting rather than a therapeutic one, the role of an educator is to create a supportive, trusting relationship through congruence, unconditional positive regard and empathy (Joseph et al., 2020; Swan et al., 2020). This means respecting each child as an individual capable of positive growth. Rogers felt that the greatest tool a therapist or an educator has in supporting the client or the child is acceptance. Acceptance of the child does not mean passivity or indifference (Joseph et al., 2020) – a lack of involvement may be experienced by children as rejection. Both Bronfenbrenner and Baumrind show that for learning to happen, support needs to be provided alongside significant challenges. What is recommended by Rogerian approaches is active engagement or, in Bronfenbrenner's terms, bidirectional reciprocity of exchange (Bronfenbrenner & Morris, 2006). In Rogerian therapy, the counsellor must assume the client's internal frame of reference to see the world as he sees it (Rogers, 1995). An early childhood educator working with young children must also try to see the world through their eyes and be clear that this is what he is trying to do (O'Toole & Hayes, 2020). This can be achieved in very simple ways. For example, rather than saying, "That's a lovely picture of a house", the Rogerian educator says, "Tell me about your picture" – it might turn out to be a giraffe! Early childhood educators should never assume he understands the child's perspective; rather, he should ask about it, remembering that children communicate their perspectives in many ways beyond language.

## REFLECTION

How well do you listen to children? Do you try to see the world through their eyes? How can you make time in your busy day to enter the 'internal frame of reference' of children? What specifically can you do to achieve insight into how they think and feel?

Rogers's concept of person-centredness has been transferred to the educational arena through these ideas of self-direction and the importance of the relationship in an approach known as 'student-centred teaching' where the aim is to create 'freedom to learn' (Rogers, 1983; Rogers & Freiberg, 1970). The educator is seen as a 'facilitator', helping children to discover learning for themselves rather than giving direct instruction (Joseph et al., 2020). Early childhood educators using this approach choose topics of interest to children rather than only those decided by adults, and they provide interesting materials for children to make sense of themselves. Such practice is inclusive and welcoming to children from diverse backgrounds and of diverse ability, and when educators actively focus on the development of relationships and on accessing the internal frame of reference of learners, student-centred approaches can be very powerful (O'Toole, 2015; O'Toole & Hayes, 2020).

Rogers (1974) describes a list of "questions I would ask myself if I were a teacher", many of which are relevant to the concept of 'the relationship', or in Bronfenbrenner's terms, proximal processes. For example:

Do I dare to let myself deal with this boy or girl as a person, as someone I respect? Do I dare reveal myself to him and let him reveal himself to me? Do I dare to recognize that he/she may know more than I do in certain areas – or may in general be more gifted than I?

*(Rogers, 1974, p. 2)*

In asking such questions, Rogers emphasises respect for children and recognises that there is risk involved in the development of true and genuine human relationships. An understanding of proximal processes can incorporate Rogers's insights into the human emotions involved in the creation and maintenance of relationships. Thus, we can value both the 'thinking life and the feeling life', as Rogers refers to a holistic understanding of children's development in the context of their relationships.

Think about how the early childhood educator in this vignette is showing respect for children, accessing their internal frame of reference and supporting them to develop self-direction.

> It is coming up to Christmas and the setting where Jenny works usually puts on a Christmas play for parents. Last year, the children did a 'nativity' play, but Jenny feels uncomfortable with this because there are children from different religious and cultural backgrounds in the setting. She asks the children if they would like to write a play together. She suggests a theme – 'celebration' – and asks each child to think of the best way to celebrate a happy occasion. The children tell Jenny about different celebrations they have been involved in. "Now let's think of a story for our play about celebration", says Jenny. "What is the name of the person in our play? What do you think they might be celebrating?"
>
> *Source: author experience in practice*

## The importance of sociocultural understandings within a bioecological framework

The vignette involving Jenny reminds us that relationships happen within the context of *culture*. In contrast to other developmental theorists like Piaget, Erikson and Kohlberg, Bronfenbrenner sought to challenge some of the idealised assumptions contributing to the notion that all children develop in similar ways regardless of their circumstances; he opposed the idea of 'the universal child'. Developmental psychology is generally recognised as having been the dominant and defining academic discourse in relation to children in the twentieth century (Woodhead, 2006). However, towards the latter half of the twentieth century, critical perspectives on developmental psychology strongly contested the focus on development in the absence of emphasis on the sociocultural contexts in which development occurred. Woodhead (2006) argues that many of the descriptions of children and childhood generated by what has been termed 'developmentally appropriate practice' (Bredekamp & Copple, 1997) have little or no relevance to the realities of the diverse nature of childhood, and they do not reflect the variance of the resources available to children and their families. Many theorists in child development drew on socially, culturally and contextually specific assumptions about the nature and composition of children's relationships and home environments, the access to resources such as books and learning materials and the value placed on independence in childhood. Nowadays, we recognise that there are multiple constructions of childhood and that the way children are viewed is deeply rooted in culture and time (O'Toole et al., 2021), and as well as bioecological theory, this dawning understanding has been largely informed by sociocultural theory.

According to Tzuo, Yang, and Wright (2011), the tendency in recent years to polarise developmental versus sociocultural understandings of childhood has been unhelpful. They identify the need for a synthesis of theory. If we are to fully understand the nature of childhood, we need to draw on a variety of theoretical perspectives. Bronfenbrenner's emphasis on development in context provides a powerful framework through which to achieve such synthesis without

**42** Proximal processes and relationships

losing coherence. A bioecological framework allows for a child-centred approach when considering individual children's development within various interacting microsystems whilst, at the same time, moving beyond this to incorporate aspects of a sociocultural perspective at the mesosystem, exosystem, macrosystem and chronosystem levels. Bronfenbrenner's concept of process allows us to consider the reciprocal impact of these factors on relationships because the bioecological model helps us to think about the child in society. Vygotsky also highlighted the interaction between the social and cultural worlds of children. He proposed that it is through social interaction that ways of thinking begin to be appropriated by children and that development is shaped and supported by the social and cultural contexts in which it takes place (Smidt, 2013). This idea is the basis of a range of approaches to understanding child development that come under the banner of 'sociocultural theory'.

## *Proximal processes and sociocultural theory*

The notion of process is consistent with sociocultural theory, particularly Vygotsky's (1978) concept of the 'zone of proximal development' (ZPD). Vygotsky defined ZPD as "the distance between the actual development level as determined by independent problem-solving and the level of potential development as determined through problemsolving under guidance or in collaboration with more capable peers" (Vygotsky, 1978, p. 86). A child working alone rarely achieves to the level that she can when interacting with a more expert other (Eun, 2019), or as Gauvain (2020) expresses it, when our social interactions are targeted toward the child's ZPD, he can engage in more advanced cognitive activities than could be undertaken alone. Children learn through problem-solving experiences shared with someone else (Smidt, 2013). This concept is supported by extensive research on the benefits of cooperative learning or learning in the context of relationships with others (O'Toole, 2014). ZPD underlies several key approaches to education in recent years, and through a bioecological lens, this reflects the use of process to support learning and development. The concept of 'scaffolding' (Wood, Bruner, & Ross, 1976) was developed from the idea of ZPD, and it involves gradual withdrawal of support as children become more skilled and no longer need as much help. This idea of 'meeting them where they are at' is illustrated by this vignette involving Lily.

---

At the beginning of the year, many of the children in Lily's class have not been potty-trained very long, and going to the bathroom independently is quite a challenge. In September, Lily reminds them when they haven't been to the bathroom for a while, brings them to the toilet area and reminds them to flush the toilet. She shows them how to wash their hands properly – "let's pull up our sleeves and turn on the water; now we'll get some soap; let's rub our fingers

> between each other; here's a song to remind us how to wash our hands". By December, Lily just reminds the children to go to the bathroom every so often, but they go by themselves. In May, Lily no longer has to remind the children about the bathroom; they just go by themselves when they need to.
>
> *Source: author experience in practice*

Ellis (2012) indicates that the concept of scaffolding has to some extent fallen out of favour in recent years because it is seen as something that the adult *does* to the child. Contemporary sociocultural ideas about adult–child interaction during learning are more consistent with a bioecological interpretation of the bidirectionality of process. They emphasise 'intersubjectivity' (Bruner, 1996), which refers to interactions in which there is dynamic and engaged input from both adults and children. What is important regarding both process and ZPD is the reciprocity (or two-way flow) between the learner and the early years practitioner.

---

## REFLECTION

How do you 'scaffold' the learning and development of children you work with? Think of some concrete examples of how you initially gave a lot of support to a child but then gradually allowed him to do more for himself as his skills developed.

---

Sociocultural theory is further explored in Chapter 4, examining the interaction between 'person' and 'context' in the PPCT model. While consistencies between sociocultural approaches and a bioecological perspective are evident, it is important to note that Bronfenbrenner's description of process goes beyond interpersonal and social relationships to incorporate "progressively more complex reciprocal interaction with objects and symbols" (Bronfenbrenner & Morris, 2006, p. 814). This leads to consideration of the cognitivist psychology of Jean Piaget, again perhaps allowing for some level of synthesis between theories that may otherwise seem polarised.

## Interaction with objects and symbols

Piaget (1951, 2001) describes how a child comes to know his world by building cognitive structures, or mental maps, schemes, and networked concepts for understanding and responding to physical experiences within his environment. The application of Piaget's theory has presented a view of a structured, predetermined and universal course of development that has been extensively criticised (Burman, 2008; Morss, 2013; Woodhead, 1999) and does not fit well within a bioecological model founded

**44** Proximal processes and relationships

on the recognition of individual differences and cultural influences on development. The timing of Piaget's developmental stages has been questioned (Aguiar & Baillargeon, 1999, 2002), and research in different cultural settings has shown that children in different cultures reach developmental stages at different ages based on their experiences (Rogoff, 2003). As Hayes (2004, p. 2) puts it, young children develop "in a far messier and entangled way" than Piaget envisioned.

Nevertheless, consigning Piaget's work to "the dustbin of history" (James, Jenks, & Prout, 1998, p. 9) may be "throw[ing] out the baby with the developmental bathwater" (Woodhead, 2000, p. 31). Piaget maintained that over time a child's cognitive structures increase in sophistication, moving from a few innate reflexes such as crying and sucking to highly complex mental activities. Piaget projected the image of an active child, constantly trying to interpret and predict the world around him (Halpenny & Pettersen, 2014). He either predicts correctly or changes his ideas to survive. Bronfenbrenner and Morris (2006) describe proximal processes between the child and 'objects and symbols' in the environment whereby the opportunity to explore, manipulate and engage with new and sometimes challenging environments leads to progressively more complex engagement, thereby significantly changing the processes involved, their outcomes and the features of the environment that become most relevant. In Piaget's terminology (Piaget, 2001), Bronfenbrenner and Morris have described 'accommodation', 'assimilation', '(dis)equilibration' and the process of child development.

Piaget's insights on how we make sense of the world around us through accommodation, assimilation and (dis)equilibration have largely been supported by up-to-date findings from neuropsychology on how information is encoded in the brain, albeit with two provisos: much neurological change happens on the *inside* before behavioural change is evident on the *outside*, and his idea of progressively more complex cognitive structures may be insufficient since up-to-date neuroimaging techniques have shown the brain to be more complex and, to some degree, counter-intuitive in its pattern of development (Berk, 2018).

In educational terms, Piaget's emphasis on the 'educator as facilitator' providing instructional materials that use demonstrations, illustrative examples and corrective feedback rather than direct instruction fits well with Bronfenbrenner's ideas on progressively more complex interaction between the child and the environment and is supported by the most up-to-date, constructivist understandings of how children learn (Berk, 2018). Considering the fact that Rogers (1974) also maintains that a good teacher should spend the majority of his time creating resources to support children's learning through discovery rather than directly transmitting knowledge, this may be one occasion where the fog of relativism clears to allow for some coherence across theories, coalesced through Bronfenbrenner's concept of proximal processes.

## Implications for practice

In summary, when we use the concept of proximal processes to make sense of other important psychological theories, it becomes obvious that interactions and relationships are vital for children's development emotionally, socially and cognitively, and building good relationships should be a central area of concern for early childhood education. The analysis in this chapter has focused largely on 'process', but the bioecological model emphasises that such vital relationships are informed and shaped by the person characteristics of the children and adults involved, the context in which they take place and the time (both of the person's life and historically) in which those relationships are embedded. Bronfenbrenner says that we must understand process, person, context and time if we are to understand the child. Chapter 4 develops this idea that children's development through relationships must be understood in context.

## Key concepts for early years practice

1   Many important psychological theories emphasise the vital nature of relationships for children's development. *All learning and development happen in the context of relationships.*
2   Positive relationships between adults and children are reciprocal: there is input from both adults and children (intersubjectivity).
3   Interactions and relationships may be more important for development than environments and experiences. Strong positive relationships may have the power to overcome the impacts of even the most damaging environments, and even positive environments may be insufficient to support positive development in the absence of warm and loving relationships.
4   Notions of 'quality' in early childhood education should incorporate relationships. Warm, caring relationships between adults and children may act as a preventative measure against systems that tolerate poor-quality provision and even abuse.

## Note

1   A deficit model emphasises what a child cannot do rather than what he can.

# 4

# UNDERSTANDING DEVELOPMENT IN CONTEXT

## Introduction

The bioecological model acknowledges that children do not develop in isolation; rather, development is embedded within and across many contexts such as family, home, school, community, society and culture. Young children learn and develop in the midst of society, and the ordinary spaces, places and people they come in contact with have a profound influence on them (Hayes, 2013; O'Toole, Hayes, & Halpenny, 2020). Each of these ever-changing and multilevel settings influences, either directly or indirectly, the pattern of child development and learning. Such contexts extend beyond the child's immediate environment (e.g. home and early childhood setting) to encompass the broader sociocultural contexts in which development is embedded.

Building on the concepts outlined and discussed in the previous chapters, we now explore the contexts that inform and guide children's learning and development. Ultimately, all the contextual factors influencing a child operate through the child's immediate environment – the people, places and things with which the child has direct contact. However, the values of a particular culture are also reflected in the structure of the settings in which children spend their time. This chapter further explores how the bioecological model can offer a framework to incorporate many sociocultural insights on understanding development in context. In particular, we interrogate the idea of 'internalisation', or the incorporation of contexts for development into the personal characteristics of the developing child.

Bronfenbrenner's theory highlights the importance of actively linking early years settings to other important environments in the lives of young children as well as understanding the rich "funds of knowledge" (Hedges, 2014; Wood, 2013) children bring with them from the various contexts in which they are developing. Increasingly, the number and range of contexts young children traverse on a

DOI: 10.4324/9781003247760-4

Understanding development in context **47**

day-to-day basis are expanding, creating a potential for 'culture shock' where these are very different (O'Toole et al., 2020; O'Toole & Hayes, 2020). When the culture of the home and that of the early years setting are different, it may be difficult for children to adjust (Brooker, 2015), and this is explored in detail in Chapters 5 and 10. Thus, the bioecological model has much in common with other well-known theories that emphasise the role of culture in development.

## Bioecological theory and sociocultural theory: learning and development in context

A reading of key components of sociocultural theory through a bioecological lens highlights several consistencies between the two approaches. As noted in Chapter 3, there is some equivalence between Bronfenbrenner's concept of proximal processes and sociocultural ideas such as Vygotsky's zone of proximal development (ZPD) and the related notion of scaffolding, 'mediated learning', 'internalisation' and 'self-regulation'.

### *Zone of proximal development*

Vygotsky's concept of ZPD is one of the most widely studied sociocultural concepts (Eun, 2019) and is relevant not only to the 'process' element of Bronfenbrenner's PPCT (Process–Person–Context–Time) model as explored in Chapter 3 but also to the person, context and time elements. Like the bioecological model, "ZPD is premised on the view that development has both a social and a psychological dimension" (Ellis, 2012, p. 532). Sociocultural theory and the bioecological model are two of the few accounts of human development that go beyond traditional ideas of 'nature versus nurture' to not only investigate how the social and the psychological interact to direct outcomes but also provide mechanisms (mediating tools and proximal processes, respectively) explaining how this happens. Both theories recognise that nature and nurture are intertwined and that development is fundamentally linked to the context in which it takes place so that "the human mind is not merely influenced, facilitated, or undermined by culture and society. Instead, it is designed and moulded by them" (Chirkov, 2020, p. 120). In other words, nature *is* nurture. Children are not all the same. As Frønes puts it: "There is not one childhood, but many, formed at the intersection of different cultural, social and economic systems, natural and man-made physical environments. Different positions in society produce different experiences" (1993, p. 1).

### *Mediated learning*

As in the bioecological model, sociocultural theory indicates that development begins with the traits and dispositions of the child – the things they have inherited biologically from their parents – but recognises that children continue to develop through the "interweaving of cultural and biological inheritances" (Lantolf & Thorne, 2006, p. 59). The child's own personality and abilities are impacted by

**48**  Understanding development in context

her experiences, her contexts and her culture to influence how she will turn out. In sociocultural terms, this is known as 'mediated learning'; in Bronfenbrenner's terms, such interweaving between person and context happens through proximal processes. Sociocultural theorists believe that "mediated minds are developed out of the social activity that is embedded in the cultural values of particular communities" (Ellis, 2012, p. 524). This means that children's and adults' thinking and development are directed by their relationships and the culture and contexts in which they find themselves (Chirkov, 2020). This is in harmony with a bioecological perspective on the child in context which, rejecting the idea of the 'universal' child, emphasises diversity and individual differences even within cultures through the concept of a web of development with interacting and multidirectional contextual influences. Recognition of this fact is important in ethical terms because when early childhood educators insist on viewing all children and parents as the same or similar and educational interventions are designed based on this flawed perception, we run the risk of inadvertently reproducing the very inequalities we aim to address.

## *Self-regulation and internalisation: the interaction between 'person' and 'context'*

According to sociocultural theory, as the child develops and becomes more proficient, she begins to depend less on adults for direction and more on internal 'self-regulation'. Vygotsky drew on findings from physiology to show how external experiences can become internal to the person, illustrating how collective activity in the zone of proximal development can be then internalised (Eun, 2019). These sociocultural concepts of internalisation and self-regulation can be readily accommodated and explained within a bioecological framework. Internalisation arises when experience in context becomes incorporated into the person characteristics of the child and so influences the direction of future development.

Like the bioecological model, sociocultural theory envisions the child as an active agent in her world, both influenced by and influencing the environment, or context, in which she is living (Eun, 2019). As we have seen, a child's dispositions may be generative, inviting positive interactions with other people, or disruptive, potentially leading to negative interactions with others. These positive or negative interactions then impact, through the power of proximal processes, on the direction that the child's development will take. This is significant since most research on child development treats personal characteristics as developmental outcomes rather than recognising that they are both outcomes and producers of development. More simply, Bronfenbrenner shows how a child's characteristics prompt certain reactions from others and those reactions then impact the future development of the child's characteristics, which, in turn, prompt further reactions, and so on. This transformative dynamic process is illustrated in the vignette involving Tania.

> Tania is three years old and attends Aileen's community-based preschool three mornings a week. Tania is bright and full of energy, and she loves to take control of her own activities. She dislikes being told what to do by adults, and when she feels her autonomy being challenged, she reacts badly, sometimes shouting and becoming quite stubborn. Aileen knows Tania well, and the two have developed a warm way of working together that meets both of their needs. When it is time for free play to end and for children to get ready for lunch, Aileen gives Tania the job of setting out the plates for everyone because she responds well to the responsibility. As a result, she usually agrees to end her play at the appropriate time, even when she is enjoying herself.
>
> On Monday, Aileen is out sick, and Christine is working with Tania. When the time comes for free play to end, Christine asks Tania to put away the doll she is playing with. Tania is enjoying herself and refuses. Christine tells Tania that she must do what she is told as it is time for lunch. Tania sits on the floor holding the doll tightly and refuses to move. Christine raises her voice slightly, warning Tania to comply. Tania throws the doll on the floor and marches over to where the plates are kept. Christine, unaware of Tania's usual job, tells her to come immediately to the lunch corner and sit down. Tania picks up the plates and in temper throws them on the ground, shouting that it's not fair. Christine removes Tania to calm down.
>
> *Source: author experience in practice*

In this example, we see how an active child with her own dispositions (in this case a *disruptive* tendency towards stubbornness and temper) provokes two very different reactions from two different educators, leading to two different outcomes. Bronfenbrenner shows how such interactions over time can influence the dispositions developed by children. The bioecological model predicts that if Tania regularly experiences calm, supportive interactions, like those with Aileen, she will learn to manage her emotions more appropriately over time. In sociocultural terms, she will learn self-regulation. Alternatively, if Tania regularly experiences interactions based on conflict, such as those with Christine, she is likely to become more prone to temper and stubborn responses. This is a good illustration of the concept of internalisation: how personal characteristics both shape and are shaped by experiences in context. These personal characteristics are described by Bronfenbrenner and Morris (2006) as 'dispositions', 'resources' and 'demand characteristics'.

## Dispositions, resources and demand characteristics

As we learned in Chapter 2, Bronfenbrenner identified three key characteristics of the developing child, which contribute to her engagement with others and her

**50** Understanding development in context

environment. Dispositions can be either positive (generative) or negative (disruptive; Bronfenbrenner, 1995). Generative dispositions involve curiosity, the tendency to initiate and engage in activity and readiness to defer gratification in pursuit of long-term goals. Disruptive dispositions, on the other hand, include impulsiveness, explosiveness or distractibility and apathy, inattentiveness, unresponsiveness or a general tendency to withdraw from activity (Bronfenbrenner & Morris, 1998, p. 1009). Positive resources relate to skills, knowledge and experience and enhance the trajectory of development. Alternatively, a child may have limited resources through their genetic endowment, low birth weight or severe illness, and this can compromise their development. Demand characteristics are reflected in the difference between people in the way they attract attention, and they relate to characteristics that might elicit a particular response such as gender, age or skin colour.

The important thing about these characteristics is that they "first appear as one of the components of the (bioecological) model and therefore as an influence on development" (Rosa & Tudge, 2013, p. 253) while, at the same time, they can be seen to be a developmental outcome as a consequence of interactive experiences. These concepts have been interrogated by authors including Bourdieu and Passeron (1977), Brooker (2015), Carr and Claxton (2002) and Katz (1988, 1993). Next, we incorporate these insights into a bioecological framework in order to elucidate the concepts.

## *Dispositions*

Early writing on the meaning of 'dispositions' fell within the traditional nature–nurture debate. Katz (1993) highlights the definition of dispositions in *A Comprehensive Dictionary of Psychological and Psychoanalytical Terms* as "the sum of all innate tendencies or propensities" (English & English, 1958, p. 158) with the implication that dispositions are solely internal to the person, little influenced by external contexts. Conversely, Carr and Claxton (2002) note the work of Lave and Wenger (1991) who argue that learning and behaviour are so situation-specific that there is no such thing as dispositions, or traits and inclinations that are stable across contexts. However, through the lens of a bioecological perspective, neither position on dispositions seems quite right. While theories of 'personality', represented by the English and English (1958) definition, overlook the effects of internalisation of experience, it seems that such polarised sociocultural thinking as that of Lave and Wenger (1991) neglects the power of the mesosystem and how individuals 'drag' their experiences with them from setting to setting (Slesnick, Prestopnik, Meyers, & Glassman, 2007).

Instead, a bioecological perspective views the development of dispositions dynamically through the power of *process*. A child's dispositions influence the way she experiences the world and so acts in it, in turn influencing the way the world responds, in turn influencing the development of further dispositions, and so on. Dispositions are seen as being operative from early infancy onward, evolving over the life course and being manifest even in old age. Experiences in early childhood are considered particularly powerful, and this has relevance for the *time* element of the model also. Dispositions are not just seen as a result of biological inheritance but, rather, reflect the interaction between innate traits and the contexts in which development occurs. The individual acts on the environment and, in turn, 'embodies' the micro and macro environment around them so that experiences and *context* become part of the *person*. This can happen at the individual level and at the level of a broader culture as sociocultural theory has shown us. Specific cultures develop individual ways "of standing, speaking, walking, and thereby of feeling and thinking" (Bourdieu, 1990, p. 70). Thus, the child develops knowledge and skills required for effective proximal processes *in a specific context* which may dictate how well a child functions in certain settings. Bronfenbrenner refers to such knowledge and skills as 'resource characteristics'.

## Resources

Some writers using a bioecological approach tend to see resource characteristics as applicable across contexts, but in keeping with the emphasis in this chapter (and this book) on the importance of context and culture, it is important to note that the knowledge and skills needed to function well in one society or context may differ from those required in another (O'Toole & Hayes, 2020; O'Toole, Kiely, McGillicuddy, O'Brien, & O'Keeffe, 2019). Remembering the importance of a sociocultural understanding of childhood experiences, we must recognise that the resources required for particular contexts may vary and are often based on what Bourdieu calls a 'cultural arbitrary' (Bourdieu & Passeron, 1977). As Brooker explains, "[c]ulture is itself arbitrary: there is no objectively right or wrong way to bring up children" (2015, p. 43). Sensitivity to cultural values and beliefs can be incorporated in early years practice, in curriculum frameworks and in national standards.

Language is a good example of how the resources required to function well may differ across contexts. A child attending an early years setting in Ireland, for instance, would benefit from possessing the resource of speaking English, but this would not be an important resource for a child attending a setting in China. Even within specific languages (like English or Chinese), there are many differences based on context, and this is particularly relevant to social class. Children with middle-class accents and linguistic constructions may 'fit in' more easily in middle-class educational settings. However, Pinker (1994) found more internal grammatical consistency in Black Vernacular English in the United States than in the language patterns of academics presenting at conferences. This shows that the style of language used by particular groups can be seen in error as somehow inferior due to prejudice or because outsiders do not always understand its complexities, and this illustrates the importance of understanding experiences in context. In other words, rather than possessing any inherent value itself, the resource characteristic of speaking 'proper' English only becomes more useful based on what is valued in certain contexts.

## Demand characteristics

Tudge, Mokrova, Hatfield, and Karnik's (2009) list of 'demand characteristics' (those which invite or discourage reactions from the social environment of a kind that can foster or disrupt the operation of proximal processes) include age,

**52** Understanding development in context

gender, skin colour and physical appearance – all characteristics that are subject to the application of prejudiced beliefs and actions in particular circumstances. This is particularly important for early childhood educators to understand considering extensive evidence that educators often misunderstand and inappropriately punish children from cultural and racial backgrounds that differ from their own (Lindsay & Hart, 2017). Since culture is in many ways invisible when we are immersed within it, educators' engagement with children is often guided by biases and assumptions of which the educator may or may not be conscious. Many beliefs and practices relevant to children's development vary across cultures – norms of behaviour, images of children and their competence and responsibilities, beliefs regarding the appropriateness of various forms of discipline, and ideas on how relationships between adults and children should be conducted. When there are differences between home and school in terms of such beliefs and practices, there can be potential for a child to be seen as misbehaving when her behaviour would be acceptable in a different context (O'Toole & Hayes, 2020).

In many countries, educators come predominantly from the dominant culture, and minority cultures are under-represented in the teaching staff. This is important to consider because children from minority cultures are often disadvantaged in such circumstances by negative stereotypes held by educators, even when educators express egalitarian and multicultural beliefs (Glock, 2016; Hachfeld, Schroeder, Anders, Hahn, & Kunter, 2012). Through a bioecological lens, in societies characterised by structural racism, it is not surprising that educational settings are not immune from racism, since features of macrosystems influence features of microsystems. It is important for early childhood educators wishing to ensure fair treatment of all young children and their families to be mindful of factors such as race, culture and socio-economic background. For example, the dispositions of a working-class child might be inappropriately seen as a 'disruptive demand characteristic' in the largely middle-class educational system. Tudge et al. (2009) describe 'resource characteristics' as those not immediately apparent but sometimes induced, not always accurately, from demand characteristics; for example, educators may assume inaccurately that the level of 'intelligence' or 'motivation' possessed by working-class children is lower than that of middle-class children. The occurrence of such unfounded assumptions by educators, based on social class, is well established. As Bronfenbrenner and Morris explain, personal characteristics

> [p]lace that person in a particular environmental niche that defines his or her position and role in society. Recognition of that ambiguity moves us to change in focus from developmentally relevant characteristics of the person to their counterparts in the structure and substance of environmental contexts as they affect developmental processes and outcomes.
>
> *(2006, p. 814)*

## Temperament

Also relevant is Thomas and Chess's (1977) concept of 'temperament'. *Temperament* refers to the child's tendency to respond to the environment in characteristic ways, regarding energy levels, persistence and the extent to which she gets upset if she cannot reach her objectives. They distinguish between 'easy', 'difficult' and 'slow-to-warm-up' babies (Thomas & Chess, 1956), similar to Bronfenbrenner's notion of generative or disruptive dispositions. Temperament may be seen as an innate part of the *person*, but its expression and its impact are portrayed as intricately bound up with the *context* in which that person is developing:

> Temperament is always expressed as a response to an external stimulus, opportunity, expectation, or demand. It can be considered a dynamic factor that mediates and shapes the influence of the environment on the individual's psychological structure. Therefore, a similar stimulus may evoke different behaviour in different individuals, and different environmental stimuli may evoke similar behavior. It follows that temperament should be primarily rated in terms of the social context within which it occurs.
>
> *(Coldsmith et al., 1987, p. 509)*

The view of person characteristics impacting on and impacted by environmental factors (context) is particularly congruent with the concept of 'goodness of fit' (Chess & Thomas, 1991). This indicates that a child born with a 'difficult' temperament can have this aspect of their personality exacerbated through inconsistent, harsh or neglectful interactions with adults or, alternatively, minimised through supportive, calm and responsive contexts, as in the example of Tania in the earlier vignette. Thomas and Chess (1977) found that the development of children's behavioural problems in later life could not be predicted from a knowledge of the child alone or for that matter, of the parent alone, but rather from the goodness of fit – or lack of fit – of the characteristics of both parties. They also established that the nature of the child's temperament right from the moment of birth was a factor. This is a hugely important concept for educators wishing to understand the dynamics of children in educational settings (Hayes, 2013; O'Toole & Hayes, 2020). The reality is that a wide variety of factors, including the temperamental nature of the child, can influence development. McLowry and Collins (2012) observes that when goodness of fit is examined through the lens of self-regulation the focus of attention shifts from the adult–child dyad to situations in which a child's temperamental tendencies have to accommodate environmental demands. This fits with a bioecological interpretation of the interaction between person and context.

## Learning dispositions

The concept of 'dispositions' has also evolved in the early childhood education literature. Carr and Claxton (2002) focus largely on 'learning dispositions', as opposed

**54**  Understanding development in context

to the wider range of dispositions explored by Bronfenbrenner, but their work is interesting and relevant, not least because they devote considerable analysis to the question of whether dispositions are innate or context-specific. Carr and Claxton (2002), in line with bioecological theory, indicate that dispositions can be transferred across domains but, at the same time, are not 'fixed'. They maintain that it is possible to support the development of positive learning dispositions within early years settings, particularly through the use of innovative methods of reflection and assessment, and that this is more important than teaching children specific knowledge or skills. They state that "[t]he manifestation of learning dispositions will be very closely linked to the learning opportunities, affordances and constraints available in each new setting" (Carr & Claxton, 2002, p. 12), highlighting the idea that learning and development happen in context. The notion of learning dispositions has extended conceptions of learning in early childhood education to incorporate dimensions such as habits of mind and patterns of behaviour (Zhao, Zhang, & Guo, 2020).

---

### REFLECTION

Think of an interaction you have had with a child that you would characterise as negative. What 'dispositions' in the child provoked a reaction from you? How might you have responded differently so as to create 'goodness of fit' in the environment and promote the development of 'generative dispositions' while minimising the development of 'disruptive dispositions' in the child?

---

## Active agents within a limited range of choices

The bioecological model foregrounds the influence of diversity and the futility of expecting all children, parents and educators to behave in the same way regardless of the individual characteristics they bring to a situation. The definition of dispositions provided by Perkins leads to intriguing questions about how much or how little we humans are in control of the way we behave and the decisions we make in life – "[d]ispositions are the proclivities that lead us in one direction rather than another, within the freedom of action that we have" (1995, p. 275). Bronfenbrenner shows that the way a child's experiences become a part of her *person* characteristics may dictate the future choices made. However, this is not to support determinism as is often charged. Rather, his theories stem from a joint freedom–determinism base, seeing the child as simultaneously in control of her behaviour and constrained by the circumstances in which she finds herself. Such a dynamic view of learning and development that is in flux, and that focuses on the child's potential rather than becoming fixated with achievement in isolation at one particular moment in time is also evident in sociocultural theory (Gauvain, 2020).

## REFLECTION

How 'free' are we as human beings? Do we make our own decisions and behave the way we do through free will? Or do the traits we inherit and the experiences we have combine to lead us in certain directions that are largely out of our control? This is known as a debate between 'freedom' and 'determinism'. Discuss with colleagues where you stand in this debate.

Even very talented children (and adults) find it difficult to achieve if they are not given the opportunity to do so through access to resources such as supportive relationships and positive learning environments. In bioecological terms, while the child is an active agent in her world, options are filtered and narrowed by particular contextual influences. This resonates with Vygotsky's (1978) ideas of the social formation of the mind and modes of thought through the mechanism of culture. In fact, it is consistent with sociocultural theory generally, particularly activity theory and the idea of 'motives': "[s]ubjects are constrained by the components of an activity system but they also possess agency and thus are able to reconstitute it to suit their own motives" (Ellis, 2012, p. 536).

This also applies to processes of educational change because individuals make choices in educational settings within the institutional norms of these settings and in the context of their own personal and cultural experiences (Downes, 2014; O'Toole et al., 2020). Therefore, while later versions of the bioecological model have somewhat moved away from a sole emphasis on *context* towards a stronger emphasis on *process* (Bronfenbrenner & Morris, 2006), there is no denying the importance and influence of context in a 'systems' approach to understanding human development. Contexts for development are still key – even in more up-to-date iterations of the bioecological paradigm – to how development happens within a relational process. Particularly, it must be remembered that young children may traverse many different contexts at any point in time, and their developmental trajectory may in part depend on the 'linkages' created between these different microsystems (O'Toole et al., 2020). This is a central consideration in Bronfenbrenner's concept of the mesosystem, explored in depth in Chapters 5 and 10.

### Context and family

Another key issue of diversity for consideration within a bioecological framework is family structure. According to Berk, "the family is the child's first and longest-lasting context for development" (2009, p. 563). The family has a strong influence on children, and most educators recognise parents as the child's primary and most important educator. Families represent the primary setting in which most children's lives are shaped and influenced. Within family contexts, children

**56** Understanding development in context

gradually internalise social standards and expectations, which facilitates, in turn, better self-regulation skills and responsibility. Central to this process are the parental behaviours and discipline responses that children experience within family settings. However, the concept of 'family' is open to a diversity of interpretations, and different parenting arrangements bring different challenges and benefits to the social and emotional development of children (Halpenny, Nixon, & Watson, 2010).

It is the relationships or process within family contexts that actually matter rather than who is a part of the family *per se*. The presence of another adult who gives support and love to the primary caregiver is supportive of positive functioning within families (Bronfenbrenner & Morris, 2006), and that 'other adult' could be a same-sex partner, a grandparent or some other close individual, not exclusively the biological parent of the child. Previously, much of what we knew about the effects of family transition (such as divorce) on children focused solely on child outcomes regarding family type or structure and emphasising parental absence. However, some research has focused on the profound importance of the quality of family processes or interactions prior to, during and following family transitions (Halpenny, Greene, & Hogan, 2008). Consistent with bioecological thought, this approach draws our attention to the importance of family interactions and how these interactions may evolve and progress over time. Proximal processes and positivity of relationships within families may be more influential on outcomes for children than whether families are structured in traditional ways.

This is important to remember with regard to the increasing culture of testing for 'school readiness' using checklists that impose a cultural arbitrary on what constitutes 'good' parents and home learning environments, disregarding diversity in families (Brooker, 2015). Early childhood educators must be cognisant of and sensitive to the needs of different types of families and different family contexts.

---

## REFLECTION

Consider this quote from Adrienne Rich:

> When those who have the power to name and socially construct reality choose not to see or hear you, whether you are dark-skinned, old, disabled, female, or speak with a different accent or dialect than theirs, when someone with the authority of a teacher, say, describes the world and you are not in it, there is a moment of disequilibrium, as if you looked into a mirror and saw nothing.

*(1986, p. 199)*

> Would all children in your early childhood setting see themselves in the 'mirror' you provide? And their parents? What assumptions do you bring to your interactions with them that are based on your own cultural, linguistic, social, class-based and gendered 'normality'? Could these assumptions create challenges for the children and parents? What practical measures could you take to minimise such challenges and instead create 'linkages' between the contexts of home and early childhood setting?

Differences based on factors such as socio-economic status, race, language, culture and religion can contribute to disjuncture in the mesosystem and can be implicated in difficulties for children, parents and early childhood educators alike. However, contextual factors can worsen or ameliorate these potential difficulties; thus, the importance of early childhood educators contemplating practice through a bioecological lens. This understanding highlights the fact that 'children' and 'parents' are not homogeneous groupings and that processes in early years settings may be extensively impacted by both person-based and context-based factors. The Diversity, Equality and Inclusion Charter and Guidelines for Early Childhood Care and Education (DCYA, 2016) provide practical ideas for the creation of contexts that fit every person.

## Implications for practice

In creating nurturing contexts in early childhood education, most important in Bronfenbrenner's eyes are the proximal processes that take place within them:

> In order to develop – intellectually, emotionally, socially, and morally – a child requires, for all of them, the same thing: participation in progressively more complex reciprocal activity, on a regular basis over extended periods of time with one or more other persons with whom the child develops a strong, mutual, irrational attachment, and who are committed to that child's development, preferably for life.
>
> *(Bronfenbrenner, 1989b, p. 5)*

Bronfenbrenner and Morris (2006) stress the importance of strong proximal processes in terms of providing a buffer in less ideal contexts. Bronfenbrenner draws on the work of Rutter et al. (1998) to show that the impact of protective forces, such as strong, supportive proximal processes with an important adult, on the development of resilience in children is even greater in 'at-risk' contexts. Therefore, while the latest version of the bioecological model does still acknowledge the importance of the micro-, meso-, exo- and macrosystems within which a child develops, such context factors are emphasised less than in earlier models, and now the relationship (process) is foregrounded. This is consistent with the maturation of

**58** Understanding development in context

developmental psychology generally and the move away from simple linear models of causality towards an understanding of the interaction of risk and protective factors (Downes, 2014).

## Key concepts for early years practice

1  *Children's development is inextricably linked with the context in which it occurs.*
2  *Children's dispositions (person) and their experiences (contexts) are reciprocal.* Children's dispositions influence how they experience the world, but children's experiences can be 'internalised', in turn influencing the development of those traits. This influences how children act in future contexts, impacting in turn developmental outcomes, and so on. In this way, children develop through their relationships.
3  *Diversity is a key feature of what it means to be human.* It is senseless to expect standardisation of outcomes for children or families, socially, emotionally, behaviourally or educationally. It is important for early years practitioners to create respectful 'linkages' between the various contexts experienced by children to avoid a sense of 'culture shock' in the mesosystem.
4  *The course of human development is neither completely free nor completely predetermined.* Children are active agents within a narrow range of choices that are defined by complex interactions between personal characteristics and the contexts and relationships in which they find themselves.
5  Less-than-optimal contexts may be overcome through the power of positive relationships, and contexts that on the surface appear to be supportive of development in fact lose their power in the absence of supportive relationships. *Resilience is best understood as being reliant on a complex interaction of protective and risk factors with the personal characteristics of the child.*

# 5

# A BIOECOLOGICAL PERSPECTIVE ON TRANSITIONS

## Introduction

In his lifetime, Bronfenbrenner called for the bioecological model to be confronted with real-world data to test its predictions and key principles (Bronfenbrenner and Morris, 2006); he wanted to know whether events in the real world could be predicted and explained by the bioecological model. This chapter draws on research to identify and animate key elements of the model impacting early educational pedagogy and practice while enhancing understanding of why the model is so powerful and how it can be realised in practice. Specifically, the chapter applies a bioecological lens to research on transitions in early childhood. There is increasing recognition of the importance of transitions for children and their families (O'Toole et al., 2014, 2020), and much work on transitions is framed within a bioecological approach. In fact, Brooker refers to Bronfenbrenner as "the 'father' of transitions studies" (2008, p. 5).

## Thinking about transitions

Young children make many transitions on a daily basis – for example, going from home to crèche, transitioning from playing with friends to eating a meal, moving from engaging in family life to going to bed. Graham (2012) distinguishes between vertical or major transitions (bigger more visible events involving transitions between educational settings, e.g. transition from preschool to primary), horizontal or minor transitions (happening in the daily or weekly routine of the child, e.g. home to day care each morning) and mini transitions (smaller, less visible transitions within settings throughout the day, e.g. transitioning from naptime to active play). Children may be somewhat vulnerable at these times, and even the most secure and confident children can experience challenges during major transitions like the transition from ECEC to primary school. In fact, this transition has been identified as one

DOI: 10.4324/9781003247760-5

**60** A bioecological perspective on transitions

of the most significant and challenging in the first years of their lives (González-Moreira, Ferreira and Vidal, 2021; Yamauchi and Sousa, 2020). In keeping with the theoretical framework provided by bioecological theory, the exploration of transitions in this chapter uses the PPCT (Process–Person–Context–Time) structure and identifies important *process* factors (like children's friendships), *person* factors (like language, gender, cultural background and socio-economic background) and *context* factors (like support structures within microsystems and across mesosystems), acknowledging that establishing smooth transitions can take *time*. Key principles and predictions of the bioecological model are in turn elucidated and confirmed by the findings of research on transitions.

However, an important concept of the bioecological model is that development is not linear and passive. On the contrary, factors influencing both developmental outcomes and experience of the educational journey are complex, intertwined and mutually influential. It is important to remember that "the principal main effects are likely to be interactions" (Bronfenbrenner, 1979, p. 38). Many of the factors explored here regarding transitions are indeed interactive and work together in nonlinear and unpredictable ways. Attempting to stay true to a PPCT framework leaves us with the near-impossible task of separating out key factors in order to study them while, at the same time, analysing and presenting them in all their complex interdependence.

## Transitions – crucial 'time's in early childhood

Experiences of transition can be crucial to outcomes socially, emotionally and educationally. Transition can bring discontinuity and may cause social and emotional turmoil as well as discontinuities in learning or even regression in development. Equally, transitions can bring many developmental, academic and social opportunities for children, and positive experiences of transition tend to position children well for ongoing positivity of educational and developmental outcomes (González-Moreira et al., 2021; O'Toole et al., 2014). Therefore, the extent to which children experience smooth transitions may have long-term implications for their future experiences and for later functioning, emphasising the importance of events in the chronosystem. For example, when children have positive experiences in transitioning from early years settings to primary school, they are likely to regard school as an important place and to have positive expectations of their ability to learn and succeed. Such positive early experiences can be influential in interrupting cycles of social and economic disadvantage and can contribute to resilience among young people. Negative or traumatic experiences of transition can have significant impacts on future self-efficacy beliefs, motivation and academic achievement (Educational Transitions and Change Research Group, 2011).

In spite of the opportunities presented by transitions, times of rapid change can be stressful for young children. Think about how you felt during transitions in your own life, perhaps when starting a new job or on your first day in college. You may have been excited about the prospects ahead of you, but also nervous about how well you would cope with challenges and whether you would make friends. Research highlights the turbulent feelings associated with transitions, with children often feeling both nervous and excited ahead of major transitions, a mix of optimism and anxiety, perceptions of a challenge and a threat (O'Toole, 2016). For example, children starting primary school may both celebrate 'getting big' and worry about what that might mean. These feelings are illustrated in the vignette involving Joshua.

---

Joshua is starting 'big school' next week. Two weeks ago he went to a shop and tried on a new uniform. His mother keeps saying that this means he is now 'big', and even though that is exciting, she sometimes looks like she is crying when she says it! Joshua wonders if there is something sad about being big. It makes him feel a bit worried. The uniform is scratchy. His dad says that he will learn lots of new things and make lots of new friends in big school. Joshua is happy about that. On the other hand, he has a lot of friends in preschool. Maybe he will just stay there instead.

*Source: adapted from O'Toole (2016)*

---

Experiences of major transition can be very positive, and children value the new educational experiences on offer as well as the extended opportunities to make new friends. However, a significant minority of children experience difficulties in vertical and horizontal transitions like during the settling in period for a new Early Childhood Education and Care ECEC setting, moving to a new room in the setting or moving on from preschool to primary school. In thinking about babies, toddlers and young children coming to ECEC for the first time, Goldshmied and Jackson state:

> We can never remind ourselves too often that a child, particularly a very young and almost totally dependent one, is the only person in the nursery who cannot understand why he is there. He can only explain it as abandonment, and unless he is helped in a positive and affectionate way, this will mean levels of anxiety greater than he can tolerate.
>
> *(1994, cited in McDermott, 2016)*

Equally, when moving on to primary school, international research (Margetts and Kienig, 2013; Ring et al., 2015; Tatalović Vorkapić and LoCasale-Crouch, 2021) identifies the stress of adjusting to a new setting that tends to be physically much larger, with strange buildings and classrooms, as well as the challenge of a new teacher, new academic and behavioural expectations and a new, more diverse group of classmates. To use bioecological terminology, vertical and horizontal transitions may lead to disjuncture in the mesosystem of the child as he moves from one familiar microsystem to a new, unknown microsystem.

**62** A bioecological perspective on transitions

Similarly, on a day-to-day basis, minor transitions between activities in early childhood settings, of course, offer a chance to experience new things, and babies, toddlers and young children need a variety of experiences both indoor and outdoor to support optimal learning and development. However, when a child is immersed in an activity and needs to make a change, he can experience stress and anxiety, and sometimes needs support to regulate his emotions and behaviours (O'Toole and Hayes, 2020). Consider how many transitions occur in a typical day in your setting. Is there consistency in how transitions are managed? How much time is spent in transition? Educators need to reflect on which transitions are a necessary, maybe even supportive, element of the day in ECEC, and which transitions may be causing unnecessary distress to children and adults alike, and so could be eliminated. For example, Early-O'Brien (2018) recommends 'seamless snack-time', using a warm, inviting, accessible snack space that children can go to when they feel hungry, rather than having to wait for a specific snack-time that may not suit their appetite or their play. Ideally, an ECEC setting should balance a predictable routine to support security for babies, toddlers and young children with the flexibility to respond to their cues when they need time to process and adjust to a change in activity (Early Childhood Ireland, 2016). This requires the development of attuned, responsive relationships as emphasised by the bioecological model.

## Proximal processes and the importance of interactions and relationships for transitions

Research on transitions has supported a bioecological interpretation identifying the central role of relationships as well as opportunities for those involved to build and maintain these relationships (McDermott, 2016; O'Toole, 2016). Bronfenbrenner identifies the potential power of *process* to overcome difficulties caused by *context*, and the literature on transitions shows the importance of interactions and relationships in this regard. Nurturing, trusting relationships are crucial for the development of smooth transitions, be they vertical, horizontal or mini transitions.

### *Children's interactions and relationships with educators*

Love and nurture are hard-wired into the brains of children, and their 'social brains' mean that they look to adults to help them figure out whether they are safe in a new setting or experience. While these skills develop further as children get older, some studies show infants extracting emotional information from interactions with adults from as young as three months (Fawcett and Liszkowski, 2015). According to Lawrence (2019), babies and small children cannot regulate emotion alone, they need adult help as cortical connections are evolving. This is known as emotional co-regulation (Lawrence, 2019) and is hugely important to understand in the context of transitions.

As noted in Chapter 3, attachment theory is identified by Bronfenbrenner and Morris (2006) as providing key insights into such processes between children and

A bioecological perspective on transitions **63**

adults, and it may have particular relevance for transitions. O'Toole and Hayes (2020) note that when babies are hungry, in pain, fatigued, or feeling threat or anxiety, they cry. Bowlby saw this as an innate instinct that babies have to call their caregiver to them and ensure the caregiver is close by to meet their needs. This instinct may have developed as an evolutionary response to encourage adults to take care of their young, dependent offspring. When the distance between the baby and the caregiver is too great, the baby experiences separation anxiety and the evolutionary urge to close the distance between himself and the caregiver is engaged, leading to a 'separation protest' from the baby (Riley, 2011). This gives us the beginnings of an attachment-based understanding of children's behaviour that may be interpreted as negative – from our earliest days we understand that when feeling anxious, protest behaviours like crying, kicking and making noise are likely to bring a response from an adult who will hopefully help us manage that anxiety (Riley, 2011). Later in childhood and in life, however, when a child is feeling anxious, like during transitions, an evolutionary response may kick in, whereby he acts out in an attempt to draw the adult to him, but this is interpreted as misbehaviour and has the opposite effect, or the attention that it does draw is negative. When children experience stress, as is perhaps inherent in any move between microsystems, or even in a disruption of activity within a microsystem, separation anxiety may be reignited, even in older children. This can explain why educators often find times of transition to be a flashpoint for children's behaviour (O'Toole and Hayes, 2020). González-Moreira et al. (2021) note that the stress of change during transitions can manifest itself in maladaptive behaviour by children. Think about how Bronfenbrenner's concept of process and theories about attachment would explain what is happening in this vignette.

---

Shira has been attending a crèche since she was 18 months old, and when she was three, she transitioned to the preschool group within that setting. When younger, she would cry every morning when her mother dropped her off, but as she got older, she no longer cried each morning. She is now five years old, and it is her first day at primary school. When her mother tries to leave, Shira holds on to her, cries and kicks, just like she did when she was a baby.

*Source: author observation*

---

In this example, the transition has provoked separation anxiety in Shira, and she seeks to maintain proximity to her primary attachment figure, her mother. Children may 'externalise' their anxiety during transitions, showing aggressive or angry behaviours; they may 'internalise' anxiety, becoming withdrawn or upset; or they can sometimes 'freeze' (O'Toole and Hayes, 2020). An individual child's response to stress linked to transition may depend on their attachment style, with a securely attached child more likely to "approach the world with confidence, and when faced with potentially alarming situations [more] likely to tackle them effectively or seek help in doing so" (Bowlby, 1973, p. 208). On the other hand, a child whose

**64** A bioecological perspective on transitions

emotional needs have not been met comes to view the world as "comfortless and unpredictable; and they respond either by shrinking from it or doing battle with it" (Bowlby, 1973, p. 208)

As noted in Chapter 3, early childhood educators play a hugely important role as 'secondary attachment figures' (Bowlby, 2007) in the lives of young children, and this can be particularly influential in supporting smooth transitions. According to Lawrence (2019), babies' three biggest fears are strangers, loud noises and being separated from their primary caregivers, and in the case of babies in day-care, these are experiences that must be endured every morning. A secure secondary attachment with an educator can help mitigate these fears, and so many settings employ a key-person approach. This means that each child is allocated a specific educator to be his primary carer to "support the child and their family when they are first integrating into the setting and … continue to be the key person for routine care and for moments of emotional intimacy, building up a secure attachment with the child" (McDermott, 2016, p. 2).

A central aspect of the relationship between children and educators is the understanding of behaviour, and changing disciplinary structures and behavioural expectations of children during vertical and horizontal transition may lead to difficulties (O'Toole et al., 2014; O'Toole and Hayes, 2020). There are varying disciplinary structures and styles in different educational settings, and behavioural expectations often vary within settings. The approaches that educators take in terms of behaviour can significantly impact on children's experiences of transition. For example, if a child encounters very different behavioural expectations from early childhood educators and primary school teachers, it can be challenging for the child to adapt.

Mirroring the application of Baumrind's ideas to parenting styles at times of educational transition, approaches to behaviour in educational settings can be related to concepts of 'authoritarian', 'authoritative' and 'permissive' styles (Gregory et al., 2010). Authoritarian practices may be highly ineffective for children at times of transition, and excessive strictness can elicit antagonistic responses from them. Such styles are also linked to decreased academic performance (Gregory et al., 2010). This makes sense when we consider the influence of brain structure on learning and emotion: the same structure in the brain (the limbic system) controls both emotion and the transfer of information from short-term to long-term memory. If children are frightened by the adults educating them, the 'fight–flight–freeze' instinct may be engaged, and the processing power of the limbic system is engaged with that, shutting down higher-level cognition and limiting the child's ability to learn.

Unfortunately, however, there seems to be a move in many countries towards more authoritarian methods as children progress through the educational system. There may be massive shifts in behavioural expectations for children once they enter primary school; indeed, the Irish National Teachers Organisation INTO characterises these expectations as "overwhelming demands" (2009, p. 45) on small children. They maintain that "the most experienced stakeholders in the transition process (the adults) [expect] the least experienced stakeholders (the children) to make all the changes" (2009, p. 45).

The effects of educator–child relationships may be particularly powerful in times of transition and positive educator–child relationships are particularly crucial when children experience factors exposing them to risks of difficulty at this time. Those who are vulnerable in transition tend to benefit most from supportive relationships with educators (Burchinal et al., 2002), and this confirms Bronfenbrenner's prediction of the increased impact of proximal processes in less optimal contexts (Bronfenbrenner and Morris, 2006).

## Children's friendships

Of course, the interactions and relationships experienced by children in early education are not just with adults, and children's friendships are important buffers for potential difficulties during transitions; for example, if children go to primary school with others that they know from preschool, linkages in this mesosystem are strengthened through maintenance of common elements across settings. Unfortunately, when preschool friends transition to the same primary school, teachers often separate them, aiming to encourage independence and the development of new friendships (O'Toole, 2016). Early childhood educators informed by a bioecological perspective are empowered to advocate for young children through their awareness of the importance of maintaining key relationships across transitions. Transition to school is a social process, and young children must engage in complex social interactions at school. Relationships with their peers may provide protection to children during transition, and it is often through friendships, particularly with older children and siblings, that children develop their understanding of school culture and norms. Peer mentoring is often presented as an effective intervention to ease the processes of transition (Dockett and Perry, 2013), and playful engagement with peers during mini-transitions may also support positive experiences. Of course, the bioecological model recognises children as active agents in their proximal processes, and children's *person* characteristics may influence the dynamic of the relationships they experience during transitions and beyond.

## Person factors impacting on experiences of transition

As explored in Chapter 4, the bioecological model emphasises diversity and the inappropriateness of expecting all children or adults to behave in the same way. This vignette involving Ava and Orla may help to explore these ideas.

Ava and Orla have attended preschool together for the past two years. Now they are five and starting 'big school'. Orla's parents both grew up in the area, and her mother attended the primary school she will be going to. Her family speak English and a little Irish, and both her parents have experienced the Irish educational system to the degree level. Ava's family are from Poland and have lived in Ireland for three years. Her parents' English is improving rapidly, but they still struggle sometimes to understand what Irish people are saying. In Poland, early education is quite different, and Ava's parents are not quite sure what to expect of primary school. They are quite anxious, and Ava is beginning to think that maybe 'big school' is something to be afraid of.

*Source: adapted from O'Toole (2016)*

Ava and Orla are both five years old, both are girls, and both have benefitted from the same preschool provision. However, their experiences of starting school may be quite different. Orla's parents understand what is expected since they have been through the Irish educational system themselves. Their communication with the school is facilitated by the fact that English is their first language. Therefore, they are less nervous than Ava's parents and are able to transmit positive messages about starting school to Orla. They both grew up in the neighbourhood and so are likely to have a network of support, friendships and family available to them. Ava's parents have no experience of the Irish educational system and only an emerging knowledge of supports available in the area. Their communication with the school is hampered by a language barrier, and while Ava herself is used to communicating in English in preschool, Polish is still her first language. Ava is becoming aware of how anxious her parents feel, and she is beginning to feel quite anxious herself. Clearly there are risk factors that make Ava somewhat more vulnerable during transition than Orla, and while, of course, Ava may have a wonderful experience of starting school, her early educators need to be aware of her needs. These are complex issues and should not be thought of in simple terms. However, as predicted within a bioecological framework depicting the child as an active agent, the literature shows that personal dispositions, skills and characteristics possessed by individual children can have a profound influence on their experiences of transitions.

## REFLECTION

What 'person' factors can you think of that might impact on the experiences that children and families have at times of transition? Write down as many as come to mind and compare your answers with the bullet points that follow.

Children's experiences of and ability to cope with transitions may be influenced by the following:

- Specific skills: Social skills, independence, language and communication skills, and the ability to take responsibility for belongings, wait and take turns, seek help when needed and cope with frustration.

A bioecological perspective on transitions **67**

- 'Self-esteem', 'self-concept' and 'self-efficacy': Children with low self-esteem and self-efficacy beliefs and poor self-concept may be vulnerable during transitions.
- Behavioural difficulties or special educational needs: Children with behavioural difficulties or special education needs (SEN) sometimes struggle during transitions in the absence of appropriate supports.
- Gender: The literature generally indicates that boys are more vulnerable than girls during some transitions, particularly vertical transitions like the move from preschool to primary.
- Previous experiences: Children's 'funds of knowledge' can be employed at times of transition. For example, children may transition to primary school more easily when they have attended a *good-quality preschool* as they may have developed social skills such as sharing and taking turns and previous positive experiences of transitions set them up for positive transitions in the future.
- Language, culture and religion: Educational settings sometimes represent the dominant culture, and depending on the supports available, where the language, culture or religion of the home differs substantially from that of the school or preschool, children may be vulnerable.
- Socio-economics: Educational systems usually represent middle-class values and culture, and low socio-economic status is associated with less positive transitions for children.
- Family structure: Children with older siblings often find vertical transitions easier as they may have already visited the educational setting, and siblings can also provide informal information and a sense of protection from older children.

However, children's experiences of transition differ based on both the intensity of the change and the intensity of the child's reaction to that change (Tatalović Vorkapić and LoCasale-Crouch, 2021). This illustrates the bioecological conception of person characteristics interacting with contexts over time to produce outcomes, and contextual supports at micro-, meso-, exo- and macro-level play a significant role in creating smooth transitions for children.

## The impact of context on transitions: Micro-, meso-, exo- and macro-systems

Bronfenbrenner's bioecological model demands that educators acknowledge and act on the importance of contextual knowledge, individual characteristics, environmental factors, and processes in relationships while also taking account of macro-level factors and the sociocultural time in which development takes place.

### *Microsystems*

Contextual factors within microsystems can aggravate or ameliorate potential difficulties during transitions. The literature identifies the vital nature of formal structural supports within early childhood settings for babies, toddlers, young children

**68** A bioecological perspective on transitions

and their families during transitions, and highlights a number of contextual considerations that may help or hinder individual children (Dockett and Perry, 2013). On a day-to-day basis, it is important to give children a sense of agency and control during mini-transitions, although approaches like giving advance warning and using visible timers so that children know when to expect a transition, allowing children to self-register their attendance by (for example) adding their photograph to a board, and maintaining a 'work-in-progress' area so that interrupting play to transition to another activity is not so challenging, since children know they can return to it later.

A playful environment can also facilitate smooth transitions, and many educators use playful routines or songs to support mini-transitions like tidy-up time. Consider how early childhood educator Ingrid uses a play episode to support an orderly transition from outdoor to indoor play:

> The children in Ingrid's preschool are playing outside drawing on the ground with chalk. It is time to move indoors, and many of the children are reluctant to do so as they are enjoying the activity, but it is almost time to go home, so Ingrid is aware that unfortunately she cannot allow it to continue for much longer. One of the children, Tom, is drawing circles with the chalk and telling the other children that they are puddles. The other children are jumping up and down in the circles, pretending to splash in the puddles. Taking a piece of chalk, Ingrid says, "Wait until you see my big puddles!" She draws a series of large circles leading towards the preschool door. The children happily "splash in the puddles" all the way into the preschool.
>
> *Source: O'Toole and Hayes (2020, p. 85)*

In this example, some educators might have scolded the children for not coming inside when she wanted them to or used star charts to reward children for formally lining up and coming inside. Instead, Ingrid tapped into children's natural wish to move and play. Turning a desired behaviour into a game is a key tool in an educator's arsenal and very pleasant way for both educators and children to achieve smooth transitions (O'Toole and Hayes, 2020).

When considering horizontal and vertical transitions, the settling-in policy for children entering early childhood settings can have extensive impact on their wellbeing, and a well-planned approach rooted in relationship building over time can be effective, with a 'short-sharp-shock' approach to be avoided at all costs (McDermott, 2016). Other approaches like the use of 'transitional objects' (teddy bears, soothers, blankets and other keepsakes) can help children bring a sense of security from home into the early childhood setting (Figure 5.1). In bioecological terms, the transitional object creates a linkage in the mesosystem as an element from one secure microsystem (home) travels with the child to another potentially less secure microsystem (the early childhood setting), but policies within specific early childhood settings (microsystems) may decide whether children can avail of such supports. Approaches worth considering within early childhood settings to support children in their transition from preschool to primary school include extensive

**FIGURE 5.1** Transitional objects
(Left) Katie picnics with her teddy Stewie who accompanies her to and from day care. (Right) Cillian and his mother use O'Kane's 'hug button' strategy to facilitate smooth transition – when missing each other they can press the hug button to feel a sense of connection

contact with primary schools by preschool children before enrolment, encouraging independence in preschool, discussion about starting primary school, and mentoring systems whereby older, more experienced children support younger children through transition.

Of course, we must engage with these ideas critically. For example, the concept of 'independence' is contested. Brooker (2008) notes that at preschool, independence tends to mean the child choosing his own activities, whereas at the primary level, independence tends to mean the ability to follow instruction and stay on task (a task chosen by adults) without intervention. In some ways, these skills are actually the complete opposite of each other, despite being given the same label of independence, and so it is little wonder that parents, preschool teachers and primary school teachers sometimes disagree on the skills required (Brooker, 2008; O'Kane, 2015). We must emphasise 'ready schools', as well as 'ready children' or 'ready families' (Brooker, 2008; Ring et al., 2015). The concept of the mesosystem in particular is very useful in explaining children's experiences as they move across contexts, and this is explored in detail in Chapter 10 but is worth consideration here regarding transitions specifically.

## Mesosystems

Transitions across settings may offer either opportunities or threats in the mesosystem, depending on various contextual factors. This can apply to movement between informal settings like home and formal settings like schools, or movement between two formal settings, such as preschool and primary school (O'Toole, et al., 2014). Sometimes the links between educational settings and other microsystems are smooth and easily traversed. Individuals can recognise familiar elements from one

**70** A bioecological perspective on transitions

setting to another and use the skills they have gained in one setting when moving to another (O'Toole et al., 2020). According to Bronfenbrenner (1979), facilitative mesosystems are created through 'linkages' that tie various microsystems together and encourage individuals to apply the learning from one setting to another. The stronger the linkages and the more consistency experienced in the mesosystem, the easier it is for learners to traverse microsystems, and learning can travel between settings. This brings to mind Jackson's (2014) idea of a self-created learning ecology, or "the means by which experiences and learning are connected and integrated across the contexts and situations that constitute a person's life" (p. 13). Bronfenbrenner proposed that a child's development will be enhanced if two settings in which he is involved are strongly linked, emphasising the importance of including families, particularly parents, in children's transitions.

One of the most important features of a child's mesosystem may be the relationships with and between their parent(s) and their early educators (Dockett et al., 2012) and research indicates that parents are a vital factor in educational success of children (O'Toole et al., 2020). Transitions offer opportunities for parents to collaborate with educational settings to strengthen and support each child's learning and development, and parents' knowledge of children may have much to contribute to facilitating smooth transitions (Mhic Mhathúna, 2011).

---

## REFLECTION

In your experience, do early childhood settings involve parents in their children's transitions? Discuss examples of how parental involvement can be facilitated and supported.

---

Family support is linked to children's achievement and the influence of encouraging parents is cumulative, supporting the bioecological emphasis on the developmental impact of early experiences. The specific parental behaviours and inputs that may be helpful in support of children's transition into primary school, for example, include promotion of children's independence, talking positively to children about their own school experiences and asking about the child's day in school, having good communication with the teacher and the school, and ensuring that belongings are child-friendly (INTO, 2009). Overall, it may be that transition is an opportunity for relationship-building between educators and parents, but just like the potential vulnerabilities of children at such times, some parents and families may be vulnerable too. Dockett et al. indicate that "the responsiveness of teachers is a key element in promoting family engagement at school" (2012, p. 58) because parents' proactivity may be limited by feelings of intimidation, especially when the culture, language, religion or socio-economic status of the home differs from that of the educational setting (Kiely et al., 2021; O'Toole et al. 2019). Early childhood educators may

A bioecological perspective on transitions **71**

have a particularly important role to play in vertical transitions because anxious parents often seek support from them during the transition to primary school if their relationships are already well established.

A responsibility rests with all educators to facilitate parental understanding of what to expect and what is expected. Settling-in policies should be clear and well explained and should be guided by the needs of children, not only the needs of the setting (McDermott, 2016). They should also be aware of and work towards a balance in power relations, and this may be particularly true for parents whose backgrounds differ from the dominant social, linguistic and cultural group. For example, approaches like home visits can help create mutual understanding between families and educators and parent–teacher relationships can impact on children's outcomes (Soule, 2020; Soule and Curtis, 2021). In bioecological terms, such approaches create linkages in the mesosytems of children, but in taking a bioecological perspective on the impact of diversity on transitions, early childhood educators must also consider how person factors might influence parents' capacity to support their children at these times.

---

**REFLECTION**

Consider the families whose children attend your early years setting. Do all parents have the skills and knowledge and the cultural and economic capital required to support their children in transitions? What factors might impact parents' ability to engage with transition? What can you do to support families? Are there any structural aspects of your early years setting that potentially empower or limit parents' capacities at these times?

---

Think about the dynamics at play in this vignette involving Jane and Lydia. How might the teacher involved interpret the situation differently, potentially resulting in more positive outcomes? Is there a role for the early childhood educators in Lydia's preschool in supporting the family through the process of transition?

---

When Jane was a little girl, she hated school. Her mother often forgot to give her lunch, and her memories of school largely involve feeling hungry, finding it hard to pay attention and being shouted at by teachers for not knowing the right answers. Jane's daughter Lydia has just transitioned from preschool into the primary school where Jane went as a child. She has received a note from Lydia's teacher asking her to call to the school to discuss a matter related to Lydia's learning, but each time she is in the schoolyard, Jane feels sick and frightened and can't bring herself to go in. After a week, the teacher phones Jane. Jane shouts at the teacher, tells her that she's just picking on Lydia, that

> she won't come up to the school to listen to them bad-mouth her daughter, and hangs up the phone. The teacher chats to her colleagues in the staffroom about how parents from Jane's estate just don't care about their children's education and there's nothing she can do to help Lydia if the mother won't fulfil her responsibilities.
>
> *Source: adapted from O'Toole (2016)*

Bronfenbrenner's bioecological model provides us with a theoretical framework to look beyond the individual person to the context in which they are developing and the relationships (processes) through which they do so. This may help to avoid a problem-focused deficit narrative whereby children and their families are 'blamed' for any potential difficulties or certain groups of parents are seen as 'not interested' in their children's education. It allows us to see a comprehensive picture of how individual characteristics interact with, are influenced by and impact the context in which they find themselves.

---

## REFLECTION

'Person' factors may lead some parents to feel excluded from the educational system and nervous when interacting with it, limiting their ability to be pro-active in creating the linkages needed for a smooth mesosystem for their children. Write down as many factors as you can, then compare your answers with the bullet points that follow.

---

Parents' experiences of and engagement with their children's transitions may be influenced by (Kiely et al., 2021; O'Toole et al., 2019):

- Socio-economics: Working-class parents sometimes feel excluded by the middle-class educational system.
- Language and culture: Parents from other countries may not understand the norms of an educational system, and teachers may not understand cultural practices that vary from the dominant culture. Linguistic differences may also lead to challenges in home–school communication.
- Gender: Early education is largely dominated by women, posing challenges to the engagement of some fathers.
- Family structure: Parents who have had a child attend early childhood settings and primary schools already may find transition easier since they know what to expect; single parents or those with poor support networks may find it difficult to engage with their children's educational setting; same-sex couples

sometimes meet with limited understandings of what 'parenthood' means, which can lead to challenges with accessing information about their children.

- Support networks: Different parents have differing formal and informal support networks.
- Employment status: Parents who work long hours may have little time to engage with their children's education. Parents who are unemployed may have little money to support it.

We need to deconstruct these statements a little; a bioecological perspective shows us that children's development is akin to a web, not a straight line. No one factor will automatically predict the behaviour and development of a child or how smooth their transitions will be. We must also consider how various factors interact. Thus O'Toole et al. (2020) outline how through a bioecological lens, factors such as socio-economic status, gender, language, culture, religion, disability and so on are seen to interact in a complex and dynamic way, potentially contributing to disjuncture in the mesosystems of some learners. However, contextual factors can aggravate or ameliorate potential difficulties. For example, bringing learners' home languages into educational settings, where possible (Skinner and O'Toole, 2018), can constitute an important 'linkage' in learners' mesosystems. Many educational settings attempt to create linkages through events such as intercultural days or educational classes for community members, but some argue that there is little evidence internationally of more than lip service to the ideals of partnership between formal educational settings and learners and communities from diverse cultural and linguistic backgrounds (Hornby and Lafaele, 2011). Support structures sometimes constitute attempts to shape attitudes and practices to meet the needs of educators, rather than attempting to shape education to ensure the creation of mainstream contexts where everyone fits in. However, some approaches to creating linkages between educational settings and traditionally marginalised groups have been successful. For example, the Delivering Equality of Opportunity in Schools (DEIS) scheme in Ireland, which is aimed at supporting the education of economically disadvantaged children, has achieved success both in measurable outcomes, such as literacy and numeracy rates (Kavanagh, Weir, and Moran, 2017), and in so-called softer outcomes, such as the development of parental involvement in children's education through the Home–School–Community–Liaison system (O'Toole et al., 2019).

From early childhood and on into primary, secondary, and third-level education, the range of contexts that learners traverse on a day-to-day basis is expanding, and there is potential for 'culture shock' within the mesosystem when those contexts are very different from each other (Brooker, 2015). Unfortunately, the structure of many formal educational settings fails to support the development of linkages across mesosystems and may erect barriers to smooth transitions. In bioecological terms, this is known as 'disjuncture' in the mesosystem. As a result, the transition to formal education can be particularly difficult for learners from backgrounds outside the dominant culture. Such learners need to come to terms with the social practices of educational settings, which are culturally embedded and may be inconsistent

**74** A bioecological perspective on transitions

with home background (Skinner and O'Toole, 2018). For example, speaking a language at home that differs from that spoken in the educational setting may lead to adjustment challenges through a degree of dislocation and difficulties in accessing academic material (Skinner and O'Toole, 2018), as shown in the vignette involving Ava and Orla above. It can be difficult for some immigrant learners to maintain their sense of linguistic and cultural identity whilst making a life for themselves and succeeding in education in their new country (O'Toole et al., 2019, 2020).

On entering formal education, children of minority groups often acculturate to the dominant culture more quickly than their parents (Kraftsoff and Quinn, 2009), sometimes rejecting the home language and culture in favour of the dominant language and culture (Machowska-Kosciak, 2013, 2019). Although encouraging close engagement with families is valuable, this must be handled with great respect and cultural sensitivity and in real partnership with parents, who are often the experts of experience regarding their own children (Gaylor and Spiker, 2012). Educators at all levels need to work with the cultural and linguistic norms of learners in planning and pedagogy, because they are central to learners' identities (Siraj-Blatchford & Clarke, 2000). However, there is evidence internationally that educational settings often fail to do so (Hornby and Lafaele, 2011). It is little wonder, therefore, that research consistently shows achievement gaps based on language and culture (Skinner and O'Toole, 2018).

## *Exosystems*

Of course, while parents may represent a key 'bridge' for children and early educators within the mesosystem, for vertical transitions relationships and communication between educators at different educational levels may be equally important. While children may not be directly involved in such relationships, they are nevertheless impacted by them, locating links between early childhood educators and primary teachers within the exosystem of the child. Transition represents an opportunity for educators at different levels to work together and draw support from each other. Good communication between staff at preschool and primary school may support a satisfactory start at school for children through the common aims, educational approaches and understanding of the two staff groups. However, the cultures of early years settings and primary schools can be very different, with the two educational sectors often developing largely independently of each other (Tatalović Vorkapić and LoCasale-Crouch, 2021). They can vary widely in their objectives and approaches to education, learning and formal outcomes becoming more central than care and attention as children progress (González-Moreira et al., 2021). Communication between the two educational levels can be limited; there may be differences in language use and cultural expectations as well as distinctions in meanings between early years practitioners and primary school teachers (O'Kane and Hayes, 2006). In many countries, educators at the two levels attend different training programmes and work with different pedagogical approaches and methods (Castro et al., 2018), and early childhood educators and primary school teachers also may have very different expectations of each other's practices and settings (Yamauchi and Sousa, 2020).

Cultural differences between the two levels are often exacerbated by systemic structures, with preschools and primary schools often falling under different administrative auspices and adhering to different regulations and inspection processes. The knowledge of early childhood educators about primary school procedures may be vague, just as the understanding of primary schools of what happens in early years settings may be unclear. This is important because it may be that discontinuities in the exosystem at times of transition are emphasised for children when professionals do not hold mutual views on what is appropriate, making poor communication and weak processes between educational levels a barrier to children's successful transition. A bioecological perspective shows how events at exosystem, macrosystem and chronosystem levels can impact such issues, and certainly mechanisms to ease transition, such as the ideas of 'key persons', 'passports' or 'snapshots', have high profile in educational policy internationally at present (Fitzpatrick, 2015; Ofsted, 2014; O'Kane and Hayes, 2013). A number of measures at exosystem level to overcome barriers to communication across educational levels have been identified in transitions research. These include joint training for early childhood educators and primary teachers (Castro et al., 2018) establishment of common policies for transition across both settings, meetings between preschool and primary school teachers and the development of 'profile forms' to explore the specific needs and interests of children, visits to the preschool by primary school staff and vice versa, and communication between the two levels regarding curriculum and teaching methods (Mhic Mhathúna, 2011).

---

## REFLECTION

If you are currently working in the ECEC sector, how much do you know about the early years of primary school, the curriculum and approaches to teaching and learning? How much contact do you have with your local primary schools?

If you are a primary teacher in the early years, how much do you know about what happens in ECEC? How much contact do you have with the early years settings that feed in to your school? What practical measures could early educators at both levels take to support children and families during the transition from preschool to primary school?

---

Bronfenbrenner's bioecological model demands that educators acknowledge and act on the importance of contextual knowledge, individual characteristics, environmental factors and processes in relationships while also taking account of macro-level factors and the sociocultural time in which development takes place, thereby supporting the potential of all learners to benefit from quality educational experiences generally and smooth transitions specifically. 'Contextual adaptation' (O'Toole et al., 2020) with depth and breadth is required, taking account not only of physical environments but also of the emotional and relational climate within them—in

**76** A bioecological perspective on transitions

Bronfenbrenner's terms, this means consideration of both context and process. The funds of knowledge that learners bring with them to educational settings can enrich the context within which learning occurs while also improving accessibility and smoother transitions for traditionally marginalised groups through the power of the mesosystem. Critical and respectful consideration of issues of diversity is required in developing supportive bioecological systems for learners. Unicultural approaches may be doomed to failure and may actually widen pre-existing gaps in experience and understanding, leading to damaging levels of disjuncture in the mesosystems of learners. The bioecological lens promotes the understanding that good educational spaces provide diverse respectful environments in which all children's funds of knowledge can unfold and grow so that children can transition comfortably across and within microsystems. Such education is reliant on the relationships and interactions that take place within social and educational contexts over time.

## Implications for practice

In summarising the research evidence explored in this chapter, we can see that positive transitions can be supported through promoting friendships; developing a structured series of peer interactions with older students; supporting students to manage the logistical demands of the new setting; involving families and communities, particularly parents; avoiding jarring cultural shifts in educational approaches and behavioural expectations; and ensuring availability of supports for children with specific vulnerabilities such as special educational needs or behavioural difficulties. At the microsystem level, smooth transitions can be facilitated by a key-person approach, the use of transitional objects, a playful environment with a balance between routine and responsiveness, and an underlying understanding by attuned educators of the potential impact of transitions on children's behaviour and well-being.

## Key concepts for early years practice

1   Transitions can represent *crucial times* for children and families, socially, emotionally and educationally.
2   Individual 'person' factors can leave some children and families more vulnerable during transitions.
3   A bioecological perspective on transition identifies a *responsibility for early childhood educators to be proactive* in developing relationships to support children during these potentially crucial times.
4   Contextual supports at micro-, meso-, exo- and macro-level can be vital in achieving this.
5   There are a number of different types of transitions, and for excellent practice in early childhood, we must consider the smaller, less visible transitions children experience within their daily routine just as much as the larger, more obvious transitions like moving from preschool to primary school.

# 6

# LOCATING THE CHILD AT THE CENTRE OF PRACTICE

Bronfenbrenner's model places the child at the centre of a complex network of family, social and cultural influences and emphasises that she actively participates in and influences the interactions within and between these settings. The young child directs her own learning through ongoing interactions with the environment – both the children and adults she shares her time and space with and the objects located in that space (Halpenny & Pettersen, 2014). Children are seen as competent social actors within a complex network of social and cultural influences, thus placing children and significant adults at the heart of contemporary educational processes:

> Our image of children no longer considers them as isolated and egocentric …does not belittle feelings or what is not logical…. Instead our image of the child is rich in potential, strong, powerful, competent and most of all, connected to adults and other children.
>
> *(Malaguzzi, 1993, p. 10)*

In this chapter, the concept of the child as an active, interested and influential agent in shaping her learning in early years settings is further explored. Drawing on key principles of Bronfenbrenner's theory, the importance of building a pedagogy promoting and respecting children in practice in early childhood is reinforced.

We begin by reflecting broadly on the term *agency* with regard to early childhood and on the different ways in which it can be supported and expressed. We then think about how, in practice, agency translates into different aspects of children's development and learning, focusing on the importance of independence and interdependence. We reflect further on how we, as adults, can develop effective strategies to deepen our understanding of children's ideas and opinions in early years settings. Finally, we highlight some of the tensions and discussions around

DOI: 10.4324/9781003247760-6

**78** Locating the child at the centre of practice

the viability and feasibility of locating the child at the centre of practice in early childhood education.

Pedagogical approaches to young children's learning have been influenced by the values and beliefs predominating at different times and across different cultures throughout the last two centuries. As noted in Chapter 4, from the beginning of the twentieth century up until the middle of the twentieth century, principles of young children's learning tended to conceptualise a universal child, passive and open to being moulded or shaped by the environment and the individuals within that environment. Some of the key principles underpinning learning included a focus on reinforcing learning through external reward. Such approaches to pedagogy placed a lot of emphasis on 'extrinsic' motivation in order to promote learning. This refers to learning that is driven by external incentives or rewards. Children typically feel encouraged to repeat actions when those actions meet with praise and approval from adults. Such motivation can be very positive and effective, but if relied on exclusively or excessively, children may not engage in these actions when the rewards are no longer present. In contrast, "intrinsic motivation has been defined variously as a tendency to engage in activities for their own sake, just for the pleasure derived in performing them or for the satisfaction of curiosity" (Covington & Müeller, 2001, p. 163). A child who is curious and encouraged to explore activities in which they have a personal interest is likely to develop these abilities further and, in this way, expand her abilities. Moreover, research highlights the important role which educator relatedness with children plays in promoting intrinsic motivation in young children's learning (Guay, Stupnisky, Boivin, Japel, & Dionne, 2019).

---

## REFLECTION

What do you understand by the terms intrinsic and extrinsic motivation? Can you think of how these terms might be applied to children's learning in the early years? How might strategies based on extrinsic motivation operate to facilitate children's learning? What are some of the limitations of facilitating children's learning through extrinsic motivation? How can educators best support and promote intrinsic motivation in children's learning in the early years?

---

In the middle of the twentieth century, the translation of Vygotsky's work into English (Vygotsky, 1978) influenced an increased focus on the child as a component in her own learning. Later theorists drew on both a social and a constructivist approach to learning based on the principle that children construct their own knowledge through observing and interacting with their environments. In contrast to previous approaches, the role of the child in constructing her experience of the world is characterised as active in that children are considered "agents of experiences rather than simply undergoers of experiences" (Bandura, 2001, p. 4).

## The agentic child in early years

In contrast to the 'universal child' typically portrayed by some of the earlier developmental theorists such as Piaget, Bronfenbrenner characterised each child as having a unique and very particular set of experiences which, in turn, generates a very particular life story. Each child is an active learner growing up as a member of a family and community with particular traditions and ways of life. In recent years, the promotion of young children's agency has been identified as foundational to learning, development and well-being (Mashford-Scott & Church, 2011). Agency in childhood is understood as a quality allowing the child to engage in 'intentional action' to achieve the particular goals valued by her. It is widely acknowledged that children learn and develop through active interaction with others and participation in their environments, and these principles have been increasingly foregrounded in early years practice. However, Greene and Nixon (2020) contest the simplistic notion of agency as "a property of the child, which needs only to be encouraged or revealed" (p. 4). According to these authors, agency can be defined as "intentional activity", which is always context-dependent and emerges developmentally from transactions with the social and material environment. Consistent with Bronfenbrenner's bioecological model, these authors emphasise that agency is constrained by "biological, environmental and temporal realities" (p. 194).

This concept of agency in early childhood provides a good illustration of Bronfenbrenner's depiction of the child at the centre of her development. The characteristics of each individual child are important to consider in the expression of agency as highlighted in the bioecological model of development. Children's agency must be carefully conceptualised to accommodate the specificity of different children's lives, what is shared between children and, finally, what is universal to children and adults (Valentine, 2009). The significant and valuable role which early years educators can play in facilitating and supporting children's agency is also important to highlight through their emphasis on each child as a unique person with a unique constellation of abilities, interests, needs and experiences. As pointed out by O'Toole et al. (2020, p. 25), Bronfenbrenner's bioecological model demands that educators "acknowledge and act upon the importance of contextual knowledge, individual characteristics, environmental factors, and processes in relationships, while also taking account of macro-level factors and the socio-cultural time in which development takes place, thereby supporting the potential of all learners to benefit from quality educational experiences". Supporting children's agency in early years practice, therefore, requires that educators are aware of the family background and particular communities and cultures in which children are growing up and negotiating their agency. It is also important to facilitate children's agency in their interactions within a group setting.

Greene and Nixon (2020) identify schools as one area where children often have little or no voice and are often embedded within a school system where they lack power and their agency is not enabled. While the authors acknowledge that certain pedagogies in early childhood settings establish frameworks which aim to promote

**80** Locating the child at the centre of practice

competent and agentic behaviours in children, the extent to which these aspirations can be realised in practice is debatable and dependent upon the choices made possible or not possible by the early childhood setting.

---

### REFLECTION

What practical measures can early years educators take to support the development of children's agency? How can we support children to become confident learners, allowing them to make decisions about what they learn and when? Think about the children you work with in early years settings and note down some of the ways in which children express their agency. What are some of the strategies they use to achieve this?

---

Consistent with bioecological theory, many writings on agency in childhood emphasise competence in individual children and draw attention to the importance of interaction between individuals and the societies in which they live. Some of the questions generated by such an approach focus on how children act to achieve their goals and what strategies and resources they use to gain control. Locating the child at the centre of her learning involves a focus on the particular knowledge, dispositions, actions and behaviours children bring to negotiate their learning experiences.

Markstrom and Hallden (2009) carried out an ethnographic study on children's strategies for agency in the context of a Swedish preschool. An interesting dilemma they highlight is the potential conflict between individual interests and collective interests embedded within institutions such as preschools. In this study, children's strategies for navigating these tensions were explored. Children's experiences of and approach to the institution, the collective, the other individuals and the daily routines were negotiated among the children themselves and between the children and the preschool teachers. The study shows that children bring certain issues into question and use different strategies when doing so. One strategy, illustrated in the vignette below involving Peter and John, is for children to negotiate with adults and other children to stay out of collective activities and to be in control and realise individual ideas about activities and everyday life. In this vignette, all the children are asked to come together and play in the play hall during free playtime.

---

Two four-year-old boys, Peter and John, express a preference for listening to a CD Peter brought with him to preschool that day. Peter asks the preschool teacher if he and John can listen to Michael Jackson on the CD player. The preschool teacher is quiet for a long while.

PRESCHOOL TEACHER: Hmm, you ask such difficult questions. Everybody is going to the play hall now. [Pause] Could you do it in this room?

> PETER: We can be in the other room so we don't disturb you.
> PRESCHOOL TEACHER: You won't disturb anyone. What do you say about this room?
>
> The boys look happy. The preschool teacher brings the CD player, starts it up and leaves the room.
>
> *Source: adapted from Markstrom and Hallden (2009)*

In the example, although the two boys are part of a collective and *all* children are supposed to play in the play hall, Peter and his friend succeed in negotiating with their preschool teacher to be allowed to follow their own ideas rather than what the schedule or routines prescribe. Markstrom and Hallden (2009) note the fact that in the interaction with the preschool teacher, they use their knowledge of the collective norms and routines to get access to time and space. In this case, Peter says that the boys can be in another room so that they do not disturb the others – the collective and the activities in the play hall. The children view themselves as competent in not only negotiating activities but also negotiating having some time and space of their own. The authors reflect on this further as follows:

> The children are actors in making time for children by navigating among the scheduled and 'predefined' activities. The actors use their knowledge about the teacher's social order in the preschool where the preschool teacher makes a suggestion and the children know that they have the choice of either accepting the decision or negotiating other options. This knowledge is used as a resource in realising their own strivings and purposes.
>
> *(Markstrom & Hallden, 2009, p. 117)*

Children in the study often help each other to get what they want. Consistent with bioecological theory, this study provides us with an opportunity to focus on how children shape their own experiences through reciprocal interactions with their environment rather than seeing children as passive products of social structures. From these examples, we can see that children's agency can be expressed in many different ways including exercising power with or over others through strategies that suggest elements of self-interest, such as refusal to play, inclusion or exclusion of peers, and drawing and maintaining boundaries. Agency can thus be expressed in multiple ways.

## Negotiating the tensions around children's agency in the early years

Along with recognition of the relationships between agency and development, the promotion of children's right to agency has received a steady increase in attention internationally. The United Nations Convention on the Rights of the

Child (UNCRC; United Nations, 1989) positions children as being entitled to fully participate in and influence matters that concern them. However, tensions exist around the extent to which young children possess agency. A key consideration reflected in these tensions is balancing the desire to facilitate children's agency and right to autonomy with their right to be protected from harmful and damaging experiences. Respecting children's competencies is not an alternative to protecting their vulnerabilities (Greene & Nixon, 2020; Woodhead, 2006). Neither is children's right to participation and agency in opposition to their right to protection (Smith, 2013). As stated in the UNCRC, "[t]he child's right to be consulted in matters that affect them should be implemented from the earliest stage in ways appropriate to the child's capacities, best interests, and rights to protection from harmful experiences" (United Nations, 1989, General Comment 7, Paragraph 14).

Beliefs and uncertainties around young children's capacity for self-regulation and self-reflection also underpin these tensions (Mullin, 2007). Such perspectives are informed by traditional discourses, typically portraying children as incompetent and immature. Contemporary, sociocultural perspectives argue that young children are highly skilled co-constructors of their own development (Ahn, 2011). However, challenges to supporting children's agency in early years practice are located in the constraints around the implementation of a particular curriculum and the associated organisational demands (Mashford-Scott & Church, 2011). The transition from early years settings to primary school provides a good illustration of this tension. As explored in Chapter 5, in primary school settings, meeting the needs of the individual agentic child may present a greater challenge than in the early years setting as educators are working with greater numbers of children within a collective context and striving to cover a more structured and demanding curriculum. More recently within early settings, greater emphasis has been placed on supporting and promoting an emergent curriculum, where the shared experiences of all participants in the setting are foregrounded, and as outlined in Chapter 4, such an approach is influenced by children's own background experiences, their dispositions and their individual characteristics (Hedges, 2014).

Consistent with Bronfenbrenner's focus on the significance of macrosystems for development, perceptions of children's competency and agency are also strongly influenced by the cultural context in which they arise (Punch, 2016). In Australian indigenous communities, young children are seen as holding the same rights and responsibilities as adults and, for example, may sleep and eat whenever they choose (Townsend-Cross, 2004). Activities like climbing, sliding, balancing, jumping from heights and hanging upside down can be considered risky in some cultures and yet be part of everyday activities in others (Tovey, 2010). Despite these differences in perception of young children's competence, there is increasing consensus across a wide range of cultural contexts that it is important to facilitate choice in young children's decisions and actions. The belief that one of the main purposes of early childhood education is to develop children's independence and self-confidence resonates across many differing cultural contexts.

## Supporting children to be active participators in learning

Bronfenbrenner's positioning of children at the centre of their development high-lights increased participation for young children in matters affecting their lives. Participation in early years practice can be broadly understood as children having the right to be supported in expressing themselves, becoming visible and having an impact in a social context. Bae (2009) notes that the overall goals of children's participation and the desired outcomes are relatively indistinct. The emphasis is on process, not outcomes. The significant role which adults play in supporting and promoting agency in childhood cannot be overemphasised. Wyness (2012) highlights that the concept of children's participation and voice cannot be fully understood unless we take on board the complexities involved and reflect on the nature of child–adult relationships. Creating an environment that invites children to participate, together with and alongside adults (Taft, 2015) acknowledges the respective roles and positions of children and adults as well as how they are connected. In a recent study of intergenerational learning in early childhood education, Fitzpatrick (2021) highlights the pivotal role of the educator in what and how they provide for the optimal development of children, including the effective promotion of agency in childhood.

Increasing policy support for early years practice is focused on preparing children for school and reducing the likelihood of later school failure. Early childhood is expected to enhance society in terms of preparing future citizens to become productive members of society. One danger of such a focus is that the lived experiences of the 'present' child in early years settings may be disregarded. While the outcomes discourse emphasises the importance of the product of early education, it distances and obscures the contribution of the day-to-day practices within early years settings (Hayes, 2015). The processes involved in such practices play an important role in developing capabilities in children that allow them to be competent, strong and active participators in their learning and development. It is therefore important for early childhood educators to recognise the value of education that is present-focused for development and learning through enhancing the well-being and mastery of children (Hayes, 2013).

## Listening to children in early years practice

Respectful listening to young children by adults is essential for engagement with children as competent individuals. To facilitate children's active participation in their early learning, we need to find ways to access and give expression to their own experiences, world views and actions. This requires a child–oriented paradigm. Sommer et al. posit that

> In being involved in caring and learning activities with infants and young children, adults are barred from directly entering the child's experience. But being 'child-oriented,' that is, in practice carefully observing a child's

**84** Locating the child at the centre of practice

patterned actions, responses and utterances and interpreting these through empathetic imagination, can be a head start in a professional journey enhancing the understanding of the child's specific perceptions of their world.

*(2013, p. 462)*

When early childhood educators take a child's perspective, they seek to understand the child's perceptions, experiences, communication and actions in the world; in this sense, the child's perspective is mediated by the adult. Sommer et al. (2013) draw attention to five principles that need to be in place if we are to implement a child perspective approach in practice:

- *Seeing the child as a person:* A child-oriented perspective sees the child as a person with the same needs as other human beings – to be seen, respected, included, loved and influenced by others. This principle highlights the significance of respecting each child as a person in her own right and responding to each child's ideas, thoughts and desires, relating to children as independent and thoughtful human beings. This requires early years educators to recognise that each child has her own set of experiences and a unique life story and is an active learner growing up as a member of a family and community with particular traditions and ways of life.
- *Empathic participation with the child:* Working with young children, educators must be able to grasp the intended meaning in a child's initiatives and respond accordingly; they must be emotionally available. Efforts to understand young children's desires and intentions include participating in conversations with babies, toddlers or young children. Skilful use of questioning during these conversations can elicit children's theories and understandings, enabling them to share feelings and engaging them in speculation and imaginative thinking. An important aspect of empathic participation with young children is the use of gestures such as imitating actions, gaze, touching and pointing. Educators and children not only co-construct meaning through words but also supplement children's linguistic resources and abilities through the use of gestures and non-verbal expression.
- *An interpretative attitude of respecting the child's utterances and world of meaning:* This involves seeing utterances as meaningful extensions of a child's way of understanding and experiencing and exploring the child's world of meaning as an object of study in its own right instead of reducing it by comparing it with adult ways of understanding. This principle emphasises the importance of educators developing strategies for deepening their knowledge and understanding of the child's world, ideas, perspectives and wisdom. Educators should develop sensitivity towards children and aim to improve their ability to conduct conversations with them and engage them in multiple activities assisting them in expressing their ideas (e.g. drawing and looking at photographs).
- *Guiding the child in a sensitive way by adjusting and expanding her initiatives and ways of understanding in the direction of the educational goal or object:* This involves supporting and encouraging interests, emotional involvement and exploration

Locating the child at the centre of practice **85**

in activities that are important for development. The importance of developing learning environments that allow children to learn at their own pace and extend their learning over time is foregrounded in this principle. Children need time and space to produce work of quality and depth. Imagination, creativity and symbolic behaviour (reading, writing, drawing, dancing, music, mathematics, role-playing and talking) develop and emerge when conditions are favourable. The most effective learning comes from simple but versatile materials and environments that extend the child's imagination and can be adapted by children to suit their own learning needs and level of understanding (French, 2013).

- *Early care and education is a dialogical process between the child and the educator:* Both contribute to the learning objective – sometimes the adult is dominant, sometimes the child. Through expressive signals and appeals, a child invites the adult to respond in a particular way. Thus, both the child and the educator are jointly responsible for the outcome – they are co-producers of the care and education that the child receives. This final principle emphasises setting up opportunities for children to participate in creating meaning about content or learning objects. The child as agent and learner constructs her knowledge through interactions with the educator and other children. These experiences are integrated and interpreted in each child's personal meaning-making. Educators, parents and other adults must develop sensitivity to the child's perspective in order to get into a dialogue with the child – a dialogue that is necessary for young children's creation of meaning.

---

**REFLECTION**

With a colleague, review and discuss the five principles of a child perspective approach set out by Sommer et al. (2013).

What aspects of your practice facilitate engagement with children as unique persons in their own right? What strategies do you use to facilitate 'empathic participation' with children in early years practice? Identify some of the potential challenges involved in accessing and interpreting young children's world of meaning. How can educators deepen their knowledge and understanding of the child's world? Think of some of the ways in which you can support children in adjusting and expanding their initiatives to encourage interest and exploration and extend imagination and creativity. Identify some ways in which early years practice is a dialogical process between children and educators.

---

## Interdependence, intersubjectivity and the agentic child

In our efforts to capture some key aspects of the central role that children play in their learning and development, we see that the concepts of sharing, negotiating and constructing meaning and knowledge are evident. It is wise to be wary of creating unnecessary conflict between the concepts of independence and interdependence (Mashford-Scott & Church, 2011). Much research on the early years shows that agency and autonomy in children are associated with more cooperative, sharing behaviours (Mosier & Rogoff, 2003). Similarly, engagement within a group can promote individual agency and autonomy (Konstantoni, 2012). In keeping with bioecological theory, children's learning and sense of agency and autonomy develop in a complex web of interdependencies. Learning and development involve establishing shared understanding or intersubjectivity, and this, in turn, is the basis for the joint construction of new and more advanced conceptual structures. Children also value interdependent relationships that reinforce their sense of identity and belonging and help them realise their desire to enjoy each other's company and support and learn from each other (Kernan, 2010).

As previously discussed, Bronfenbrenner drew our attention to the importance of proximal processes – reciprocal interactions which are repeated and endure for substantial periods of time. Now we consider the importance of play as a vehicle for the expression of children's agency and child-centred learning. Play also provides us with an excellent opportunity to see proximal processes at work.

## Play as a vehicle for agency and proximal processes in early childhood

Models of learning in the early years provided by thinkers such as Froebel, Montessori, Steiner and Malaguzzi focused on the active playing and learning child. Unlike teacher-based curricula aimed at instruction and the transmission of knowledge, 'play curricula' were (and are) seen as being more holistic, inclusive and participatory.

Internationally and in the UNCRC, play policies propose that choice is characteristic of play, and research on children's perspectives consistently shows that they value freedom from structure, making choices and having time to themselves (Wood, 2014). The inclusion of play is a key component of the unique nature of early years practice. Children are viewed as active, inquisitive and playful, and therefore it seems natural to have play-based learning as central to early years practice. The underlying assumption is that play forms the basis of childhood development. Research also indicates that children learn best in an environment that allows them to explore, discover and play (Neaum, 2020). Therefore, many early years curriculum frameworks have incorporated play as a means of learning for children.

Play typically involves an intense relation with the immediate social and physical environment (Singer, 2013). A child actively chooses to play with a friend or an adult, and she plays with objects from her environment. The child is active also in the creation of a play-world, distinct from the 'normal world', in which rhythms, rules and structure play an essential role. Even the youngest babies participate and share in the creation of this play-world. Observations of caregiver–baby interactions show that both partners create a play-world together by imitating each other, through eye contact, and in taking turns repeating, varying and improvising sounds (Trevarthen, 2011). There is also a structure of repetition in play with the physical environment, and this is emphasised in Bronfenbrenner's theory. Children can influence these repetitive series of actions so that they grow into a more comprehensive ritual. For instance, Corsaro (2010) introduces us to a lunch that is concluded with singing, clapping of hands and, finally, letting the heels drum. A shared play-world often has the character of a 'magic circle' (Huizinga, 1950) where children create their own images and narratives while listening to a story being read aloud. Children easily become totally absorbed in their play with cars or dolls, or in their role as a tiger or a dog. Consider how the adult in the vignette involving Isabelle and Sophie has misinterpreted the shared play-world of these children. The adult is outside the magic circle.

> Sisters Isabelle and Sophie have constructed a tent out of blankets in their bedroom. Their mother enters the room, and noticing that the side of the 'tent' has fallen down and one blanket is caught behind the bed, she tries to help by fixing it. The children are annoyed because that side of the tent has been torn by a giant, and he hid their door, turning it into a magic portal to his world. It took them a long time to get the tent just right and now their mother has ruined it.
>
> *Source: author observation*

In this case, the adult has transgressed the 'rules' of the play-world. Young children also love to play with the rules of their caregivers by transgressing them for fun (Corsaro, 2010). One example from Corsaro's ethnographic research involves children slapping loudly and screaming and all the while looking to see whether the educator has seen what is going on and laughing even louder if it has not been noticed. What he illustrates so colourfully in the studies he has carried out (see Corsaro, 2010) is that children, even very young children, direct their play activities to explore the boundaries of their world – boundaries typically drawn by adults. Thus, play allows children a very effective means of bridging the great difference in power that exists between them and the adults in their world. Through play, agency can be expressed in different ways by children through their knowledge, dispositions, actions and behaviours. As Wood (2014, p. 15) puts it, "agency can thus be expressed in multiple ways within the many paradoxes of play such as seeking order and disorder, creating and subverting rules, being inclusive and exclusive and being sociable and unsociable".

In our exploration of how children are located at the centre of their learning and development in early years practice, and consistent with Bronfenbrenner's theory, it is also important for us to consider the tension in practice between supporting and promoting children's agency and the need to provide appropriate boundaries to support the development of self-regulation and positive social and emotional development within early years settings. A child's ability to learn and to function as a contributing member of society rests heavily on the development of social competency and emotional health, which begins at birth and is greatly influenced during the preschool years (Domitrovich, Durlak, Staley, & Weissberg, 2017). ECEC programmes that pursue the highest standards of quality will contribute substantially to this development.

Corsaro (2010) describes how rituals help children reconcile themselves to the inevitable. Rituals include such daily occurrences as, for example, children taking leave of their parents, sitting at table for lunch or the activities that take place at the beginning and end of the day. An example of educators using play and humour to soothe and influence children's behaviour is provided in the vignette involving Nicola.

---

Nicola is roaming around the room although she has been asked by Donna (teacher) twice to remain seated until she has finished her lunch. Nicola ignores both requests and heads in the direction of the kitchen. Donna asks her once again to sit down but this time with smiles, saying: "Nicola, you have a carrot, a big juicy carrot. You will be the envy of all the rabbits in the world". Nicola grins and sits down at the table.

*Source: adapted from Brennan (2005, p. 116)*

---

In this way, the educator draws on the magic of pretend play to create a shared reality in which both adult and child can share in freedom. Children are not simply influenced by their environments but act in ways that change and even transform those environments. What better illustration of this acting on and transforming environments than pretend play. By creating imaginary roles and events, children choose to write the script for endless situations, challenge the logic of adult rules and develop their own internal logic. These opportunities to direct and control scenarios in pretend play allow children to exercise and affirm their agency. Wood captures the power of proximal processes in pretend play when she writes:

> Through such meditational means and activities, children exercise individual and collective agency because they are learning about the internal rules that govern play, the self-control and self-regulation that are needed to sustain play, and ways of resisting adults' rules or boundaries. These processes therefore have particular significance as forms of affirmation for children as agents in their ability to change their circumstances, and in their learning and development.
>
> *(2014, p. 14)*

## Locating the child in early years assessment

We conclude this chapter with a brief focus on the role children can play in assessing their own learning and skills in collaboration with educators in early years settings. Assessment of children's learning typically involves using a range of tools at different times to generate a comprehensive picture of the learning and development that is emerging (Dunphy, 2008). Assessment must also take account of the multimodal dimension of children's learning, as we have seen in the earlier sections. Documenting children's use of imitation, gesture, facial expression and other features to supplement their linguistic resources demands sensitivity by the educator to recognise these skills and competencies. Regarding children's role in the assessment of their learning strategies, the Mosaic Approach developed by Clark and Moss (2001) provides a very effective illustration of how we can use a variety of tools to facilitate children in conveying their ideas and feelings to early years educators. Children can communicate their ideas and opinions on their learning in a range of symbolic ways involving multiple methods and encompassing a variety of media (Halpenny, 2021). Such strategies include drawings, photos, mapmaking, child-led tours, and through drama and storytelling strategies. Relevant here also is the work of Carr and her colleagues in which, working *with* children, they develop 'learning stories' to document children's learning. These learning stories are used in many ways, both as assessment *of* and assessment *for* learning (Carr & Lee, 2019). Discussions with children about their drawings or listening to children explain their drawings to others can give the educator rich insights into children's understandings, preoccupations, sense of identity and interests.

Another creative way of drawing children into the assessment process is the use of portfolios. Portfolios involve gathering together evidence of early learning and development and of children's progress in relation to learning goals. When compiling portfolios on younger infants and toddlers, the educator in collaboration with parents selects materials from which they draw a range of information on the children's learning. It is beneficial to encourage children as early as possible to play a role in assessing their learning.

> As soon as they can, children should be encouraged to participate in the selection process with adults. The processes of compiling, talking about and sharing portfolio work will also contribute to children's ability to think and talk about their own learning and that of others – helping them to become meta-cognitively aware. It also involves children in the process of self-assessment wherein they begin to be aware of goals for learning and of the possibility of setting their own goals, and reflecting on and making judgements about their own progress towards those goals.
>
> *Dunphy, 2008, p. 32*

## Implications for practice

Bronfenbrenner's bioecological model positions the child at the centre of her learning and development in early years practice. The unique constellation of dispositions and characteristics that individual children bring to their early years settings influences and shapes the experiences they have within these settings. Early years

**90** Locating the child at the centre of practice

educators play an important role in facilitating and supporting children's agency and participation in their learning and development. Children's agency must be carefully conceptualised to accommodate the uniqueness of different children's lives, what is shared between children and, finally, what is universal to children and adults.

## Key concepts for early years practice

1   *Locating the child at the centre of her learning involves a focus on the particular knowledge, dispositions, actions and behaviours that children bring to navigate and negotiate their learning experiences.* Early childhood educators facilitate and support children's agency through their emphasis on each child as a unique person with a unique constellation of abilities, interests, needs and experiences.

2   *It is important to facilitate children's agency in the context of their interactions within a group setting.* Children learn to negotiate with adults and other children in order to have some control over their actions and realise individual ideas about activities and everyday life. In keeping with bioecological theory, children's learning and sense of agency and autonomy develop in a complex web of interdependencies.

3   *Tensions exist around the extent to which young children can be considered to possess agency.* It is of paramount importance that we balance children's right to agency with children's right to be protected from harm. Beliefs and uncertainties around young children's capacity for self-regulation and self-reflection also underpin these tensions. Educators can provide appropriate boundaries to support the development of self-regulation and positive social and emotional development within early years settings.

4   *Through play, agency can be expressed differently by children through their knowledge, dispositions, actions and behaviours.* Such expression can include exercising power with or over others through strategies that suggest elements of self-interest, such as refusal to play, inclusion or exclusion of peers and drawing and maintaining boundaries.

5   *Educators working with young children must be able to grasp the intended meaning in a child's initiatives and respond accordingly, being emotionally available.* Efforts to understand young children's desires and intentions include participating in conversations with babies, toddlers or young children and being able to enter into a dialogical process with children.

# 7
# CREATING RICH LEARNING ENVIRONMENTS

One key component of children's microsystems in the early years is the learning environment, which plays a central role in supporting children's development and learning. Context is extensively elaborated in the bioecological model and is identified as central to understanding development and informing good-quality practice. The importance of the environment as the 'third educator' in the early years setting is highlighted by, among others, those who follow the Reggio Emilia model of early education. The early childhood educator can be a creative architect of learning and development, with careful environmental planning creating points of interest, exploration, quiet, creativity, safe risk and aesthetic pleasure for the child. This chapter considers how to provide a learning environment that contributes to children's development and wellbeing. However, in keeping with bioecological theory, the early years setting must also be understood in terms of the other contexts in children's lives, including those contexts beyond the early years setting. Therefore, it is necessary for early childhood educators to take account of the contexts from which children come, working at building strong bridges between these contexts. This is particularly relevant in situations where children of diverse cultural backgrounds attend the setting. From a bioecological perspective, the early learning environment can be understood as a complex, interrelated set of elements and relationships. Moreover, learning environments linked to and extending beyond the early childhood setting are important to highlight with an emphasis on the ECEC setting as an interactive relational space which can activate and support links among people, places and resources. Throughout this chapter, we apply a bioecological lens to identify some of the features that may create a rich learning environment for young children.

DOI: 10.4324/9781003247760-7

## Creating an invitation to learn

Perhaps the most important feature of any learning environment is that it is welcoming – not only a space where children feel a sense of security and belonging but also a dynamic and stimulating space that offers the child an invitation to explore and discover. Curtis highlights the importance of creating responsive environments allowing for "co-operative play, large muscle activities, high drama, messy play, the sounds of childhood, working through conflict and the importance of family engagement ... offering children rich childhood experiences where children can build their passions and attention over time" (2001, p. 42). Spaces carefully designed and drawing on children's perspectives are welcoming and encourage children's natural responses of curiosity, exploration and communication. Inviting surroundings also enhance children's positive learning dispositions and sense of belonging. Children love to create their own worlds at their own pace and their own scale in any environment they can manipulate or modify (Strong-Wilson & Ellis, 2007). Spaces allowing for experimentation and transformation of the environment are also likely to be rich in learning experiences.

Young children thrive in calm and predictable early learning environments that give them opportunities, encouragement and time to develop and learn, where the pedagogical process is relational, responsive and reciprocal. Key features of rich learning environments include

> [s]patiality; placeness; materiality; affordances of the environment; everyday life and design concepts such as aesthetics; orientation for solar gain and natural light; introverted spaces; indoor circulation; flexibility, transparency, indoor-outdoor connectedness; compatibility of building with natural terrain and the architecture of the surrounding neighbourhood and meeting places, which enhance our knowledge of children's wellbeing and experiences of learning.
>
> *(Kernan, 2015, p. 6)*

Our exploration of rich learning environments is guided by Bronfenbrenner's PPCT (Process–Person–Context–Time) structure, highlighting important process factors (e.g. affordances for reciprocal interactions with people, objects and symbols in the environment), person factors (e.g. age, language, gender, cultural background and socio-economic background) and context factors (with an emphasis on the mesosystem and 'softening boundaries' between early childhood settings and home and community contexts). The implications of historical time (macrotime) are also considered with particular reference to children's interactions with technology in early years settings and the implications of potential future changes in features of early learning environments. The significance of informing learning environments through a focus on mesotime and microtime is also explored.

## Proximal processes and learning environments in the early years

As we have explored in previous chapters, the bioecological model sees development as a process of interaction between an individual and the environment. These interactions occurring regularly and over extended periods are termed proximal processes. Implicit in rich learning environments in the early years is the provision of opportunities for children to engage in progressively more complex reciprocal interactions with the people, objects and symbols in those environments. One concept which helps to bring together Bronfenbrenner's proximal processes with the notion of a rich learning environment in the early years is that of 'affordances' – features of the environment that contribute to the positive interactions which occur within these environments (Greeno, 1994). The concept of affordances is used increasingly in research on early years practice to gain insight into the relationship between children and their environment (Kernan, 2007). Heft (1988) developed a functional taxonomy of children's outdoor environments that subsequently became influential amongst some play environment designers and researchers. This highlighted the quality of surfaces available to children – objects which could be grasped, attached and non-attached objects, climbable objects and so on – and each category was further defined in terms of its affordances. The value of this approach is that it offered a way of thinking about environments that was fundamentally active and goal-directed and which supported children's activity, curiosity, exploration and creativity (Kernan, 2007).

Lynch and Hayes (2015) explored how very young children learn to negotiate objects and spaces of everyday life in the home. One aim of this study was to identify some of the affordances of the physical environment that influenced the child's learning. The physical environment was identified as a learning environment when it provided affordances for interactions meeting the needs of children's play interests and choices. Consistent with Bronfenbrenner's concept of proximal processes, as these young children's play interactions developed over time, the function of the play spaces became more complex, affording opportunities for climbing and sliding. A range of physical features are, therefore, required to afford multiple play opportunities. The significance of proximal processes for guiding learning opportunities is underscored by the study's identification of a "just-right environment" including transactions between the infant, the physical environment and the social environment. This requires the ability of an adult "to orchestrate the environment for available affordances … in a way that maximises successful interactions" (Lynch & Hayes, 2015, p. 22).

Guerrettaz and Johnston (2013) further conceptualise affordances as the potential starting point of the meaning-making process, involving active engagement between the child and the environment. Affordances that enhance children's experiences in early years settings can perhaps best be understood as those features of the environment that children value and which allow them greater possibilities for furthering skills of exploration and imagination. A key feature of designing and shaping a rich learning environment for children in the early years is the ability to tune in to and perceive the environment from the perspective of the children inhabiting their space, thereby generating shared moments of discovery (Kernan, 2015). Significantly, drawing deeply on how young children perceive and use space to create meaning, in keeping with a bioecological approach, positions the child at the centre of his learning environment.

---

## REFLECTION

Discuss with a colleague/fellow student your understanding of the concept of 'affordances' in learning environments in early years practice. To what extent are you aware of the affordances that may enhance learning opportunities for children in their early years setting? How can we learn to better perceive affordances from children's perspectives?

---

Early learning environments inviting complex reciprocal interactions are designed to capture children's interest and curiosity and challenge them to explore and share their adventures and discoveries with others. Such environments can stimulate thinking, imagination and creativity, thereby enriching communication. Kernan (2015) identifies features that contribute to rich learning experiences and support positive proximal processes within a learning environment. Specifically, she highlights designated interest areas providing opportunities for choice of activity and manipulative materials; these should be plentiful and freely accessible to children, and there should be a high level of child–material interaction. Children benefit from rich and stimulating play choices both outdoors and indoors.

## Rich outdoor learning environments

Finding the balance between indoor activities and outdoor explorations is also part of a purposeful planning process. Access to outdoor play opportunities can be influenced by educators' views on their benefits and challenges. Kernan and Devine (2010) explored outdoor experiences in early years settings in Ireland, identifying three key discourses: a discourse of freedom and spontaneity in childhood, a discourse of 'naturalness' and rich sensory experiences in childhood and a discourse of safety in childhood. Interviews with parents, educators and policy officers generated a construction of the outdoors as simultaneously a space of freedom and of risk for children. The former was spoken of in terms of spontaneity and freedom to explore; the latter reflected concerns around traffic, 'stranger danger' and a fear of litigation in the event of personal injury. The authors conclude that in an increasingly risk-averse society, especially regarding children, this construction of the outdoors means it has become marginal in the experiences of many children in early years services, leading to the invisibility of children in outdoor spaces. A more recent qualitative case study carried out in the United Kingdom explored how early childhood teachers' beliefs and practices influence the function of preschool outdoor play (McClintic & Petty, 2015). Key findings included the perception that the physical design of the outdoor environment posed significant limitations for planning, preparation and implementation of meaningful outdoor play and learning. Moreover, despite the belief in and acknowledgement of the importance of outdoor learning, there was minimal evidence of the necessary knowledge and motivation among staff members needed to promote it.

## Naturalness and risk-taking

In addition to the benefits of outdoor play in general, a relatively small but growing body of research suggests benefits specifically related to play in *natural* outdoor environments. The rich multi-sensory experience of being outdoors appears to encourage children to be more observant of and curious about their surroundings, leading to a desire to explore, investigate, and make sense of their observations (Thomas & Harding, 2011). Other findings comparing natural versus less natural areas of outdoor play environments found that children not only spent more time playing in the natural area and utilised the traditional equipment less but also engaged in more social interaction within these more natural spaces (Kemple, Oh, Kenney, & Smith-Bonahue, 2016). Bronfenbrenner's bioecological model – and, most specifically, the chronosystem – draws our attention to the importance of time in terms of the changes and continuities which take place over time and which may impact a child's learning and development. The COVID-19 global pandemic represents a potentially significant event, specific to a particular period of time in historical time, and with the potential to impact development and learning. The potential impact on access to resources for children and their families with a particular focus on early childhood education has been explored (Pattnaik & Jalongo, 2021). The associated pressure on families and intensification of inequities were highlighted, reflecting the need to make the care and education of all young children a top priority, regardless of racial, ethnic, cultural and geographic boundaries. An adverse effect on physical movement and play among children was also identified (Carroll et al., 2020). However, it is also worth considering that in some countries, greater emphasis was placed on organising activities in the outdoors, including outdoor learning in ECEC settings, as a result of the COVID-19 pandemic.

The extent to which outdoor learning environments offer affordances for risk-taking and physical activities was also explored in Australian early years settings (Little & Sweller, 2015). In this study, despite educators' firm beliefs that the environment in their settings supported children's engagement in moderate to vigorous physical activity, insufficient space and regulatory restrictions relating to recommended height limits on climbing apparatus were identified as factors limiting opportunities for challenging, physically active play. Outdoor space and adult

**96** Creating rich learning environments

support were also identified as important factors in early learning environments to promote physical activity and risk-taking. Affordances for risky play create invitations for children to challenge themselves and extend boundaries within a setting where the safety and wellbeing of the child are paramount.

Risky play has been defined as thrilling and exciting forms of play that involve a risk of physical injury (Sandseter, 2007). In keeping with bioecological theory, affordances for risky play involve interactions between the environment and the child. These affordances are unique for each individual and correspond with the child's size, strength, skills, courage and fear. Armitage (2011) suggests that children should have access to four types of risky play experiences: experience of height and depth, experience of movement and speed, experience of den buildings using tools and experience of fire. To provide access to experiences of height and depth, equipment like climbing frames and slides provide opportunities for children to climb up, jump down, slide and generally explore the sensation of height and depth. Climbing frames designed with multiple platforms and levels allow children to experience different levels of height, which provides multiple opportunities for challenge. Affordances for experiencing movement and speed can be provided through spaces that allow children to run around freely without constraints. The experience of moving through the air is also facilitated through the provision of swings. Providing children with access to the natural environment and constructing tree swings is an exciting alternative (Armitage, 2011). Experiences of building dens and using tools create invitations for children to change and transform their physical environment, and many early years settings provide access to this form of play by providing materials such as old sheets, netting, rope and poles.

Generating affordances for experiencing fire could involve constructing a well-sited firepit and allowing children to experience fire in a controlled way. Activities such as cooking around the fire pit and storytelling by the light of a fire are activities that provide children with unique and pleasurable learning experiences. The question as to whether there are greater affordances for risky play activities in natural settings rather than in preschool play spaces was explored by Sandseter (2007) in one traditional and one nature preschool in Norway. Findings suggest that the nature playground does not afford a higher frequency of risk-taking play among children but, rather, a higher level of risk in children's play. Children seek out risky experiences in most play environments. However, experiences of risky play in natural settings are likely to provide greater opportunities for more intense, exhilarating and thrilling play situations than the ordinary playground. The importance of mesosystem connections and communication is emphasised throughout discourses on promoting and supporting outdoor learning environments. Early childhood educators have the opportunity and a responsibility to reframe the importance of outdoor play and learning environments by demonstrating to families and their communities the benefits and value associated with the outdoors (McClintic & Petty, 2015).

Creating rich learning environments **97**

---

**REFLECTION**

Taking Armitage's four types of risky play (experience of height and depth, experience of movement and speed, experience of building dens using tools and experience of fire), reflect on how your learning environments might provide affordances for such play. List any changes you might make to enhance the opportunities.

---

A rich learning environment also optimises opportunities for generating interactions with the people who share these spaces. The design of learning environments in the early years should encompass spaces and resources encouraging children to cooperate with each other, thereby stimulating and fostering connection and communication. An example of such spaces is 'experiential centres' in which children can choose to gather together to explore their interests and discuss and plan their play explorations. Rich early learning environments support engagement with the people and objects within them. Providing invitations to experiment together, share curiosities, stimulate and support cooperative ventures, and negotiate roles and routines can deepen children's sense of self-worth and belonging. Belonging is about having a secure relationship with or a connection to a particular group of people (NCCA, 2009). This can be nurtured within a learning climate which allows children to feel the security of their connections with other children and adults. Research has shown that rich learning environments in early childhood can help children to become emotionally strong, self-assured, and able to deal with challenges and difficulties, creating an important foundation for learning and development (Harper, 2017). Spaces that invite children to interact with each other also provide invaluable opportunities for them to manage and regulate their emotions in situations of conflict and disagreement.

Flexibility in learning environment designs is also an important consideration. As children's interests change, possibilities for transforming their surroundings contribute significantly to extending learning experiences.

---

**REFLECTION**

How does your early years setting help to generate a sense of belonging and self-worth for children? To what extent is the learning environment flexible enough to allow children to transform surfaces and materials?

---

Learning and behaviour in any setting is a function not only of experiences in that setting but also in the full range of settings experienced by individuals (O'Toole &

**98** Creating rich learning environments

Hayes, 2020). The importance of connections between the child, ECEC setting, home and community is emphasised in Bronfenbrenner's bioecological model, highlighting that children's development and learning are enhanced through strong connecting links between all the microsystems in which children participate (Hamer & Loveridge, 2020; McLachlan, Fleer, and Edwards, 2010). Increasingly, greater emphasis has been placed on children's learning in environments linked to but *beyond* the early childhood setting, with particular emphasis on communities surrounding the setting. Related to this, the view has been expressed that children may have become more separated from relationships and life in the wider community as a result of childhood being perceived as a special period in life with its associated emphasis on children spending time in segregated child-centred spaces (Fitzpatrick, 2021; Gray, Geraghty, & Ralph, 2016; Kernan, 2010). Early years settings provide a particularly important connective or networking service for families within communities (Fleer, 2003; O'Toole, Kiely, McGillicuddy, O'Brien, & O'Keeffe, 2019).

One example of rich learning environments beyond ECEC settings is provided in a recent study of intergenerational learning and practice (IGL) in the context of Irish ECEC settings (Fitzpatrick, 2021). This study evolved from a larger European Union–funded European study in 2012 (The Together Old and Young [TOY] project) which began in response to the situation that many older people and young children were having less and less contact with each other. The aim of TOY is to bring young children and older adults together to share experiences, have fun, learn from each other and develop meaningful relationships (Gallagher & Fitzpatrick, 2018). Through IGL, children have opportunities to form relationships with older people of mixed ages, abilities, cultures and risk-rich experiences that may be quite different to the relationships typically experienced within the ECEC settings (Fitzpatrick, 2020). Such an approach is consistent with Bronfenbrenner's view (1971a, 1971b) that child-care centres should be located in or near schools and other services or settings within their communities, with a view to encouraging adolescents, adults, and older persons to engage as much as was feasible with young children. According to Tudge et al. (2021), the benefits of such an approach for children and adults are important to highlight. Bronfenbrenner also placed an emphasis on the concept of the chronosystem – describing time as an element that may impact development over the life span and across generations (Bronfenbrenner & Morris, 2006), and these principles are reflected in IGL. Further details of intergenerational learning and practice in the context of ECEC are outlined in Chapter 10.

## The role of the educator in rich learning environments

Early childhood educators play a central role in building and developing an environment that motivates children to interact with each other, with the participating adults and with the objects within their space. These early experiences support children in becoming confident and competent communicators. Well-designed early learning environments can promote positive learning dispositions in children. As outlined in previous chapters, learning dispositions are characteristics, innate or

Creating rich learning environments **99**

acquired, that facilitate rich learning experiences for children. Such dispositions include curiosity, playfulness, perseverance, confidence, resourcefulness, risk-taking, social competence and the ability to work with others (Mitchell, Wylie, & Carr, 2008). By capturing children's interest and curiosity and reflecting these in both indoor and outdoor environments, educators play an important role in fostering positive learning dispositions in young children. Through their interactions with other children, with adults, with materials and with concepts, children learn about the world and their place in it. As adults, we have a powerful role in facilitating this development through providing good-quality early learning environments that encourage children to develop positive, generative dispositions of curiosity, persistence, responsiveness, the tendency to initiate and engage in activity, alone or with others, and inhibit the more disruptive dispositions of impulsiveness, explosiveness, distractibility or, at the opposite pole, apathy, inattentiveness, unresponsiveness, a lack of interest in one's surroundings, feelings of insecurity or shyness (Hayes, 2013). Observing, listening to and creatively documenting children's activities in their daily routines provides unique insights into their collective interests and pursuits and also their individual curiosities and learning dispositions. Significantly, documenting children's ideas and activities generates new information about additional props and resources for extending learning.

## Transforming the environment through interactions

As noted in previous chapters, bioecological theory emphasises the dynamic nature of development. Children are not simply influenced by their environments; they also act in ways that change and even transform those environments. With progressive, reciprocal interactions with objects, symbols and people in their learning environment, children have possibilities for transforming their environments and this, in turn, impacts on how they respond to and develop through the changing nature of the milieu in which their learning occurs. Through their interaction with the environment, children change it (as a result of actions and interactions) and the environment influences what they can accomplish. Rogoff (1998, p. 691) describes development as "transformation of participation", and Dunphy explores this further:

> Transformation occurs at a number of levels: for instance, the learner changes at the level of their involvement, in the role they play in the learning situation, in the ability they demonstrate in moving flexibly from one learning context to another, and in the amount of responsibility taken in the situation.
>
> *(2008, p. 14)*

Transformation can occur to a greater extent if we can develop learning environments rich in opportunities for children to become involved in their learning, to be active and directive in their learning experiences, to have access to different contexts for their learning and to have the potential for increased responsibility.

**100** Creating rich learning environments

Implicit in this is an understanding of early learning as an active, social, dynamic and transforming process and the role of the adult as responsive and flexible (Hayes, 2007).

A key feature of children's play is spontaneity, and it is this that allows children the freedom to explore and make connections between familiar and novel information. Pretend play requires the ability to transform objects and actions symbolically, it is furthered by interactive social dialogue and negotiation and it involves role-taking, script knowledge and improvisation (Bergen, 2002). One of the earliest sources of creative imagination is the ability of the child to substitute one object for another in pretend play. Research has highlighted many aspects of play that feature in spontaneity, including enhanced social and emotional skills, language and communication skills, imaginative and divergent thinking skills and problem-solving (French, 2007). However, while acknowledging the importance of spontaneity in children's play, the value of providing a rich environment in which children can become confident players and learners is equally emphasised. Early childhood educators manage the learning environment to optimise the quality of pedagogical learning through play for children. The material resources (toys, furniture, props), as well as the opportunities for social interaction and varying activities, are typically chosen by adults, and these may influence both the opportunities and limitations for learning (Tajik & Singer, 2021). Educators can facilitate learning through play by planning an environment that provides a wide range of play possibilities, structuring both the indoor and outdoor environments to reflect children's individual strengths, interests, abilities and needs (NCCA, 2009). Through careful documentation of children's activities, we can identify the types and quality of children's play and reflect these in the learning environment by providing relevant props, toys and objects. Play can be quiet or noisy, messy or orderly, funny or serious, strenuous or effortless. It can take place inside or outside, and it develops as children grow and change.

## Person factors and rich learning environments

Child characteristics considered most significant for their potential to influence future development are called 'active behavioural dispositions'. As explored in Chapter 4, children's dispositions are environmentally sensitive. They are acquired, supported or weakened by interactive experiences in an environment with significant adults and peers (Bertram and Pascal, 2002). Significant adults obviously include educators in early years settings. For example, in Reggio Emilia–inspired schools, educators purposely integrate materials from nature into activities. An ordinary tree branch can become the core for cooperative ribbon weaving, and this sort of activity is an invitation to children's dispositions, such as cooperation, creativity, problem-solving and inventiveness.

An interesting study of learning dispositions and the role of mutual engagement in early years settings examined relationships between learning dispositions and what is termed 'learning architecture' (Duncan, Jones, & Carr, 2008). This research explored how children's dispositions 'travel' between the various settings

Creating rich learning environments **101**

and activities the children participate in, such as home, their early years setting and then later in school. The authors argue that dispositions can be described as "attunement to [the] constraints and affordances" (2008, p. 108) in any given setting. Furthermore, dispositions can be seen to "reside in the reciprocal and responsive relationships between children and other people, places and things, or in participation in activities of various kinds" (Carr, 2004, p. 6). Reflecting bioecological theory, Carr emphasises that dispositions are both shaped by and shape the interactions that children have with others – people, places and things. An extract from Duncan et al.'s study (the vignette involving David) provides a good illustration of Bronfenbrenner's construction of development as an interactive process between the child and the learning environment.

> David attended his early childhood centre one day a week. He had been going to the early childhood centre for two to three years on a part-time basis. The centre was licensed for 25 children aged two and a half and over.
>
> … A house was being built a few doors down from the centre and, on this particular morning, a concrete mixer had arrived to pour the floor. The building process had been watched very closely by the children at the centre over a number of weeks and so very quickly the decision was made to all go down and have a closer look – but not too close – at what was happening. David was very interested in the concrete mixing…. He described to the teacher the use of 'cement' and water in the making of concrete and demonstrated prior knowledge of the whole process.
>
> Back at the centre, David says to his friend, "I'm going to start making concrete. Do you want to help me start making concrete?" His friend agrees and they run off to the sandpit. David obviously has a very clear objective in mind as he starts to dig a hole and then look around for some water. He says:
>
> > You go and get the normal buckets and I'll pour it in then I'll come back over. I'm making concrete. Could you get me water …?
>
> The teacher helps them organize the water and then move things around in the sandpit to give them more room. Over the next few minutes more children start to join in the activity and soon concrete making takes over the whole sandpit.
>
> During all the digging and mixing with water, another child makes a suggestion which David responds to immediately and which is followed up on by the teacher …:
>
> CHILD 1: You need some flour, but not real flour. [*Imitates, offers expertise*]
> DAVID: Just pretend flour. [*Agrees*]
> TEACHER: Pretend flour, what do you think the pretend flour would do? [*Extends*]
> DAVID: Just make different colour. [*Responds*]

**102** Creating rich learning environments

---

TEACHER: Oh, we could add some flour and see what happens to your texture, couldn't we? Should I get some? [*Offers to help*]

DAVID: Then get some, get some flour. Look out, I've got a mixture [*as another child blunders into his hole*]. [*Instructs, protects the task/agenda*]

CHILD 1: We're going right down to the bottom, eh? [*Seeks clarification*]

DAVID: No, I'm not. We need just concrete mixture and don't put sand in the concrete mixture. [*Adds expertise, clarifies the task – not digging a hole – and protects the task/agenda*]

CHILD 1: Na. [*Agrees*]

DAVID: She's going to get some concrete flour, I think. It's going to be fine, we don't need to dig. We don't need to dig. [*Reminds, reassures, instructs*]

At this stage the field observation notes read: "David is putting everything into mixing his concrete, he is using his whole body to mix it. His technique looks like he has watched/done this before."

*Source: Duncan et al. (2008, p. 113)*

---

Duncan et al. identify how the learning architecture in this situation supported David's interactions by drawing attention to the following features within the environment:

> *Time for interaction – mutual access by participants*: ... children were invited to decide for themselves if they wanted to stay or do other things. Thus, David was not kept from his desired objective – mixing concrete – for a long period of time....
>
> *Joint tasks and activities – negotiable enterprises with common meaning*: Throughout the concrete-mixing episode, David interacted closely with the other children and adults. The teacher supported the children in their negotiations with each other in sharing the resources and ideas. Ideas expressed by other children were listened to and taken up....
>
> *Opportunities for peripheral participation and multiple entry points*. Children came and went throughout the whole sandpit activity. Some [worked] on the edge of the activity; others were attracted by the action but then played their own games in the water trough that was being used. If others wanted to join in but were unsure of what to do, they were invited to ask David to help, and he did so very willingly....
>
> *Tools and artefacts that support communicative competence*.... there was a big sandpit with a multitude of containers, shovels, tubing, pipes and water troughs – enough for everyone to have a turn. Again, negotiations with turn taking were necessary, and the [educator] modelled and suggested strategies for the children to use in order to achieve this.
>
> *(Duncan et al., 2008, p. 115)*

Drawing together some of the key messages from this observation and analysis of David's interactions and how they were supported by the learning environment, Duncan et al. (2008) suggest that through the success of his engagement in episodes such as this, David strengthened his dispositions of reciprocity, expecting tasks to be mutually meaningful to participants, and moving from the periphery to the centre of deep engagement. Earlier in this chapter, we explored the importance of a learning environment that creates an invitation to learn. This resonates with Wenger's (1998) notion of a 'community of practice' or perhaps in this case a community of learners:

> Children enter a community of practice, such as the early childhood centre or the new entrant classroom, and through their engagement in the various activities, with the people in the setting, and using the tools and resources available to them, they come to belong to that community of learners. The learning architecture of the educational setting can work either to support or inhibit this.
>
> *(Duncan et al., 2008, p. 115)*

Consistent with bioecological theory, 'dispositions' evolve in a dynamic pattern through the power of process. A child's dispositions influence how he experiences the world and so influence the way in which the world responds, which affects the development of further dispositions, and so on.

Children have diverse needs and belong to different cultures and social groups, resulting in their participating differently in early years settings. Providing access to a wide range of learning opportunities and activities is a defining feature of rich learning environments, but it is also important that environments are open to all the person characteristics children bring with them. A welcoming learning environment invites and accommodates individual differences in abilities, skills and competencies, including an emphasis on engaging with and across different age groups. Rich learning environments reflect diversity in family types and differences in socio-economic class and culture. Early years settings allow children to actively construct images of themselves through interactions with people and materials in their immediate environments. There are many ways of reflecting the diversity of young children's lives – displaying children's artwork and reflecting the diversity of the world through a variety of toys, books, magazines, pictures and musical instruments. Drawing on what they see around them, children access essential information about who and what is important. Therefore, every effort should be made to create a setting that is rich in possibilities for exploring diversity (Robinson & Jones-Diaz, 2006). Creating a learning environment that respects diversity sets the scene for fostering children's positive self-concept and attitudes. Assisting children in developing positive ideas about themselves and others allows them to initiate conversations about differences and generates possibilities for them to compare, explore and become familiar with diverse beliefs, lifestyles and cultural contexts.

## REFLECTION

In what ways can the planning and resourcing of early learning environments contribute to ensuring diversity and equality of opportunity in children's activities? What materials can be used to promote positive identities and attitudes to diversity? How can we empower children and foster feelings of confidence through the careful design of early learning environments?

Rich learning environments also encompass features relevant to person characteristics, such as a child's age. Such environments support the abilities of children and include features to invite learning for very young babies and toddlers, as well as children of preschool age. Some affordances within the learning environment for younger children include opportunities for gross and fine motor development, hand–eye coordination, language and communication development, emotional expression and social competence, imagination and creative skills (Bradford, 2012). During the first three years of life, children's brains are highly active, and brain development needs "affection, stimulation, and meaningful interaction – language, touch, eye contact, exploration, play" (Early Childhood Matters, 2013, p. 5). The profound importance of young babies' interactions with adults for developing language acquisition has been demonstrated in fascinating research in the field of developmental neuroscience, providing substantial evidence for the complex interaction of nature/nurture influences on human development (Kuhl, 2010).

Person characteristics also include gender, and children sometimes show different kinds of behaviour and make different choices in their play based on their gendered experiences. Being attentive to the different play areas and how they might be used differently by girls and boys can help to challenge some of the limitations caused by the provision of gender-specific resources. For example, traditionally, the home play area is often characterised as being dominated by girls, while boys choose more risky outdoor play (Nutbrown & Clough, 2009). Girls may need support to extend their play activities beyond the home corner and to take risks outdoors, and boys may need help in negotiating their way to engage with and enjoy domestic play. Representing each child in the early years environment involves more than simply adding a range of diverse resources. Resources need to be discussed and explored with children, and educators should tune in to, listen to and observe how children are interacting with them.

An inclusive learning environment should, wherever possible, make the usual range of play and learning opportunities offered indoors and outdoors accessible to children with additional needs (Kernan, 2010), ensuring that they have the freedom to explore, create, take risks, make choices, accept challenges and develop friendships (Sayeed & Guerin, 2000). Learning environments must be inviting for children with additional needs, providing a space where they are relaxed and valued, enhancing their opportunities to engage in, initiate and sustain play.

## Context factors and rich learning environments

Bronfenbrenner is probably best known for highlighting the many and multi-layered levels of influence on development associated with the different contexts in which children develop and learn. In this section, we reflect on some of these contextual influences with an emphasis on the mesosystem (links across microsystems), the exosystem (more indirect environmental influences that have a profound influence on a child's development, even though that child is not directly involved with them) and the macrosystem (broader social and cultural influences). The final sphere of influence within bioecological theory is the chronosystem, which focuses on the influence of time.

In the second level of contextual influence on development, the mesosystem, Bronfenbrenner draws attention to interactions and interdependencies between the elements within the child's microsystems. There are many ways in which interactions within and across different microsystems operate to impact the early learning environment. A particular focus in this chapter is on the possibilities for designing learning environments to maximise opportunities for bridging communication between children's home and early childhood education settings. A number of studies have identified the profound influence of children's home environment on their wellbeing in early years settings and more broadly. The Effective Provision of Pre-School Education (EPPE) study (Melhuish, Phan, Sylva, Sammons, & Siraj-Blatchford, 2008; Sylva, Melhuish, Sammon, Siraj-Blatchford, & Taggart, 2004) found that a home learning environment where parents were actively engaged in activities with children promoted intellectual and social development in children. Although parents' social class and levels of education were related to child outcomes, the quality of the home learning environment was more important. The importance of enhancing continuity and alignment between learning environments offered by the home and early years settings is emphasised in these research findings. Drawing attention to the notion of the malleability or fluidity between home and early years settings, Kernan talks of "softening the boundaries" (2015, p. 6) between these environments and reinforcing the connections between children's families and communities and the learning environments they inhabit.

Increasingly, the early care and education of babies, toddlers and young children are shared among parents, families and educators. By working together and sharing information, adults can help to facilitate access to valuable information contributing to more meaningful experiences for children in both home and early years settings. Another aspect of softening the boundaries between these settings is the practice, where possible, of home visits. Home visits are part of the mesosystem, promoting interaction between home and early years settings. They allow educators to learn more about the child's exosystem and macrosystem, especially regarding parents' occupations, family culture and parental attitudes and beliefs. This can provide important contextual information for enhancing children's learning and development.

**106** Creating rich learning environments

---

> ## REFLECTION
>
> How can early childhood educators gather and exchange information with children's parents and families to improve the early learning environment? How can early childhood educators help parents to support their children's learning and development?

---

Bronfenbrenner also highlights the many contexts in which children are not directly involved but which significantly impact on their wellbeing and development. He called this level of influence the exosystem. A number of factors play a very significant role in shaping the design, layout and intention of early years settings and practice, though some of those involved in the design of the physical environment have little connection with the needs of the children they are designing spaces for. Lippman describes a "responsive approach" (2010, p. 1) to designing environments that asks how does the environment shape the learner and, in turn, how does the learner influence the environment.

The designer can then create a learning environment that is more responsive to the needs of children and that is more aligned to the needs of twenty-first-century education. Policymakers, who play a significant role in influencing the quality of provision of early years practice, could also be considered as part of the exosystems that influence the development of rich learning environments. Policy design and decisions around early years practice do not happen in a vacuum but, rather, are ideologically and culturally specific, reflecting the social, political, cultural, economic and historical context in which they are derived (O'Donoghue Hynes & Hayes, 2011; O'Toole et al., 2021).

Learning environments are also culturally shaped and moulded. Attitudes to the design and development of learning environments are typically affected by the sociocultural values and beliefs that inform them. One example of this is how we perceive and construct indoor and outdoor learning environments. Early years settings are an important context for children's engagement in physically active play. The emphasis on outdoor play in Nordic countries has prompted early years educators in different cultural contexts to establish greater fluidity between indoor and outdoor learning environments. Fjortoft (2001) explored the relationship between environmental affordances and children's play and development, particularly outdoors; findings suggest that environmental complexity and diversity in nature are highly associated with increased play opportunities and activities.

## Time factors and rich learning environments

We saw in Chapter 2 that within the bioecological model, time is conceptualised at three levels: microtime, mesotime and macrotime (Bronfenbrenner & Morris, 2006). *Microtime* refers to what is happening during specific episodes of proximal

Creating rich learning environments **107**

processes. *Mesotime* refers to the extent to which processes occur in the person's environment, such as over the course of days, weeks or years. *Macrotime* refers to historical time and how proximal processes may be affected by the changing times in which development takes place.

One key feature of rich learning environments referred to throughout previous chapters is a calm, unhurried environment where children have space to interact with objects and people in their surroundings. The term *microtime* evokes this sense of attending to what is happening in the moment – the child's 'now' activities – rather than focusing on what might be the outcome of these activities. Rich learning environments informed by the concept of microtime emphasise opportunities for children to respond to the affordances present in their surroundings without limiting those opportunities by excessive structuring of the time available for exploration. The term *microtime* also evokes the *being* child rather than the *becoming* child – the child who is actively engaged in the present moment in the construction of their learning and experience of childhood. The term *mesotime* refers to broader intervals of time, over days and weeks, in which proximal processes can develop and become more complex, consistent with bioecological theory. A focus on the relevance of mesotime to early years learning prompts us to think about the central role of the educator in facilitating meaningful learning experiences through planning and the provision of rich learning opportunities over time. Time must be made available for planning rich learning experiences:

> Practising a nurturing pedagogy both challenges and permits educators to give time to planning for the 'soft' and messy aspects of early learning and to encourage playful interaction, exploration, dialogue and collaborative learning to encourage and support babies', toddlers' and young children's learning. The learning environment, and children's interaction with it, should be challenging and rich in both language and content. This can be either directly, in terms of the content of social interactions with an adult or advanced peer, or indirectly, through the carefully considered provision of materials, objects, activities and opportunities.
>
> *(Hayes, 2007, p. 16)*

---

## REFLECTION

Work with a colleague to identify what you understand by the terms *microtime* and *mesotime*. Think about the ways in which you provide opportunities for children's learning and development to take place in an unhurried way. Identify some barriers to providing these opportunities for children in early years settings. How can early years educators play a central role in providing meaningful learning experiences through a focus on mesotime? Identify some barriers to providing these experiences in early years settings. How might we begin to overcome these barriers?

## 108  Creating rich learning environments

*Macrotime* refers to historical time and some of the changes in lifestyles, values and beliefs that accompany the passing of time from one generation to another. Many aspects of macrotime are relevant to early learning environments. As noted previously in this chapter, the COVID-19 global pandemic represents one such influence. However, one of the most significant fields of change, and one that impacts on all our lives, is the field of information technology. Developments in this field prompt examination of the roles of educators and children as they constitute wider societal influences that inform and shape learning environments. Changes in information technology impact on children's learning and their lives, and they are often quick to embrace the possibilities for how we live and learn in the twenty-first century. Creating rich learning environments in the early years necessitates focusing on the potential impact of technology on methods of teaching, modes of learning and connections to societal and global contexts (Warger and Dobbin, 2009). The rate of change in this area and the extent of the reach of this change require early years educators to be alert, informed and ready to adapt.

Technology and its role in early years practice tend to generate tensions and fears around the risks and dangers that children may be exposed to through access to the internet and to technology more broadly. Some educators fear that technology in early years settings may threaten children's desire for active, physical exploration of their environments. Alternatively, technology has been welcomed in the early years as empowering children, and the use of new technologies is facilitated in positive and meaningful ways. Buckingham (2008) suggests that these two competing perspectives of concern and celebration are symptomatic of viewing children in a sentimental way, especially in Western society. He emphasises that new technologies in fact rely on many of the forms and conventions of old technologies. However, he also notes that while much research refutes the idea that computer games, for example, are antisocial, very little is known about how children perceive, interpret and use new media. Palaiologou (2016) develops this point, showing how even children younger than five are immersed in technology at home so that the discussion about the use of digital technologies in education must shift from debate on whether they are 'good' for children to how they can be used in order to enhance children's learning.

The importance of connecting macro and micro perspectives, locating children's relationships with media within the texture of their daily lives while also understanding economic and political forces at stake, is foregrounded in these arguments (Kewalramani, Palaiologou, Arnott, & Dardanou, 2020). Current tensions between proponents of established forms of literacy like reading, writing and numeracy and proponents of new forms of literacy are very real and it is interesting to explore how these tensions may be resolved in future early learning environments. For the early years educator, it will be important to strike a balance between incorporating technological advances into settings while also ensuring high-quality social and interactive learning environments. Further exploration of technology and digital learning is outlined in Chapter 10.

## Implications for practice

In this chapter, we focused on the importance of creating a welcoming learning environment where children encounter invitations to learn in a space that not only provides them with a sense of security and belonging but also offers dynamic and stimulating opportunities for them to explore and discover new experiences and concepts. Guided by the PPCT structure, we explored the concept of rich learning environments through a focus on the process, person, context and time factors that may influence the development of such environments.

## Key concepts for early years practice

1  *Rich early learning environments provide affordances for children's learning that invite and support complex reciprocal interactions* designed to capture children's interest and curiosity and challenge them to explore and share their discoveries with others. Such environments can stimulate thinking, imagination and creativity, thereby enriching communication.

2  *A number of features contribute to rich learning experiences and support positive proximal processes within a learning environment.* These include designated interest areas providing opportunities for choice of activity and manipulative materials that are plentiful and accessible and where there is a high level of child–material interaction. Children benefit from rich and stimulating play choices both outdoors and indoors.

3  *Flexibility in the designs of learning environments is an important consideration.* As children's interests change, possibilities for transforming their surroundings contribute significantly to extending learning experiences. Greater emphasis on access to outdoor learning environments and connecting indoor and outdoor spaces is important to highlight. Moreover, a focus on facilitating access to nature and natural spaces in the outdoors is recommended.

4  *By capturing children's interest and curiosity and reflecting these interests in both indoor and outdoor environments, educators play an important role in fostering and promoting positive learning dispositions in young children.* Through their interactions with other children, with adults, with materials and with concepts, children learn about the world and their place in it.

5  *Transforming the environment through interactions can occur to a greater extent where learning environments are rich in opportunities for children to become involved in their learning,* to be directive in their learning experiences, to have access to different contexts for learning and to have the potential for increased responsibility.

6  Learning environments that connect to and extend beyond the ECEC setting are important to highlight. Creating opportunities for children to engage with and connect to their wider communities, as, for example, through a focus on intergenerational learning and practice, is invaluable in developing rich learning environments.

7  *Through careful attention to and documentation of children's activities, we can identify the types and quality of children's play* and reflect these qualities in the learning environment through the provision of props, toys and objects aligned to the differing interests of children.

8  *Rich learning environment is one that invites and accommodates individual differences in abilities, skills and competencies.* Rich learning environments reflect diversity in family types and differences across socio-economic classes and cultures.

9  *Creating rich learning environments focuses on the impact of time on learning experiences.* This influences micro and meso-levels, where it is important to plan and provide for calm and extended periods for play and learning in early years settings. Influences may also be at the macro level, where changing values, developing technology and societal expectations impact the educator and learner roles and modes of learning and discovery.

# 8

# EARLY EDUCATION AS A DYNAMIC PROCESS

## Introduction

Different theories of development illuminate different aspects of development with varying challenges for educational principles and practices. System models like Bronfenbrenner's have been criticised as being either too focused on context (Downes, 2014) or exhibiting a preoccupation with individualism and ignoring the power of interactions (Penn, 1997). However, Bronfenbrenner's model provides a comprehensive framework, allowing visualisation of the complex dynamics of development in different contexts incorporating social, cultural and temporal elements.

Although most well known for his nested systems model of human development, Bronfenbrenner's contribution to our understanding of the role of interactions and relationships in children's development is of particular significance. A feature of the final iteration of his model (Bronfenbrenner & Morris, 2006) is its focus on the role of the interactional, relational process. He defined the model as "an evolving theoretical system for the scientific study of human development over time" (Bronfenbrenner & Morris, 2006, p. 793). His theoretical system conceptualises the dynamics of development as the interplay between the four key elements of development: process, person, context and time (PPCT). Bronfenbrenner emphasises the importance of interactions between the individual and the social, spatial and temporal contexts. This construct of a dynamic and reciprocal relationship between individuals and their contexts is central to the pedagogy of early education. It foregrounds learning as a complex, dynamic and interactive process in which knowledge is created through the transformation of experience (Hayes, 2013).

The construct of proximal processes and their role as engines of development is important. The quality of proximal processes is mediated by social interactions, and this provides a link between the structure and the processes of development,

DOI: 10.4324/9781003247760-8

**112** Early education as a dynamic process

with implications for practice in the early years. This harmonises the view of the child as a biological reality – a 'structure' – and the view of the child as a participant in the environment – an 'agent'. Neither is sufficient in itself. The bioecological framework provides a model within which different educational approaches can be considered, drawing on a multi-theoretical perspective. Proximal processes have certain distinctive properties and depend on the activity of the developing person as well as the context. You will recall from Chapters 3 and 4 that proximal processes are more likely to lead to positive outcomes for children when they occur in sensitive, responsive and stable environments. Bronfenbrenner proposes that if early learning environments are chaotic or seriously disadvantaged, the presence and impact of high-quality proximal processes, parental and/or educational, might act as an important protective feature. To be effective, proximal processes must occur on a regular basis over an extended time. Activities must continue long enough to become increasingly more complex; mere repetition does not work. Equally, developmentally effective proximal processes are not unidirectional; they are bidirectional, interchanging between the givers and receivers. In interpersonal interactions, this means that initiatives do not come from one side only; there must be reciprocity of exchange between, for instance, the adult and the child. The child or adult can initiate the interaction and should be allowed time and space to do so. Finally, proximal processes are not limited to interactions with people but can involve interactions with objects and symbols. Children respond to and act upon the environments surrounding them, and so they alter these environments. For effective reciprocal interactions to occur, the objects and symbols in the immediate environment must be of a kind that invites attention, exploration, manipulation, elaboration and imagination.

Adults have a profound impact on the learning experiences of children. Research tells us that effective early childhood educators reflect on their practice and quality of provision for young children in order to create experiences in early years settings that are affirming for all involved. The contemporary view of children as active agents in learning and development requires educators to understand that even very young children contribute to their own development. This is not to underestimate the vulnerability of the child or the very powerful protective role of the adult. It does, however, challenge adults to reconsider the child as competent, to reflect on practice and recognise the diverse nature of each child when planning early care and education, designing learning environments and providing learning opportunities. It also provides a context within which children can be valued for their own sake in the present, the here and now. Focusing on the present moment allows the development of meaningful engagement and extended learning. The present moment, microtime within Bronfenbrenner's chronosystem, is that moment-to-moment connection where sustained shared thinking (Siraj-Blatchford, 2009) can occur – where the adult sets the scene for children's engagement with the world.

In this chapter, Bronfenbrenner's emphasis on development as a dynamic process is explored with reference to a pedagogy of early years practice that values the present moment for its immediate developmental contribution while also acknowledging its potential in respect of later development.

Early education as a dynamic process **113**

## Considering development and learning

Katz and Chard (1994) introduce the reader to two aspects of development: the normative and the dynamic. They note that, traditionally, early years practice has drawn heavily on psychological research, studying the child in isolation from everyday life. Such studies focus on normative development, providing us with a general descriptive guide of what children at particular ages can be expected to achieve and how they can be expected to behave; such descriptions are often called milestones. While useful as general points of reference, developmental milestones can become problematic if we depend on them to guide early years practice with groups of young children. Features of normative development fail to take account of the diversity of individual children and the importance of context. Each child presents with different capabilities, interests and experiences. Katz and Chard (1994) identify three interrelated dimensions of dynamic development:

1 developmental change over time with experience;
2 delayed impact of earlier experiences affecting later functioning;
3 long-term cumulative effects of repeated or frequent experiences.

This reminds us that children's early experiences have potential long-term consequences.

The idea of normative development has been particularly influential for curriculum development and practice in early education. In early years practice, for instance, we see the focus on normative development when we observe educators offering the same activity (e.g. making a snowman mobile using materials prepared by the adult) to all children for a particular length of time. While this might keep children busy, it shows limited understanding of the capabilities and interests of each individual child in the group and limits opportunities for them to imagine and create their own response to the idea of a snowman mobile.

The normative dimension of development addresses the question of what most children can and cannot do at a given age and draws on the work of Gesell in child study and Piaget in studies of cognitive development. The influence of consideration of development from a normative perspective alone is evident in the publication *Developmentally Appropriate Practice in Early Childhood Programmes* (Bredekamp & Copple, 1997). This presents a variety of early education materials and activities and identifies them as either 'appropriate' or 'inappropriate' for children at different ages and stages of their lives. The description (or prescription) of 'appropriate' here is closely tied to the contribution these materials and activities make to the development of the child towards operational thinking and conceptualises development as continuous progress toward adulthood.

The Developmentally Appropriate Practice DAP approach to early years practice has been criticised (Dahlberg & Moss, 2005) because it suggests that all children develop in a predictable way. While this may appear to be the case over time, at an individual level, on a daily basis, things are far messier and more entangled.

An overemphasis on milestones in early childhood results in less attention being given to the dynamic dimension of development and the learning opportunities that arise in children's day-to-day lives (Hayes & Filipovic, 2018; Navarro, Doucet, & Tudge, 2020).

Research indicates that dynamic development matters most when considering young children's learning and the early years environment that is provided. 'Childish' behaviours should be regarded as adaptive to the period or situation and not presumed problematic or imperfect; rather, they are important responses to the particular 'niche' of childhood:

> The idea that a behaviour, such as play, has immediate rather than deferred benefits is consistent with the view that development is an adaptation to the specific demands of a niche, such as childhood. The important point to stress here is that behaviour may serve different functions at different periods of development.
>
> *(Pellegrini & Bjorklund, 1998, p. 17)*

Sometimes, there is continuity of behaviours over time; for instance, a physically active infant is likely to be active during her preschool through into her school years; the continuity of development is clear. However, there can also be a developmental link across time between two apparently dissimilar behaviours, and this is more difficult to track. For example, the ability to engage in make-believe play at age three is closely related to word reading at age five; thus, make-believe or pretend play can be seen as evidence of developing literacy skills (Pellegrini & Bjorklund, 1998). Make-believe play and word reading look very different and involve different response modes, but they are theoretically related in that they both involve the manipulation of symbolic representation. The essence of 'being developmental' in practice challenges early childhood educators to value the moment for its immediate developmental contribution to the individual whilst acknowledging (but not overemphasising) its potential for later developmental outcomes. Viewing development as a dynamic and discontinuous process allows one to view behaviour in early childhood as being adaptive to the demands of childhood.

Sensitivity to both the normative and dynamic dimensions of development is critical in early years practice. The distinction between what young children can do and what they should do is especially serious in the early years because most children appear willing, if not eager, to do what is asked of them. They are often willing to attempt to meet even the most unrealistic expectations when encouraged by important adults in their lives. Therefore, many authors (Pramling-Samuelsson & Asblond-Carlsson, 2008; Singer, 2015) caution against adult-led, prescriptive models of early years practice. Such approaches are designed towards the achievement of specific learning outcomes in, for instance, literacy or numeracy rather than attending to the process of how children become literate and numerate. Evidence suggests that it is more important to attend to the process of the present and the dynamics of individual development in everyday practice. During the early years, it

Early education as a dynamic process **115**

seems that *how* children learn rather than *what* children learn matters most. When early years educators are too concerned with what a child should be learning at a particular stage, not only may they miss the learning/teaching moments of every day, but they may also act to inhibit the child's learning. Researchers have found that toddlers often blur the boundaries between play and not-play activities even though adults see a clear distinction. This can result in children experiencing confrontations and commands from adults with many comments like 'no, don't do that' and 'put that down' (Singer, 2015) when adults misinterpret adaptive processes of learning as misbehaviour.

Consider the behaviour of the children in the vignettes involving Ilinka, Eyad, and Annelise and Ruby. How does the environment facilitate interactions? Are the materials available to them contributing to their play? What role has the adult?

---

Nine-month-old Ilinka is in a high-chair being fed by early childhood educator Ella. Ilinka repeatedly puts her hands into the bowl of food, squashes it with her fists and throws it onto her tray, squealing each time it makes a noise – 'splat!' Ella is irritated because she needs to get Ilinka fed and the eating area cleaned up before it is time for 'messy play'.

*Source: author observation in an early childhood setting*

---

Ten-month-old Eyad is playing on the floor while his father cleans the house. He is very interested in a plant in the corner of the sitting room because it has a leaf that hangs down; Eyad likes hitting it to see it going back and forth. Every time he crawls over to it, his father lifts him away and says, 'Ah-ah, dirty, you'll spill the dirt all over yourself'. Eyad has lots of toys on the floor to play with, but he really wants that plant.

*Source: author observation*

---

Three-year-olds Annelise and Ruby are playing dress-up. They have discovered their childminder's make-up bag and decide that some lipstick would really make them look like princesses.

*Source: author observation*

---

## Interactions in development

Increasingly, we are coming to understand the powerful role that children themselves play in their own development. Bruner (1996) identifies the goals of adult–child

**116** Early education as a dynamic process

interactions as joint problem-solving, intersubjectivity, warmth/responsiveness and promoting self-regulation. He argues that if pedagogy is to empower young children to achieve their potential, it must transmit the tools of the society in which they live. This includes helping children to explore their own way of thinking and problem-solving. One of the critical features of children's developing identity and self-esteem is the extent to which they exhibit agency or consider themselves to be in control of their own actions. Agency can be observed when children take the initiative in their behaviour, form opinions or structure their experiences. To assist such positive development, Bruner stresses the importance of intense interactions in language-rich environments, reflecting the proximal processes proposed by Bronfenbrenner.

As mentioned in Chapter 1, the 'turn taking' or 'serve and return' relationships commonly seen in the interaction between very young children and adults in games like 'peekaboo' seem to have a critical role in development through their influence on brain development. Effective interactions are positive and occur on a regular basis over extended periods. Young children benefit most from relationships when they occur within stable, caring and interactive learning environments. As previously explored, the quality of interactions is closely related to the development of generative dispositions (Bronfenbrenner & Morris, 2006). What seems to be most important to effective early years practice is the quality of the relationships between children, adults and learning environments. It facilitates 'created understandings' that flow across the 'in-between' – the physical and psychological gap between people, particularly in interpersonal interactions. Engagement across this gap provides critical spaces for learning. Everyday interactions in everyday contexts can be enriching, and we should not underestimate the power of the ordinary. Studies on intersubjectivity have promoted a more respectful pedagogy, seeing the child as an active participant in the learning process. Bidirectional, transformational interactions facilitate children in explaining their ideas to others, negotiating and clarifying their thinking. Collaborative learning between peers is particularly important in early childhood where collaborative opportunities in safe environments enhance children's opportunities to refine their cognitive and metacognitive (thinking about thinking) skills (Hayes, 2007).

The importance of relationships and interactions for development is highlighted by research showing the powerful role that social context plays in the lives of young children. Support for the notion of collaborative learning derives from a theoretical stance recognising the social nature of learning and the social construction of meaning. It is based on the belief that participation in shared activities plays a key role in development. Working on problems together is particularly valuable in assisting young children to explain their thinking, to make their reasoning about things visible, even if it may not always result in enhanced performance, particularly if the more competent peer lacks confidence (Rogoff, 1998).

Children's capacity for intersubjectivity has developmental value, enabling participation in joint attention whereby an expert adult and novice child work together and develop a shared understanding (Bruner, 1996). Today, terms such as sustained shared thinking (Siraj-Blatchford, 2009), dialogic teaching (Alexander, 2004), nurturing pedagogy (Hayes, 2007) and extended purposive conversations (French, 2014) are used to describe such joint activity, and these ideas are recognised as being central to educationally supportive adult–child interactions. Sustained shared thinking is an interaction that "involves an adult being aware of the child's interests and understandings and involves the adult and the child interacting together to develop an idea or skill" (Siraj-Blatchford, Taggart, Sylva, Sammons, & Melhuish, 2008, p. 29). It has been linked to improved cognitive outcomes for children and is recognised as one key element of high-quality early years practice. Educators who are sensitive, attuned and responsive to children's cues, applying a nurturing pedagogy, are better able to engage in sustained shared thinking, assess what assistance children need, if any, and ensure their responses are respectful of the child.

Sustained shared thinking underpins a range of techniques for educating young children, such as constructing understanding, philosophising and scaffolding their learning, amongst others (MacNaughton & Williams, 2009). This view recognises the young social child as being capable of reasoning, making sense of the world and using higher-order functions such as thinking about thinking, connecting ideas through reflection or "going meta" (Bruner, 1996, p. 57). The process of sustained shared thinking is valuable beyond the early years setting, offering a blueprint for interactions with peers, teachers and work colleagues: "[i]n terms of competence, progression goes from mastering the very informal and strongly improvised *sustained and shared* interactions to more highly structured and much more formal *sustained and shared* interactions in adult life" (Siraj-Blatchford, 2009, p. 81, emphasis her own).

---

**REFLECTION**

Taking a recent experience you have had with young children, reflect on opportunities for sustained shared thinking. In what way did you extend the moment through your practice? Were there other learning/teaching opportunities? How best might they have been exploited?

---

The extent of development that typically occurs in the first six years of a child's life is striking. They develop physically from being tiny babes in arms at birth, unable to move from one place to the next, to crawling, then toddling and on to the competent physical child we see at six years of age. Language development is also visible as a child changes from a being with a limited range of sounds (the cry, the laugh, the coo) to a two-year-old making sentences to a six-year-old with a vocabulary of anything from 1,500 to 5,000 words or more. We see the influence of good food, exercise and language opportunities in the children we know and those we work

**118** Early education as a dynamic process

with. What is less visible and even more amazing is the development of the brain; brain research suggests that early experiences can affect the architecture of the brain 'by establishing either a sturdy or a fragile foundation for all of the learning, health and behaviour that follow' (National Scientific Council on the Developing Child, n.d. p. 1).

Thus, current research supports Bronfenbrenner's contention that proximal processes are the engines of development. It confirms that it is not simply the opportunity for interactions but also the *nature* and *quality* of the interactive process itself that is important. Research particularly highlights the value of dynamic, bidirectional social interactions as being crucial to early development (National Scientific Council on the Developing Child [NSCDC], 2020). These bidirectional, transformational interactions facilitate children in explaining their ideas to others and clarifying their thinking, thus refining their social, cognitive and metacognitive skills, the skills of thinking about thinking (Hayes, 2013). Early years programmes with a strong emphasis, both curricular (content) and pedagogical (practice), on the nurturing of affective development and support for social and emotional learning positively influence children's overall development, including their academic cognitive development. Good-quality social relationships are central to the positive wellbeing of both adults and children in early years settings. Positive learning environments provide secure relationships to facilitate children's exploration, play and learning. This is as true for the child of five months of age as it is for the child of five years. Educators who provide for these learning opportunities rather than focusing too closely on the development of academic skills are supporting the development of the fundamental, foundational aspects of learning. Positive and supportive adult–child interactions enhance children's security to explore and experience connectedness to peers and are important to wellbeing and flourishing as well as to the development of literacy and numeracy dispositions and skills. Blakemore and Frith highlight the danger of introducing academic training too early, noting that "there is no biological necessity to rush to start formal teaching earlier and earlier. Rather, late starts might be considered as perfectly in time with natural brain and cognitive development" (2005, p. 460).

Good-quality early years practice with children requires the attention of the adult *in context* to the whole child *in context*, highlighting the importance of being present in the now and not thinking of what you will be doing once the activity is over. Working professionally in the early years means being willing to recognise that there is always something more to learn about child development, learning environments and practice in general. A reflective practitioner monitors their practice and questions it: Why am I doing this? Why is this of value to the child, the group, my colleagues, parents, the community? A questioning approach to practice is key in sustaining quality. It challenges educators to evaluate the quality and relevance of early years practice to children. It is through asking and answering the 'why' questions that educators begin to consolidate a shared understanding and language of early years practice.

# Early education as a dynamic process  **119**

---

### REFLECTION

Busy early childhood educators often find themselves planning for the next activity rather than fully attending to the activity they are engaged in or the child with whom they are engaged. Do you recognise this tendency in yourself? What can you do to help remind yourself to be present with children in the moment in spite of the pressures of a busy working life?

---

In reflecting on why early years experiences are so important to a child's development, research findings from a range of disciplines including developmental psychology, education and neuroscience are relevant, highlighting the connectedness between various experiences of young children in different developmental domains such as the physical, linguistic, cognitive, emotional and social. The cumulative knowledge of decades of research has contributed to a greater understanding of development in the early years and supports the complexity of development captured by Bronfenbrenner in his dynamic model of human development. The NSCDC (nd) argue that research into early brain development confirms the importance of early life experiences and their impact on the basic architecture of the brain. They present evidence that brains are built up over time, beginning before birth and continuing into adulthood:

> Scientists now know a major ingredient in this developmental process is the "serve and return" relationship between children and their parents and other caregivers in the family or community. Young children naturally reach out for interaction through babbling, facial expressions, and gestures, and adults respond with the same kind of vocalising and gesturing back at them. In the absence of such responses – or if the responses are unreliable or inappropriate – the brain's architecture does not form as expected, which can lead to disparities in learning and behavior.
>
> *(NSCDC, nd, pp. 1–2)*

Infants particularly benefit from the undivided, uninterrupted attention of adults. A key ingredient in the process of brain development is the quality of early relationships between children and their parents and other significant adults. From the start, even very young children, infants, are equipped with the skills necessary to initiate and maintain communication. Reflect on the way in which Cillian, the baby in the vignette, is the central active component in the interactions, first engaging his two sisters and then his parents until all family members are participating in an activity which he initiated.

---

Ten-month-old Cillian is sitting on his mother's knee. The family are tired after a day out and are resting. Cillian, his mother and his sister Katie (seven) are watching television. His sister Saidbhín (three) is playing a game on the

> computer, and his father is tidying up. Cillian notices a strand of Katie's hair hanging down, reaches out and pulls it. Katie laughs, tickles Cillian's tummy and says, "You cheeky monkey, did you pull my hair?" Cillian giggles, and because Katie likes the sound, she tickles him again. Saidbhín moves away from the computer and joins her brother and sister in the fun. Soon the attention of the whole family is on Cillian's giggles, and instead of their solitary pursuits, they are all laughing together with the baby at the centre of their interactions.
>
> *Source: author observation*

Responsive adults reply in kind with vocalisations and gestures of their own, and children then reward such adult attention by responding, smiling or mimicking behaviour, such as sticking out their tongue. This is why it is so important for adults working with children to give their full attention to them and not become distracted by, for example, checking their mobile phones.

We have long known that children who grow up in depleted environments such as some institutional settings or chaotic and impoverished homes show signs of developmental delay from very early on. We now know that this is, in part, because of the absence of close, stable relationships – the proximal processes described by Bronfenbrenner. Considering the brain as a 'social brain' strengthens our understanding of the importance of interactions and relationships to brain development. This may be a useful concept for those working directly with young children as it provides a clear link between the environment (the space, materials, people, time) and the learning, developing child (Molapour et al., 2021). We also know that the brain is most flexible in early years and, therefore, more responsive to a range of environmental and interactional influences (Center on the Developing Child, 2016; Maconochie, 2019). As the child grows, this flexibility diminishes, and it is more difficult to change existing brain circuitry. Take language development for instance. In the first months of life, the baby responds to a wide range of sounds and begins to differentiate and specialise in those sounds she is exposed to. At the same time as this discrimination and specialisation is happening, the brain is already starting to lose the sounds of other languages. "Although the 'windows' for language learning and other skills remain open, these brain circuits become increasingly difficult to alter over time" (NSCDC, n.d., p. 2). For a rich example of the linguistic power of young babies, you may like to access the TED Talk given by Patricia Kuhl (2010, October) titled *The Linguistic Genius of Babies*.

In summary:

- *Brains are built over time from the bottom up:* early experiences strongly influence the development of a child's brain architecture and this, in turn, can influence the strength or weakness of the foundation for future learning, development and behaviour.
- *The interactive influences of genes and experience shape the developing brain:* interactions are central to this developing architecture. The active agent of influence

is the turn taking, 'serve and return' nature of interactive relationships. It is important therefore that adults are attuned and responsive to signals from children. Young children need positive relationships, rich learning opportunities and safe environments in their early years settings.

- *The brain's capacity for change decreases with age:* the brain is most responsive to change during the early years, and so this is a crucial period. However, we still have a great deal more to learn about the brain, how it develops and what role the environment plays.
- *Cognitive, emotional and social capacities are inextricably intertwined throughout the life course:* as research grows, so too does our understanding of the complex, interrelated and dynamic nature of development. From a practice point of view, we need to be aware that everything we do with and for children may have an impact, so we need to be alert and present in our practice.
- *Toxic stress damages effective brain architecture, leading to lifelong problems in learning, behaviour and physical and mental health:* we know that children who grow up in poverty or in chaotic households need a great deal of support directly and indirectly to overcome the stresses they are living with. However, we must also recognise that while early years settings can provide a nurturing, safe and secure space for young children and a protective context within which they can develop and learn, such settings are only one of a number of supports that may be needed for children.

*(NSCDC, 2007)*

Brain research has confirmed that the brain is complex and interconnected; social, emotional and cognitive (or thinking) capacities are intertwined. Positive early experiences contribute to wellbeing and the development of social skills. Both well-being and social competence contribute to a child's sense of self-confidence, which, in turn, contributes to learning and cognitive development. "Above and beyond well-known impacts on early brain development, increasing evidence is also pointing to the importance of the prenatal period and first few years after birth for the development of core immune functions, metabolic regulation, and other physiological systems that can affect long-term well- being" (NSCDC, 2020, p. 15). The evidence also indicates that stress associated with poverty, neglect, abuse or poor parenting can compromise the positive brain development so essential to later achievement and success. In such cases, high-quality early years settings can counteract – to some extent – the impact of negative stressors and set the child on a more positive developmental path. This happens not only through direct impact on children but also through indirect influences on parents and the home learning environment (Melhuish, 2014). This draws attention to the powerful role the mesosytem, the communication pathway between home and setting, can play in the overall development of the child.

The basic principles of neuroscience indicate that early preventive intervention produces more favourable outcomes than remediation later in life. Supportive relationships and positive learning experiences begin at home and are also provided in

**122** Early education as a dynamic process

high-quality early years settings. Babies and young children require secure, caring, interactive relationships with adults for healthy brain development. For babies and young children experiencing poverty, abuse or stress, additional specialised and supportive interventions may be needed to address, insofar as possible, the cause of stress and protect the child from its consequences. Bronfenbrenner (1985), writing about policy and the future of childhood, emphasises the need to counteract hectic or chaotic life experiences young children may have through the provision and support of good-quality early years services.

Thus, it is clear that the early years of children's lives are crucial to brain development, in turn influencing the trajectory of overall development and learning (O'Toole & Hayes, 2020). Supportive relationships and positive learning experiences are key, and the role of the early years educator cannot be overstated. Through good-quality practice, they provide learning environments that stimulate and challenge children and give them a sense of wellbeing and belonging within which they can explore, play, learn, develop and strive to reach their full potential.

Of course, there is a distinction between the brain and the mind. While the terms are often used interchangeably, there is a difference; the brain is a physical, observable organ, whereas the mind is a philosophical concept. The mind manifests in our thoughts and words and is unlocked within the social world. We are born into relationships and created through relationships. Our physical brain develops within our own individual skull, but "a mind only exists within a network. It is the result of interactions between brains, and it is important not to confuse brains with minds" (Brooks, 2011, p. 43). Although we know more about how relationships and interactions affect the architecture of the physical brain, we are still a long way from understanding how the brain actually works in the manifestation of mind and behaviour.

---

**REFLECTION**

Identify five key activities conducted within your early years setting on a daily basis, from play experience, care opportunities and social situations. Consider the role of social interactions in the value of these activities for education and development. How could you create further opportunities for social interaction and learning within these everyday activities?

---

## Developing executive functions

Child development is a complex process involving the interrelationship between genes, the brain, the body, behaviour and the physical and social environment. The brain is only partially mature at birth and continues to develop over the first years of life. Why are proximal processes so important to development, and what is it about positive brain development that influences an individual's learning? For optimal

Early education as a dynamic process **123**

development, babies and young children require calm, caring, interactive relationships, and healthy brain development depends on, and enables, complex social interactions. The quality of early experiences can determine how sturdy or fragile the foundations are for learning and behaviour over time.

The skills necessary to control and coordinate information, critical to success in life in general and school success in particular, are developed in the early years and provide the foundation for later learning and development. These skills are called the 'executive functions', and we use them to manage behaviour, emotions and attention (Diamond, 2013; Howard & Vasseleu, 2020). 'Executive function' describes the set of mental processes that help us organise and order our actions; this involves both concrete behaviours and abstract concepts. Children who have good executive function and self-regulation do better both academically and socially. The development of executive function depends on the biological maturity of the child, but the process is heavily influenced by environmental experiences (O'Toole & Hayes, 2020). Through their early learning experiences, children access opportunities to develop these functions, and the adults in their lives are of critical importance in facilitating this. These more recent understandings of the link between brain development and the experiences of children reflect Bronfenbrenner's bioecological argument that persons and environment, in and over time, work together to influence learning and development.

Different authors characterise the elements of executive function in different ways, but they generally include (1) working memory and recall; (2) activation, arousal and effort; (3) mental flexibility; and (4) self-control (Diamond, 2013). According to Bronfenbrenner, the extent to which individuals develop these skills depends on the dynamic and quality of proximal processes and the influence of (and on) the person characteristics of the child – that is, their dispositions, resources and demand characteristics. We look more closely at these four elements in the following discussion:

- *A working memory and recall* involve problem-solving, reasoning and planning. Through our working memory, we make sense of things over time. It requires that we hold in mind what has happened and relate it to what is happening now. It assists recall. In the HighScope model of early education, this is foregrounded through the *plan/do/review* process. Adults respond to children, give them time to talk about their ideas and plans, allow them space to actively explore their environment, create opportunities for them to review their plans and encourage their thinking and recall. Working memory is also necessary to connect ideas, to link what you have done, heard or read with what you are doing, hearing or reading right now, and to remember instructions and carry them out in the correct order. Additionally, our working memory helps us understand cause and effect.
- *Activation, arousal and effort* refer to the child's willingness and ability to start something, pay attention to the activity and put in the effort necessary to complete it. Such skills only develop where the child is comfortable, secure and has

**124** Early education as a dynamic process

a sense of belonging. Providing children with opportunities, materials, time and space to make choices in their activities while facilitating them in thinking about what they are doing is a key role for the early educator – it is the essence of high-quality early childhood education and care.

- *Mental flexibility* includes being able to switch perspectives, to see things in a new light, see opportunities and take advantage of them and be willing to change course if what you are doing is not working. This flexibility of mind allows people to think outside the box and be creative. It also helps us understand things from another person's viewpoint.
- *Self-control* is crucial to successful learning and development. It allows us to stay focused, avoid distraction, stay on task and limit impulsive behaviour. When children are impulsive, they are less likely to persist at an activity or to pay attention, and this can lead to later difficulties in school and in adulthood. Children with good self-control were less likely to drop out of school, smoke or become teenage parents. Research has also found that children in settings where early years educators encourage the development of self-control and self-regulation are more likely to experience school success (Blair, 2002). Apart from these later impacts, children who have self-control are more likely to have enjoyable and satisfying everyday experiences; their childhoods are more likely to be happy and content than fractured and stressful (Howard & Vasseleu, 2020).

We know that development progresses through feedback loops. The messages we get back from the environment (social, cultural or material) inform the view we have of ourselves, which then influences the extent to which we see ourselves as masterful or helpless, trusted or mistrusted. Poor executive function can lead to troublesome behaviour, whereas good executive function leads to greater cooperation, caring and responsiveness in children. Through observation, adults can see executive function at work in children's play when they are talking themselves through an activity as they move objects around or place things in a particular order. Understanding the power of process and the *dynamic* dimension of individual development helps foreground interactions as a central aspect of development over time. It also highlights the complexity of development as there can be a developmental link between two dissimilar behaviours. Earlier in this chapter, we noted that children's make-believe play at three is related to word reading at five. So, we see how important free pretend play is in any literacy strategy – even though pretend play rarely looks like reading!

## Implications for practice

Viewing development as a dynamic and discontinuous process allows us to view behaviour and development in early childhood as being adaptive to the immediate demands of the child in context. This approach to early education is not tied to the age and stage of development of the child but, rather, to the sociocultural context of development for the child in the present. It is exemplified by the internationally

Early education as a dynamic process **125**

recognised practices at Reggio Emila in Italy and the *Te Whāriki* early years curriculum of New Zealand in which pedagogy is directed by the connections, interactions and relationships between children and the wider world and by social, physical and emotional elements as opposed to any prescribed expectations of developmental outcome. There is increasing evidence from psychological research and neuroscience to support Bronfenbrenner's contention that proximal processes are crucial engines of development. Evidence also suggests that these interactive processes are particularly important in early childhood given the role of interactions in facilitating the development of thinking skills (cognitive and metacognitive) and affective skills (dispositions), that is their role in developing knowledge and skills, knowledge about knowledge and the inclination and readiness to apply knowledge. Furthermore, research emphasising the importance of the home learning environment supports Bronfenbrenner's contention that the mesosystem, the connectivity between microsystems such as the home and the early childhood setting, is a crucial element of his model of development and one that early childhood educators should not ignore.

## Key concepts for early years practice

1 A feature of the final iteration of the bioecological model is its *focus on the role of the interactional, relational process in driving development.*

2 *The quality of proximal processes is mediated by social interactions* and provides a link between the structure (or biology) of development and the processes of development. It harmonises the view of the child as a biological reality and an 'agent', neither being sufficient in and of itself. This has implications for early educational practice.

3 Adults have a profound impact on the learning experiences of children. *Effective early years educators reflect on their practice and the quality of provision for young children* to create experiences in early years settings that are positive and affirming for all involved, children and adult alike.

4 *Sensitivity to both the normative and dynamic dimensions of development is critical in the early years.* The essence of 'being developmental' challenges early years educators to value the moment for its immediate developmental contribution to the individual whilst acknowledging (but not overemphasising) its potential in respect of the child's later development.

5 *Children's capacity for intersubjectivity has developmental value* as it enables them to participate in episodes of joint attention where an expert adult and novice child work together on a task and develop a shared understanding (Bruner, 1996). Today, terms such as sustained shared thinking (Siraj-Blatchford, 2009), dialogic teaching (Alexander, 2004), nurturing pedagogy (Hayes, 2007) and extended purposive conversations (French, 2014) are used to describe such joint activity.

6 *A key ingredient in the process of brain development is the quality of early relationships* between children and their parents and other significant adults. Babies and

## 126 Early education as a dynamic process

young children require secure, caring, interactive relationships with adults for healthy brain development.

7 *Early preventive intervention produces more favourable outcomes than remediation later in life.* Supportive relationships and positive learning experiences begin at home and are also provided in high-quality early years environments.

8 The skills necessary to control and coordinate information, critical to success in life in general and school success in particular, are developed in the early years and provide the foundation for later learning and development. These skills are called the *'executive functions'* – *the functions we use to manage behaviour, emotions and attention.*

9 *Children with good executive function and self-regulation do better both academically and socially.* Poor executive function can lead to troublesome behaviour, whilst good executive function leads to greater cooperation, caring and responsiveness in children.

10 Understanding the power of process and the *dynamic* dimension of individual development helps foreground *interactions as a central aspect of changes in development over time.*

# 9
# NURTURING CHILDREN'S LEARNING AND DEVELOPMENT

According to Rosa and Tudge, it "is easy to argue that persons and environments are mutually implicated in human development, but it is more difficult to explain how that functions" (2013, p. 255). In this chapter, we use the bioecological model to consider high-quality early years practice and the central role of early childhood educators in nurturing children's learning and development. In particular, we explore the dynamics of development and the power of a nurturing pedagogy, which emphasises the importance of relationships. We also consider mechanisms and approaches to sustaining quality and the importance of pedagogical leadership and play to quality practice.

Concentrating more on dynamic development than on normative expectations highlights practices most beneficial to individual children at particular moments within particular contexts. Viewing development as a dynamic and discontinuous process facilitates a pedagogy attuned to the connections, interactions and relationships between children and the wider world while being sensitive to social, physical and emotional learning opportunities (Hayes, 2013). This particularly resonates in settings including children from diverse backgrounds who may be experiencing learning environments that do not reflect the expectations or experiences of their culture or family. This illustrates the multiple microsystems influencing development. To grasp why certain early years practices are more successful than others in facilitating children to achieve positive outcomes, researchers and educators seek to understand the mechanisms of development and learning. This is particularly important where investments are made to support early education as an intervention to counteract educational disadvantage.

The bioecological model introduces the new domain of process into the microsystems of development, emphasising the distinctive contribution of proximal processes to development – those close interactions that individuals have with other people, materials and ideas that occur in day-to-day life (Bronfenbrenner &

DOI: 10.4324/9781003247760-9

**128** Nurturing Children's Learning and Development

Morris, 2006). For young children, the opportunity to experience and participate in these interactions is facilitated in calm, unhurried environments where adults are attuned to children's need for time and encouragement. Bronfenbrenner and Morris recognise the negative influences of limiting contexts, increasingly present in the lives of contemporary children, with "growing hecticness, instability and chaos in the principal settings in which human competence and character are shaped – in the family, child-care arrangements, school, peer groups and neighbourhoods" (1998, p. 995).

The potential of proximal processes for combatting such negative impacts has important implications for the early years, highlighting the power of interactions and the role of adults. Nurturing children's learning as part of a caring educative process requires adults to develop skills of observation and reflection, allowing for non-intrusive planning and provision of learning environments that support and extend children's learning and opportunities for good-quality interactions. To those outside early education, including parents, the complexity involved in early years practice may not be immediately obvious. There is a continuing tendency to underestimate the educative role of caring and the importance of high-quality early education to children's happiness and well-being (Wood, 2014). Hayes (2008), writing about the contested concept of care, proposes that there is a need for a significant shift towards explicit acknowledgement of the critical contribution of the interpersonal and relational aspects of early education.

Emphasising the often misunderstood educative role of care, Hayes (2008) argues for the reconceptualising of care as nurture so that its status as an educative dimension be enhanced. She introduces the concept of a 'nurturing pedagogy', recognising the educative role of care as nurture, the importance of relationships and the role of playful interaction, exploration, dialogue and collaborative learning in supporting young children's learning. Pedagogy provides a unique integration space for care and education and is, itself, a form of assessment and a guide to an emergent and responsive early years curriculum. Characterising good-quality early years practice as a nurturing pedagogy moves understanding of practice beyond simply minding children and watching them play. The role of the adult is one of low intervention and high response, conveying a more powerful level of interaction and requiring the early childhood educator to have specific skills, actively nourishing and educating the child. Effective, learning environments of a good quality are stimulating and challenging, risk-rich, respectful and reflective. The pedagogical process is relational, responsive and reciprocal, reflecting the importance of proximal processes as the engines of development, particularly in the early years.

Skills of observation and reflection are central to a nurturing pedagogy (Palaiologou, 2019). They enhance practice and planning, are manifest in well-managed yet reasonably flexible practice and assist in providing learning environments that include children as active agents, supporting and extending learning. This allows for attention to the quality of interactions between children and the social, spatial and material learning environment. It also allows for planning by the adult for future opportunities to extend learning, taking the child, rather than prescribed curricular content, as central. Furthermore, reflective observation encourages movement away from traditional organisational/management roles, strengthening the educational, pedagogical role of the adult. Relationships and interactions are central to a nurturing pedagogy (O'Toole & Hayes, 2020). There is a rich tapestry of relations across different microsystems, facilitated by enhanced communication and rich mesosystems, between children themselves, between adults and children, between adults and their colleagues and parents of the children they work with and between learners and the environments where learning takes place. Interactions are the critical spaces for learning individually and in groups. To create a signifi-cant shift to understanding the educative role of care in practice, it is necessary to explicitly acknowledge the critical contribution of this interpersonal aspect of early education, to make it visible, to realise it as the practice of everyday interactions, the proximal processes.

A nurturing pedagogy is a different style of practice compared to that many of us have experienced in our own education. It demands that adults let go of some traditional ideas about the educational relationship between adult and child where the adult was the source of knowledge and children were expected to pas-sively receive this knowledge. Good-quality early years practice relies less on a content-led curriculum and direct instruction and more on a framework of values and principles, respecting the process underpinning an emergent or enquiry-based curriculum. An emergent curriculum is one that grows from the shared experi-ences of all participants in a learning environment. It is influenced by the layout and routines of the setting, the activities and materials available and the intentions of adults. It is also influenced by children's own background experiences, their dispositions and their individual characteristics, as discussed in Chapter 4. Thus, the content of a curriculum derives from daily interactions with others and playful, meaningful interactions with materials, objects, symbols and ideas (Hedges, 2014). Many authors recognise the value of such a pedagogical approach, acknowledging that it "incorporates children's cultural practices, meanings and purposes" (Wood, 2013, p. 72).

In such interactive and integrated settings, children come to develop work-ing theories about the world – material, social, physical and emotional. Children thereby make connections between everyday things and actions, forming the basis of knowledge relevant to different discipline areas – almost unaware that they are doing so (Fleer, 2010; Fleer, Fragkiadaki, & Rai, 2020). It is the skill of an excellent educator that they can identify and exploit learning moments and draw children's attention to them or work in partnership with children to extend oral language and expression while enriching their knowledge base. Through reflecting on and engaging with children's working theories as they explore, play and create, the attuned early childhood educator can unlock curriculum content and expand chil-dren's knowledge and understandings.

**130** Nurturing Children's Learning and Development

---

A few four-year-olds were sitting together. Three of the children were wearing trainers that would light up when they stepped down on them.

TEACHER: Wow! Look at your shoes! That is so cool. They light up when you step down.

CHILD 1: Yes, they do this. [Jumps up and down several times] *Teacher:* How does that happen? How does it light up?

CHILD 1: Because they are new.

TEACHER: Um. Mine are new too but they don't light up.

CHILD 2: No, because they light up when you step down on them [Steps down hard several times]

TEACHER: [Steps down hard several times] That's funny. Mine don't light up when I step down.

CHILD 3: No, no, no, you have to have these holes. [Points to the holes]

TEACHER: [Pointing to the hole in her own shoe] But I have holes and mine still don't light up, and Josh has holes in his trainers too and his do not light up either. I wonder why?

CHILD 4: I think you need batteries to make them work. [Thinks for a while] But I did not see batteries when I put my toes in.

CHILD 4: I think they are under your toes.

CHILD 2: I can't feel the batteries under my toes.

TEACHER: I wonder how we can find out about this?

*Source: with thanks to the 'collector', Lilian Katz*

---

Try to identify the key pedagogical moment in this vignette when the teacher moves the conversation about trainers into an educational conversation, extending the children's thinking. What moment do you select and why? Does she redirect the conversation or build on the children's contributions? (See note 1 for feedback on this task).[1]

Engaging children, respecting them and integrating learning opportunities across time and across the care and educational dimensions is central to effective practice. Traditionally, children were seen as adults-in-waiting, expected to be quiet in the presence of adults and the responsibility of their parents or guardians. Chapter 6 explored how our current understanding recognises children as full individuals with rights who should be consulted in matters affecting them. This image of children reflects many contemporary writings on the philosophy and practice of early childhood education, including that underpinning Reggio Emilia. Using a rights-based lens to inform early years practice allows us to recognise children as being competent, strong, active and participatory, and as meaning-makers and fellow citizens. This approach to practice builds on the individual capabilities and dispositions of the child within the social context and emphasises close interactions, proximal processes, between children and their early learning environments,

Nurturing Children's Learning and Development **131**

driving development and learning. Our understanding of early child development can guide us towards prioritising relationships and interactions over direct instruction as the cornerstone of early educational practice. Reflecting on practice thus provides a common language for discussing the central features that make early years practice unique and which are evident when observing a skilled educator at work.

Respecting children as having rights makes demands on adults. It requires that adults trust children and empathise with them, which in turn requires an understanding of children's cultural and developmental contexts. Manifesting trust in children translates in practice to providing, through nurturing environments, opportunities for them to recognise their own achievements and space for them to problem solve and resolve conflicts. Throughout childhood, children experience disappointment, frustration, failure and disapproval. They may also experience exclusion by peers. In healthy development within supportive relationships, children recover from these experiences. When children, even very young children, learn through experience that their feelings and concerns will be appreciated and understood, their emotions become less urgent. In the security of predictable responsiveness, children learn to regulate their emotions, confident that their feelings will be heard.

Children's curiosity and desire for knowledge and understanding are evident in their play, exploration, questions and behaviour. Young children need adults who trust that when provided with the opportunities, time and support, children will learn – adults who are excited, inspired and challenged by them. However, adults also need to set clear boundaries with rules that are sensible, understandable and consistent. Rules should not be extensive but, rather, few, fair and clearly explained; indeed, they are often most effective when developed with children themselves (O'Toole & Hayes, 2020). Where the child is at the centre of early years practice, the day-to-day curriculum reflects this; adults actively include children in the regular experiences of the setting, engage with them and learn from them while also enhancing their learning opportunities. This approach to practice is informed by a belief in the dynamic nature of child development and reflects a shift away from more traditional didactic practice to more integrated, social and interactive approaches.

High expectations are also important; children learn best when we 'expect' them to succeed (Boylan, Barblett, & Knaus, 2018; Galinsky, 2010). High expectations enhance children's motivation, self-belief and resilience, whereas low expectations undermine self-confidence and compromise self-belief. Children who develop strong self-esteem, motivation and a sense of agency are more likely to achieve their potential at school and be resilient to risk factors throughout their education. Expectations that are high assist children to achieve a growth mindset rather than one that is fixed (Dweck, 2007). Mindsets refer to beliefs we have about ourselves and our abilities. In a growth mindset, children recognise that their abilities and talents can be developed by persistence and hard work, and they enjoy solving problems; in a fixed mindset, however, where children cannot succeed at a task, they see themselves as the problem. The role of adults is crucial here as self-image develops through feedback. Adults can create learning opportunities that enhance the

**132** Nurturing Children's Learning and Development

development of a growth mindset and provide attractive and challenging opportunities for children. Where attuned to children, early years practitioners can extend learning moments created when the child needs a nudge to surmount a challenge.

Within the bioecological model, the processes mediating developmental pathways are influenced not only by the child's own interactions but also by features within the interacting individual, such as his beliefs and opinions. For high expectations to have a meaningful effect, early childhood educators must believe that every child is capable of learning, take responsibility for encouraging learning and communicate their belief to the child and to parents. This requires that they consider multiple ways of learning, value children's strengths and differences and use these in assessment and planning (Cigala, Venturelli, & Bassetti, 2019). They must find new ways to reflect on best practice and should employ a curriculum based on strengths and interests, allowing each child to experience success at his own level (Saffigna, Church, & Tayler, 2011). This means explicitly creating situations that build up children's resource characteristics so that they will be able to say, and believe, "I can".

## Sustaining good-quality learning environments

While process and person(s) are key elements of development, so too is context – the early learning microsystem, including its activities, materials, relationships and roles. The quality of everyday experiences in early years environments has a profound influence on them. Young children are not merely recipients or consumers of a service but are deeply influenced, individually and collectively, by their early years experiences. Children learn in context; the ordinary spaces, places and people they encounter make up that context. Adults who are attuned, 'watchfully attentive' and mindful in their day-to-day practices with children can make important contributions to learning and development. There is no need to distance children from society in an effort to enhance their learning and development. Indeed, creating active and effective links between early years settings and other important environments in the lives and communities of young children (strengthening the mesosystem), carefully managing the various transitions they make, is an important dimension in quality early years practice. Early years practice is the curriculum made visible – even where the curriculum may not be readily definable.

Consider the dynamics in the vignette concerning the European Together Old and Young project. How might you create opportunities for children to link with community-based services? How can you create opportunities for cross-generational connections?

> We witnessed many examples of seniors teaching skills and sharing their hobbies in the initiatives studied: seniors introducing children to local history through examining artefacts or seniors teaching children gardening, food production and cooking skills. The destruction of the piazza, the traditional

> meeting and play space for all generations in Poggio Picenze, Italy and the heart of the town, prompted the instigation of a programme whereby old people passed on the collective cultural memory of the town [to young children] by demonstrating traditional crafts and telling stories from the past.
>
> *Source: The European Together Old and Young project*
> *(The TOY Project Consortium, 2013, p. 18)*

Exploring understandings of how early years practices impact on children's learning and development can act as a stimulus for reflection on the quality of provision for young children so that experiences in early years settings will be affirming for all involved. The adult, and their style of engagement, seems to have a significant impact on the learning experiences of children. The Australian Early Years Learning Framework introduced the idea of 'intentional teaching', which is thoughtful, informed and deliberate and "is the opposite to teaching by rote or continuing with traditions because things have always been done that way" (Commonwealth of Australia, 2009, p. 15). Intentional teaching must be consciously developed. It "requires wide-ranging knowledge about how children typically develop and learn … a repertoire of instructional strategies" (Epstein, 2007, p. 1). Furthermore, educators must know when and how to use these strategies to benefit individual children in different content contexts. The intentional educator is not only aware of the importance of proximal processes but also knows how to maximise the possibilities of those interactions. We must consider the rich and diverse nature of each child when planning early care and education, designing learning environments and providing learning opportunities (Lewis, Fleer, & Hammer, 2019). The adult sets the scene for engagement with the world and provides contexts within which children can be seen and valued for their own sake in the here and now. The contemporary view of children as active agents in their learning requires educators to respond to the reality that even the very youngest children contribute to the context and content of their own development. This is not to underestimate the dependence of the child or the very powerful, protective role of the adult. The earliest playful interactions are context-specific and require supporting, intimate relationships (Parker-Rees, 2014).

The vignette involving Tony and Salima illustrates how early childhood educators can create opportunities for children to solve problems themselves and experience success. Report on two situations from your own practice where such opportunities were present.

> Preschoolers Tony and Salima are sitting on the floor, playing with the acorns Salima collected outside. Salima divides the acorns evenly between them. Their teacher sits on the floor next to them. Tony piles his acorns together, while Salima forms a large circle with hers. Tony says, "Hey, you got more than me!" Salima responds, "No, I don't. We each got the same." The teacher wonders

**134** Nurturing Children's Learning and Development

aloud how they could find out whether they have the same number, and the children suggest counting the acorns.

TONY: 1, 2, 3, 4, 5, 6, 7, 8, 9, 10, 11, 12, 13, 14. (He lines up his acorns in a row as he counts.)

SALIMA: 1, 2, 3, 4, 5, 6, 7, 8, 9, 10, 11, 12, 13, 14. (She also lines up her acorns in a row.)

TEACHER: You each have 14.

TON: Yeah. We got the same.

TEACHER: (Spreads Tony's acorns across the floor and puts Salima's in a pile.) Now who has more?

TONY (SMILES.): I do!

SALIMA: No, you don't. We each got the same. See? (She counts her acorns and puts them in a row, then counts Tony's acorns and puts them in a row as well.)

TEACHER: (This time she puts Tony's in a pile and spreads Salima's out across the floor.) Now who has more?

TONY: (Thinks for a moment.) Nobody's got more. We got the same!

*Source: adapted from Epstein (2007)*

How we consider the child in relation to the world impacts how inclusive we are in our planning and practice. Our own history and experiences of learning – even (or perhaps especially) if we are largely unthinking about them – inform and influence our practice in ways that are not always useful. Fleer (2003) has written about the unintended constraints brought to our work by assuming a shared understanding of commonly used terms, references or constructs. She argues that we need to give more attention to our 'taken-for-granted', consider how it can impose on our practice and challenge it in order to enhance our day-to-day practice. To sustain good-quality pedagogy, it is important to adopt criticality in approaching language and take time to consider the assumptions we make. Unless we are willing to challenge, explore and reflect on our own assumptions, we may never really provide children with the rich learning environments they need. In her work, Fleer (2003) identifies four tacit assumptions that influence early years practice and are often thoughtlessly accepted rather than critically reflected upon. These assumptions have significant impacts on how we create and sustain learning environments and, thus, influence children's development and learning.

The first assumption relates to how we position the child – do we see the child as part of the wider world or essentially as part of the early years setting? How we view the child, discussed in Chapter 3 when considering the work of Carl Rogers, has important implications for early years planning and practice. Fleer suggests that educators should reflect on the environmental organisation in early years settings and question it. Are we placing restrictions on children, limiting learning opportunities by creating 'corners' that we consider an essential element of the early years experience for those attending? Should we give children more freedom to circulate and choose their learning spaces and materials, placing less emphasis on these corners? Should we present a broader range of materials with a wider selection of objects representing more of what is ordinary and familiar to children?

The second assumption she considers relates to our view of children as learners – do we consider children as actively constructing knowledge, or do they learn from being told? The meaning of 'active' needs careful consideration here. It is not simply about physical activity alone; it includes being actively engaged in whatever is happening, active listening and careful, active observation – from such focused behaviour children may expand what they are doing. Early childhood educators are models for learning here, showing rather than telling, listening actively to children. Understanding children's active engagement allows us to see where and how we might provide them with challenges and work with them.

The third assumption identified by Fleer relates to the balance between the individual and the social orientation, the child alone or in a group. While it is important to understand the child as an individual, especially his particular learning style and needs, it is also important to recognise the child as a learner within a group. While individual development and learning are important, we know that children are social beings, social learners, that while they are independent, they are also interdependent. Children like to be with other children, sharing knowledge and so extending it. They enjoy succeeding in groups, and there they learn how to cope with failure too (Kernan & Singer, 2011). As adults, we understand the value of working as a team. It is similar for even very young children, and so we should plan for both the individual developing child and for the interdependent child.

Finally, Fleer challenges us to question the assumptions underpinning how we consider communication and conversation. Children are embedded in the social world and are active in their communication through various verbal and non-verbal processes. Do we see both child and adult as partners together in learning or separate from each other with the adult in the powerful position? While there is of course inequity between the child and the far more experienced adult, this should not negate the value of considering children as partners and working to manifest this. The process of distancing children, of treating them as a separate 'other', is well embedded in Western society, and so there is a need for explicit consideration and for creating occasions, spaces and time for meaningful communication or what Fleer (2003) calls "conversational opportunities". Carefully planned child-friendly environments facilitate social and collaborative learning. Real communication, that is, meaningful, between adults and children (and children and children) is not simple; it takes thoughtful planning and goes beyond reading stories or asking questions. Limiting conversation and dialogue to a question-and-answer style of communication is insufficient and disrespectful to children. It runs contrary to the inclusive and respectful early years pedagogy that underlies a democratic approach to practice, which equips children with important developmental proficiency (Mitchell, 2011).

**136** Nurturing Children's Learning and Development

We referred earlier to the fact that children come to early years settings with "funds of knowledge" (Hedges, 2014). Similarly, we need to recognise what early childhood educators bring to their practice with regard to the taken-for-granted.

---

### REFLECTION

Think about the four tacit assumptions that Fleer identifies. What might they mean to your practice in light of some recent example you can bring to mind? Discuss this with a colleague to identify if there is room for change.

---

Quality early childhood education and care practice has been more frequently observed and sustained within settings where there is strong evidence of pedagogical leadership, alongside management leadership (Siraj-Blatchford & Mani, 2007; Fonsén, 2013; Heikka, Pitkäniemi, & Kettukangas, & Hyttinen, 2021). Pedagogical leadership shifts the focus from more administrative and management tasks towards educational responsibilities and the learning environment. As such, it requires specific skills and knowledge. However, as Palaiologou and Male (2019) contend, pedagogical leadership is perhaps best considered as context-dependent rather than based on a specific model:

> Pedagogical leadership is rooted in its specific context and pays attention to its own environment through engaging with the historicity, culture and subjective perspectives/realities of the contexts that are involved.
>
> *(2019, p. 31)*

Reflecting the bioecological model, Fonsén (2013) identified four inter-related and interacting dimensions of pedagogical leadership. In addition to the importance of context the overall organisation culture of a setting, the professionality of the team and the pedagogical understanding of the setting management emerge as central. The unique features of pedagogical leadership are critical to supporting improvement, promoting the value of self-reflection and encouraging staff to continue to develop and strengthen their own practice. This, in turn, impacts the quality of the learning environment and the relational context of children's early learning.

Increasingly, families share the early care and education of their children with different types of early years settings. These settings are part of society and have links with other educational, social and cultural settings in local communities. They provide an important bridge for children and parents alike, from the seclusion of home through the early years setting and into the local community and wider society, and this is explored in detail in Chapter 10. Early years settings provide a particularly important connective or networking service for all families but particularly for minority or marginalised parents and their children. While the direct role of the educator is often characterised by their work with children attending their settings, it is important to recognise the indirect role they play, within meso- and exosystems, in creating these links. This becomes particularly important in supporting the home learning environment, which has a significant impact on the development of children (Siraj & Mayo, 2014). While encouraging close engagement with families is valuable and can sometimes lead to improvements in home learning environments, this is an issue to be handled with great cultural sensitivity and in real partnership with parents who are the experts of experience regarding their own children (Gaylor & Spiker, 2012; Kiely et al., 2021; O'Toole, Kiely, McGillicuddy, O'Brien, & O'Keeffe, 2019).

Children are motivated to learn, to seek meaning in their world, and they depend on the adults they meet to assist them in this endeavour. It is within immediate, day-to-day experiences that children learn about the world around them; the ordinary things in their lives are often new and curious and have the potential to be extraordinary, to act as the foundation for new knowledge and understandings. Children have a right to expect that early childhood settings will challenge and excite them, provide safety and security and enhance their overall development and learning. The adult can contribute by making experiences of the ordinary rich and meaningful through careful observation and reflection to inform their practice. Informed and attuned adults can expand children's language and thinking, fire curiosity, imagination and creativity, and extend skills through encouraging mastery and positive learning dispositions.

Children bring these funds of knowledge to and from different learning environments. Such knowledge is situated in children's everyday environments and provides a link across home learning and early years settings for both children and adults (Wood, 2013). Funds of knowledge are akin to the resource characteristics Bronfenbrenner identified as contributing to development, and they also echo Rogoff's (2003) idea that culture is embodied within us in terms of our beliefs, influencing the very way in which we approach making sense of the world. Adults can make these ordinary experiences rich and meaningful for children by tapping into their curiosity.

## The importance of play

Bronfenbrenner wrote extensively about the important role of the child in his own development and about the centrality of proximal processes in particular. However, his writings focused mainly on the importance of interpersonal proximal processes, giving few examples of the developmental influence of individual interactions with materials, objects and symbols. It is in play that we see the power of this type of interaction in action. When exploring and playing, children make discoveries about the world and their place in it. Early childhood educators resource play in intentional ways to ensure that children encounter positive learning experiences rich in content, challenge and risk and in which learning is consolidated. Play is recognised

**138** Nurturing Children's Learning and Development

as a key process through which children extend their learning and development during early childhood:

> [P]lay is about creating a world in which, for that moment, children are in control and can seek out uncertainty in order to triumph over it – or, if not, no matter, it is only a game.... it is primarily behaviour for its own sake, for the pleasure and joy of being able to do it. Yet play is more than mere indulgence; it is essential to children's health and wellbeing.
>
> *(Lester and Russell, 2010, p. x)*

However, play suffers from being simultaneously over-referenced in early education yet poorly understood. It is often characterised as unimportant, trivial and lacking in serious purpose, especially when compared to work. Wood, 2013 notes the ambiguous position of play in educational discourse, which is dominated by an outcomes agenda, particularly given that the outcomes of play are often not visible and certainly not measurable. Wood argues that "there is a general mistrust of play in educational contexts" (Wood (2013), p. 42) and reminds us that contemporary discourse on play in early childhood reflects little understanding of its powerful role in learning and development. Play continues to be seen as preparatory to the real learning that will occur when children transition to school. The distinction does a disservice to the important role of play in early years practice. In fact, play "is one of the highest achievements of the human species, alongside language, culture and technology" (Whitebread, Basilio, Kuvalja, & Verma, 2012, p. 3).

While children are, from birth, biologically equipped to play, they need sensitive adults to guide them through their frustrations and share in their satisfactions (Bruce, 2001). Generally, children are curious and interested in the world, and through play they become competent and confident learners, prepared to take risks and challenge themselves to learn more. However, children growing up in poverty or in stressful situations may be deprived of ordinary opportunities for play; here, the role of high-quality early childhood educators becomes more important and influential. Effective play is promoted and nurtured by adults who provide high-quality learning environments, objects, activities, time and encouragement. Through play, young children explore, create, imagine, experiment, manipulate, negotiate, problem-solve and consolidate their understandings. Play provides a safe 'magic circle' (Huizinga, 1950) within which they can struggle, strive and succeed; it is the space that allows them to explore feeling, test their fears and find their own language of expression; it is through play that they come to experience the nature of materials, such as water and sand, and begin to explore the foundations of science and mathematics. Wood (2013) cautions against being too simplistic in considering play. Not everything children choose to do is play, and children can step in and out of play. We may consider children's activities in early years settings as following a continuum from pure play through to non-play (Broadhead, 2010).

While adults prepare environments to encourage play, there are times when it may also be appropriate for them to participate in play. Participating in play with

Nurturing Children's Learning and Development **139**

children can provide valuable opportunities for early childhood educators to elaborate a particular theme through guidance or the introduction of new themes or new materials. Care needs to be taken, however; participating in play is most successful when educators are invited into a play situation and respect the direction of children in order to avoid intruding or interrupting the flow.

According to Lester and Russell (2010), common characteristics of play include being

- based on a sense of free will and control, either individually or within the group;
- motivated for its own sake rather than any external reward;
- pleasurable and positively valued;
- flexible and adaptive, using objects and rules in a variety of changing ways;
- non-literal, 'as if' behaviour – it can rearrange or turn the world upside down;
- unpredictable, spontaneous, innovative and creative.

A long-standing challenge has been identifying more precisely what children learn through play and how that learning occurs. With careful support from attuned adults, children move through play from simplistic, sometimes magical, understandings of the world towards greater mastery of scientific concepts (Fleer et al., 2020). Self-regulating functions fostered through play include working through ideas, surmounting obstacles, problem-solving and managing intense emotion. These facilitate careful, observant and scientific exploration of the world and objects therein. Play scenarios require children to devise and follow social rules. In enacting 'bedtime', 'school', or 'a rocket launch', children learn to overcome their immediate impulses and increasingly understand and commit to the rules of social life. Pretend play and role-play provide particularly rich contexts through which children can develop self-regulation skills and socially responsible behaviour. Through playing with substitute objects in imaginary situations, children become adept at distinguishing symbols from real-life objects and better able to use words, gestures and other symbols as tools for controlling reality, including managing their own behaviour and attending to others. Pretend play is a rich context for learning to resolve differences of opinion, interact cooperatively and solve social problems while also facilitating curiosity, interrogation and scientific reasoning.

Play makes major contributions to developing regulation of emotion, building strong attachments and peer friendships, engendering positive feelings and enabling children to cope with stressful situations. Play also helps build resilience – the capacity for children to thrive despite adversity and stress in their lives. But not all play is positive. Young children's play can reinforce social and cultural divides and power inequalities, for example, through teasing, bullying, unkindness and isolating games. There are a number of reasons why children may be excluded or isolated by other children – gender, social class, ethnicity, disability and so on (Grieshaber & McArdle, 2014). With support from adults who demonstrate inclusive values, children learn about playing fairly and how to build relationships within diverse groups.

**140** Nurturing Children's Learning and Development

Play also has a role in developing spatial reasoning or cognition, the type of reasoning used to judge where things are in relation to other things. Spatial reasoning is applied when making decisions about crossing a road or placing a kick for a goal, but it is also critical for more complex behaviours, such as reading and interpreting maps and graphs. The development of spatial reasoning contributes to children's mathematical ability, and the level of spatial skills children have may predict those who pursue STEM (science, technology, engineering and maths) careers (Newcombe, Uttal, & Sauter, 2013). Through careful observation of play-based opportunities, adults can help children develop their spatial reasoning skills, for instance, in block play, giving children spatial language, such as "show me the piece with the curved edge", or by encouraging children to draw simple maps from one place to another. Hiding things and giving directions for children to follow – 'over', 'under', 'up' and 'down' – encourages the development of spatial reasoning. We should also ensure that there are books and other materials available that use the images and language of space.

Children's play reveals their thinking to an observant adult whose guidance can support them in engaging with the forms of knowledge valued in the curriculum and society. Adult support for play allows children to develop new conceptual networks. Through observing play, adults can also see children's executive function at work when they talk themselves through an activity as they move objects around or place things in a particular order. The vignette involving Gabrielle is an illustration of a young child at play. If you follow closely, you will see the different elements of executive function in action and the early childhood educators' role in extending the opportunities presented.

---

At planning time, Gabrielle says, "I'm going to play with the doggies and Magnatiles in the toy area. I'm making a tall elevator." At work time, Gabrielle builds with the magnetic tiles while playing with the small toy dogs, as she planned. She stacks the tiles on top of one another in a tower-like form—her "elevator"—then places some dogs in it. The elevator then falls over. She repeats this several times but the elevator continues to fall over. Gabrielle then arranges the magnetic tiles into squares, connecting them to form a row. Gabrielle says to Shannon, her teacher, "I'm making doghouses because the elevator keeps falling down." Shannon says, "I was wondering what you were building, because you planned to make a tall elevator going up vertically, and now you are using them to make doghouses in a long horizontal row. You solved the problem by changing the way you were building." Gabrielle uses pretend talk while moving the dogs around. At one point she says, "Mommy, Mommy, we are hungry" and opens one of the doghouses and moves the dog inside where a bigger dog is placed. Gabrielle says, "Mommy says the food's not ready, so go play."

While moving the dogs around, Gabrielle says to herself out loud, "We have to find something to do until the food is ready." Gabrielle says to Shannon,

> "Let's pretend we are going to the park." Shannon agrees and says, "I'm going to slide down the slide three times and then jump off the climber." As Shannon pretends to do this with one of the dogs, Gabrielle watches then copies her and says, "My dog jumped higher than yours." She then says, "Mommy says we have to go home now. We need to move our dogs over there so they can eat." The pretend play continues.
>
> At recall time, Gabrielle is using a scarf to hide some objects she played with. When it is her turn to recall, she gives clues about what is under the scarf. She shows the group a couple of magnetic tiles and dogs. Shannon asks her what she did with these materials during work time. Gabrielle talks about the problem with the falling "elevator" and then recounts the story about the doggies.
>
> *Lockhart (2010, pp. 1–2)*

With the careful intervention of Shannon, the early childhood educator, Gabrielle was made aware of the fact that she had solved a problem. Later she was given the opportunity to see planning in action when Shannon talked through her plans for sliding on the slide. Finally, we see Gabrielle being given the opportunity to recall and share her activity with others. Where playful everyday experiences are available in well-designed and interactive early years settings, children have the time, encouragement and context within which to develop the dispositions and skills necessary to function competently and effectively at their own level. The presence of observant, attuned and engaged educators enriches experiences, strengthening learning and development

The design, organisation and resourcing of the early years setting is central to practice and the early learning process. Settings, both indoor and outdoor, should be safe whilst also providing rich and varied opportunities for exploration, play and risk-taking. However, while the planning and organisation of settings is important to early years practice, it is insufficient. Settings meeting the static requirements of quality may not be effective in enhancing children's learning and development. It is the process, as Bronfenbrenner would point out, what actually happens on a day-to-day basis, that is at the heart of good-quality early years practice (Hayes, 2019). The most effective practice is found in settings with well-trained, well-informed staff, familiar with child development and subject material, who recognise and respond to the dynamic and individual nature of development in the early years and who can work with an emergent curriculum driven by the interests and experiences of children and the opportunities afforded by the environment (OECD, 2006). Curriculum frameworks such as *Te Whāriki* (Ministry of Education, New Zealand, 1996), Aistear (NCCA, 2009) and the Victorian Early Years Learning and Development Framework (Marbina, Church, & Tayler, 2011) provide a rich basis for effective practice. Cultivating positive learning dispositions in children leads to positive outcomes in social, linguistic and cognitive development and the skills

**142** Nurturing Children's Learning and Development

necessary for later school success. It is a holistic, adaptive and, ultimately, more effective approach to early education. The process of good-quality practice is nurturing, dynamic and interactive, reflecting the dynamic and interactive nature of learning and development. Such a complex nurturing pedagogy requires that educators are responsive and reflective throughout both their planning for and their engagement with children.

## Implications for practice

Implicit in good practice is a commitment to democratic principles that recognises the need to respect and engage meaningfully with children. This identifies early years settings as sites of democratic practice where children and adults can participate collectively in interpreting experiences and shaping decisions affecting children's own development and the nature of the context within which development occurs. Changing early years practice to meet this new vision is not an easy task. It requires ongoing practice, learning and reflection.

## Key concepts for early years practice

1   Viewing *development as a dynamic* and discontinuous process facilitates a pedagogy attuned to the connections, interactions and relationships between children and the wider world while being sensitive to social, physical and emotional learning opportunities.

2   There is a continuing tendency to underestimate the *educative role of caring*. The concept of a *nurturing pedagogy* recognises the educative role of care as nurture, the importance of relationships and the role of playful interaction, exploration, dialogue and collaborative learning in supporting young children's learning.

3   Skills of *observation and reflection* are central to a nurturing pedagogy. They enhance practice and planning, are manifest in well-managed yet reasonably flexible practice and assist in the provision of learning environments that include children as active agents.

4   Good-quality early years practice relies less on a content-led curriculum and direct instruction and more on *early years frameworks* of values and principles, respecting the process underpinning an emergent or enquiry-based curriculum.

5   An *emergent curriculum* arises out of the shared experiences of all participants in a learning environment. It is influenced by the layout and routines of the setting, the activities and materials available and the intentions of adults. It is also influenced by children's own background experiences and their dispositions and individual characteristics.

6   Using a *rights-based lens* to inform early years practice allows us to recognise children as being competent, strong, active and participatory, and as meaning-makers and fellow citizens.

7   When children, even very young children, learn through experience that their *feelings and concerns will be appreciated and understood*, their emotions become less urgent.

## Nurturing Children's Learning and Development 143

8   *High expectations* are important for positive development in young children. Children learn best when we 'expect' them to succeed.

9   *Mindsets* refer to the beliefs we have about ourselves and our abilities; in a growth mindset, children recognise that their abilities and talents can be developed; in a fixed mindset, however, children see themselves as the problem.

10  *Pedagogical Leadership* is an important dimension of high-quality practice which requires unique skills and knowledge.

11  Creating *active and effective links* between early years settings and other important environments in the lives and communities of young children strengthens the mesosystem.

12  *Intentional teaching* is thoughtful, informed and deliberate and is a key dimension of an effective nurturing pedagogy.

13  Pay attention to the *tacit assumptions* unthinkingly brought to our practice.

14  *Play* suffers from being simultaneously over-referenced yet poorly understood. Children's *play reveals their thinking* to an observant adult whose guidance can support engagement with the forms of knowledge valued in the curriculum and society.

15  *The most effective practice is found in settings with well-qualified, well-informed staff, familiar with child development and subject material*, who recognise and respond to the dynamic and individual nature of development in the early years and who can work with an emergent curriculum driven by the interests and experiences of children and the opportunities afforded by the environment.

## Note

1  The key pedagogical moment is when the teacher says – "Um. Mine are new too …", moving the focus beyond the specific and providing the opportunity to expand the discussion beyond the immediately observable.

# 10

# RELATIONAL SPACES LINKING PEOPLE, PLACES AND RESOURCES

## Positioning early childhood settings

### Introduction

Jackson and Barnett (2020, p.1) state that

> the act of learning is an ecological phenomenon that brings forth new meanings and understandings of the world and of one's own being and identity in and with the world. The very act transforms us and the world around us. It is a learning ecology.

Such a conceptualisation of learning and learning spaces requires us to reconsider and review concepts of educational spaces beyond a more limited understanding of early childhood settings, schools and other educational institutions as fixed spaces, the sole providers of education for learners and exclusively responsible for providing access to education and learning. In contrast, a greater focus on a learning ecology draws attention to a more complex network of people and places which the learner, in this case, the young child, engages with as part of their learning process.

As emphasised in Chapter 6 and throughout this book, Bronfenbrenner placed great emphasis on the child as learner being located at the centre of their learning process. Within Bronfenbrenner's bioecological model, the importance of real-world contexts for children's learning and development was highlighted with particular emphasis on the dynamic and complex interactions occurring between developing individuals and the world around them (Tudge, Navarro, Merçon-Vargas, & Payir, 2021). Ensuring and promoting connections between and among the various settings and contexts in which children are situated provides opportunities for encouraging and strengthening proximal processes. Bronfenbrenner was one of the first psychological theorists to emphasise children's development in the midst of families, communities and societies. Considering these views, it could

DOI: 10.4324/9781003247760-10

be argued that educational settings such as Early Childhood Education and Care (ECEC) settings occupy a unique space in the lives of children and families, with the potential to provide a nexus or hub through which they can form a network of supports across communities and societies. The concepts of the mesosystem and the exosystem are particularly interesting to consider in this regard.

In this chapter, we begin with a focus on early childhood settings as potentially providing opportunities for creating linkages and connections across contexts, beginning with a particular focus on the mesosystem. We explore possibilities within settings for strengthening communication across the various microsystems in the child's life. Opportunities for educators to build up reciprocal relationships between the setting and home learning environments are outlined. The chapter then moves to a focus on the exosystem, exploring how early childhood settings can act as a bridge between individual children, families, the wider community, and the world beyond the early childhood setting, in addition to approaches to supporting parent–parent interactions. Strategies to draw community into the life of the setting so that it becomes a central hub in the lives of the neighbourhood and the wider community are explored. As one example of this, the potential for intergenerational learning and practice to enhance such connections is highlighted. The chapter finally moves to consider how new technologies have generated possibilities for children's learning and development to connect with an expanding world, within early-years settings. We examine the notion that new technologies impact children's lives in ways which require us to consider introducing the concept of an encompassing meta-system – a system external to, but including, the bioecological model, which may have consequences for all systems.

## ECEC as a key, linking meso-system[1]

In considering the ecology of learning across settings, both formal and informal, Bronfenbrenner's concept of the mesosystem offers particular explanatory power. With its focus on interactions and relationships across contexts, it shows how learning in any setting comes not only from experiences in that setting but from the full range of settings experienced by the person. The majority of people simultaneously inhabit many different microsystems, and the intermingling of these spaces underlies learning, both formal and informal, across time (Jackson, 2011). Different microsystems may operate under different religious, moral, ethical and social norms. Thus, a multitude of narratives is continually negotiated by children and their families, regarding who they are and who they are becoming within potentially contrasting roles, relationships, expectations and experiences (O'Toole, Regan, & Nowak-Lojewska, 2019). For example, it can be difficult for children to figure out how they are supposed to behave in an ECEC setting if expectations at home are very different (O'Toole & Hayes, 2020).

Children's learning and sense of agency and autonomy develop within complex webs, and interdependent relationships can reinforce their sense of identity and

**146** Relational spaces linking people, places and resources

belonging (Kernan, 2010). Increasingly, families share the early care and education of children with various early childhood settings. Parental involvement in children's education is one way to facilitate supportive activity in mesosystems in early childhood and beyond (O'Toole, Kiely, McGillicuddy, O'Brien, & O'Keeffe, 2019), and Chapter 5 explored how the creation of linkages between families and the setting can be crucial for positive transitions. Equally important is actively working to break down potential barriers within the mesosystem that may make it more difficult for families to engage with the setting, thereby creating disjuncture for children.

However, what we mean by the concept of 'parental involvement' is not always clear (O'Toole et al., 2019), and often the relationship between parents and educators is defined and boundaried by the educational setting, without any clear input from parents themselves on how they see their role (Wolf, 2020) or what they want or need from the relationship (Devlieghere, Li, & Vandenbroek, 2020). Parental involvement initiatives have traditionally centred on increasing children's academic achievement, providing free labour or fundraising for educational settings or seeking support for programmes to shape children's behaviour towards that deemed more appropriate or manageable by educators (Devlieghere et al., 2020; Hornby & Lafaele, 2011). Informed by our understanding of power dynamics and the concept of the 'mesosystem', we could predict that such approaches are likely to be unsuccessful at best and damaging at worst. They fail to recognise the personhood of the parent and child and the fact that families may have their own needs and wishes invested in the involvement. A healthy mesosystem for children requires a reciprocal flow of communication and regard, not a one-way directive in which power is held only by one party.

Devlieghere et al.'s (2020) call for "a shift from instrumentalizing and silencing parents towards a reciprocal, symmetrical dialogic relationship between teachers and parent" (p. 1) is consistent with Bronfenbrenner's ambition for early education. Head Start, informed by his vision, aimed to develop early education that was culturally responsive to the communities it served, and for the communities to have an investment in its success (Head Start History | The Administration for Children and Families; hhs.gov).

---

## Challenge

Over the course of two weeks, observe your interactions with parents and note the following in your reflective journal:

– How often you engage with parents.
– What format that engagement takes (face-to-face, phone, digital, etc). Why do you use these forms of communication? Do they suit the setting? Do they suit the parent? Are they limited by setting policy (e.g. COVID-19 safety procedures)?

Relational spaces linking people, places and resources **147**

- What is the communication about? Are you only providing information or are you also listening?
- What are the aims of the communication? Is the agenda set by you (e.g. letting the parent know how the child has met the learning goals you have set), or is there a 'reciprocal, symmetrical, dialogic relationship' (e.g. setting learning goals together)?

In recent years, discussion of working with families has moved beyond 'parental involvement' to begin to think about 'parental engagement' and even 'parental partnership' (Goodall & Montgomery, 2014). For example, in recent years the work of Joyce Epstein, one of the seminal researchers on parental involvement in children's education (Epstein, 1995) has favoured the idea of 'school, family and community partnership' (Epstein & Sheldon, 2016). Kiely et al. (2021) found that in forming partnerships with families, it is crucial to understand that not all families are the same. Each has its own individual needs, strengths, challenges and capacities, and what works in creating partnership with one family may not with another. For example, many parents are intimidated by educational settings and need multiple, warm invitations to draw them into the life of the setting. On the other hand, multiple invitations could be experienced as pressure by busy parents with extensive calls on their time like long working hours or other caring duties. Kiely et al. (2021) recommend that educators use multiple means of communication, tailored to the individual needs of families, with strategies for creating links with parents rooted in relationship building. In bioecological terms, this means that educators are taking 'person' factors into account and leveraging the power of 'process' in the meso-system. Sometimes the simplest of approaches can be the most effective – in the following (in abridged form) Jane Jackson describes how the introduction of a couch at the door of her setting changed interactions with families for the better:

The couch was a welcome addition to the setting some years ago and the impact it has had on relationships between children, staff and peers cannot be overemphasised. The couch has been moved around the setting several times according to the changing needs of the children and curriculum. It is more recently that we have begun to consider the potential impact of the couch in the context of parental engagement. We decided to locate the couch closer to the entrance of the setting and the importance of positioning was immediately evident. The couch, in this case, symbolises the value placed on the voice of the parents. The couch is important in and of itself, an object that speaks to us, a symbol of welcome, inviting us to sit.

… Relationships with parents and families cannot be hurried; they require adequate space and time. The accessibility of the couch provides space for parents to spend time in the setting without feeling hurried or in the way, providing parents with an opportunity to see what takes place in the early years setting. We are also provided with an opportunity to discover ways in which parents and families can contribute to the setting. This process actively engages families, builds trust, and creates a much more welcoming environment. Our language and culture and the way we think, can make some factors visible to us and others easier to overlook or never see at all. This perspective provokes us to think about the elements of our settings that give the symbolic message 'come on in' or elements that may give the symbolic message 'stay out, this is not a place for parents'.

**Access the full version: *Jackson (2020)*** The Couch – Scéalta Blog | Early Childhood Ireland https://www.earlychildhoodireland.ie/scealta-blog/the-couch/

What elements in your setting say 'come on in'? What elements (perhaps inadvertently) say 'stay out, this is not a place for parents'?

## Beyond immediate contexts: ECEC in the exosystem

Bioecological theory illustrates that the total ecology at work is complex, with the intermingling of various ecosystems, encouraging a nuanced approach to understanding educational processes (O'Toole et al., 2019). In simpler terms, this means that early childhood settings can act as a bridge between individual children or families and the world beyond. Remember that the *exosystem* refers to links between those systems of which the child has direct experience and those settings which the child may never enter but which may nevertheless affect what happens to them. Consider the power of the exosystem in the following vignette.

Amira left her family behind in Syria some time ago and came to Europe as a refugee. Today she is taking her daughter Fatima to her first day of preschool, and like many parents, she feels anxious about how the day will go for her little girl. This is more intense for Amira than for some parents, because she does not have many friends yet in this country and she does not know what to expect from the preschool here. They are a little early, and as they wait at the gate for the preschool to open, Fatima begins to play with another little girl, Anya. "First day is nerve-wracking, isn't it?" Anya's mother Faye says to Amira. They begin to chat and by the time the girls have gone into the preschool, Faye has invited Amira to join her for coffee with a group of mothers she knows from a baby and toddler group in the local community centre.

This is a good example of the exosystem: Fatima will not be present at the coffee morning in the community centre, but yet one can imagine that it may yet impact

Relational spaces linking people, places and resources **149**

her through the positive effects of community connections and friendships on her mother. Bronfenbrenner viewed raising children as the job of the whole community, and Amira will be in a much better position to be an attuned, responsive parent if she is supported herself. Early childhood settings provide a particularly important networking service for families, and while this is important for all parents and families, it could be crucial for potentially vulnerable or isolated parents like Amira. Such interactions can be informal, happening organically, but many early childhood settings, like Jane Jackson's earlier, mindfully create spaces for parents to connect to each other as well as to the setting. Actively linking formal educational settings to other important environments in the lives of learners allows recognition of the rich 'funds of knowledge' (Hedges, 2014) they bring with them from the various contexts in which they live.

Furthermore, linkages across exosystems can be more formal, putting families in touch with other services like speech and language therapy, psychological support and so on. An example of this is provided by the Access and Inclusion Model (AIM) in Ireland (https://aim.gov.ie). The idea behind AIM is to create more inclusive ECEC settings, providing universal and targeted supports, focused on the needs of the individual child, without requiring a diagnosis of disability (DCYA, 2016). Echoing the bioecological approach, it provides supports for children across seven levels, ranging from a generally inclusive early educational environment and direct additional supports for children who need them (microsystem), to information for parents provided by a qualified and competent workforce and connections to other services such as therapeutic intervention (mesosystem), to expert advice and support for early childhood educators (exosystem). Also consistent with bioecological theory is the focus within AIM on the needs, strengths, challenges and capacities of each child, seeing each child as an individual (resource characteristics, dispositions and demand characteristics) rather than allocating supports across the board according to a specific diagnosis. The early childhood educator is usually the person responsible for accessing external support for a child through AIM, requiring engagement with both families and external experts (O'Malley, 2020). If early childhood settings are to act as a hub for a network of supports for families, early childhood educators occupy a critical role within them.

Despite some criticisms (Department of Children and Youth Affairs [DCYA], 2019), AIM provides an example of how ECEC settings can potentially act as the hub or nexus for a network of supports for children and families, from micro-level, through meso- and exosystems and out into society as a whole (macro-level). Of course, the development of such models depends on good policymaking (another element of the child's exosystem), and not every jurisdiction will have such structures in place. However, an early educator who is aware of the important role they play within the wider bioecological structures of the children they work with can mindfully nurture links across meso- and exosystems.

**150** Relational spaces linking people, places and resources

---

### Activity

Map the links between your community and your ECEC setting. Are there other groups, supports or networks in your community that you could create new links with?

Consider community groups (care homes, school classrooms, etc.), services that may be of interest to families (e.g. social welfare, therapeutic services, etc.), opportunities for civic engagement (e.g. community gardens), public resources (e.g. libraries) and any other ideas of relevance.

---

## Learning ecologies

The notion of a learning ecology encompasses opportunities for learning through engaging with people and resources across a number of contexts, both immediate and more remote (Jackson, 2014). Increasingly, the role which ECEC plays within local and wider communities has been explored (Hamer & Loveridge, 2020). Moreover, consistent with Bronfenbrenner's bioecological model, the view that the socio-emotional development and learning of children is influenced and supported by the community in which settings are located has been highlighted (McMurray & Clendon, 2011). Some studies have found that connecting ECE settings to the broader community, as for example, arranging excursions with children into the local community helped children to make connections between their home, the setting and the wider physical and social community that they lived in and to make sense of their wider world (Fitzpatrick, 2021; Hamer & Loveridge, 2020).

Viewed through the lens of Bronfenbrenner's bioecological model, the community can operate as part of the mesosystem, in particular where social services may be provided and accessed by children and their families. Similarly, the community may involve influences more representative of the exosystem, where children have no direct role yet when more distal influences operate to affect children's lives, both positively and negatively. Research has identified some of the key benefits for young children in having access to and participating in the broader community within which their learning and development is embedded (Alverson, Ginn, & Gilbert, 2019). As highlighted by Fitzpatrick (2021, p. 62), extending young children's learning and development to the community and beyond ECEC settings "has the potential to acknowledge and create educational spaces that are more diverse, versatile and inclusive than formal, centre-based ECE services ... and, in the process, it can enrich children's sense of belonging, citizenship and visibility". Moreover, these benefits can be reciprocal insofar as ECEC settings have the potential to actively support local communities in which they are located through working in partnership with other social support services to provide wraparound support for families (Hamer & Loveridge, 2020), as in the earlier example of AIM.

An interesting illustration of the potential for learning environments, and for facilitating connections to the community beyond the ECEC setting is provided in the concept of intergenerational learning (IGL) and practice, briefly introduced in Chapter 7. Building and developing relationships and reducing the separation between generations is one of the primary goals of IGL. In relation to IGL involving younger children, Gallagher and Fitzpatrick, (2018, p. 29) highlight that "one of the most effective ways of building relationships is through shared activities. Spending time in each other's company doing simple activities and having fun is the focus of many successful IG projects". The core principles of IGL echo Bronfenbrenner who argued for greater emphasis on learning between and among various age cohorts, drawing attention to the potential for learning ecologies involving younger and older participants, with a view to creating opportunities for exchanging and transmitting invaluable lived experience and associated knowledge (Tudge et al., 2021). A recent study of IGL in the context of ECEC was carried out in Ireland, drawing on the experiences of early childhood educators, young children and their parents (Fitzpatrick, 2021). As noted in Chapter 7, this exploratory study evolved from a larger international study – Together Old and Young – funded by the European Union (http://www.toyproject.net). Research findings from children, educators and parents indicated that IGL as a pedagogical strategy supported children's happiness, socio-emotional competencies and executive functions. Furthermore, children's participation in and engagement with the broader community beyond the ECE setting created rich opportunities for children's participation and contribution as citizens in communities. Interestingly, children's parents also indicated the positive gains they themselves experienced through connecting to some of these settings as a result of their children's engagement with IGL. A significant finding in this study was the invaluable role which early childhood educators played in facilitating children's opportunities to engage with IGL.

Bronfenbrenner's bioecological model places emphasis on how proximal processes can be encouraged or strengthened by ensuring connections between and among the various settings in which children are situated. However, as Tudge et al. (2021) point out, person characteristics are also essential in generating and supporting these connections effectively. In keeping with this, Fitzpatrick's (2021) study of IGL as a pedagogical strategy also drew attention to the significant impact of the educator on all aspects of children's development and foregrounded the autonomy of the educator in brokering experiences offered to children (Kilderry, 2015; Mentha, Church, & Page, 2015). Person characteristics highlighted as important for educators facilitating programmes such as IGL included having extensive and specialised knowledge and skills, expertise in considering the particular requirements of children and the potential of IGL to be of value to specific children.

As previously highlighted in Chapter 7, concerns about the significant amount of time young children spend within ECEC centres, segregated and separated from older peers and adults and the wider community have been expressed and discussed (Holmes, 2009; Kernan, 2010). Likewise, the excessive compartmentalisation of educational places and spaces is called into question, in light of Bronfenbrenner's

**152** Relational spaces linking people, places and resources

emphasis on an ecology of learning and the connections across the micro and macro contexts of children's development. Fitzpatrick (2021) has drawn attention to the increasing privatisation and institutionalisation of contemporary childhood which may serve to constrain opportunities for children to develop relationships with a greater variety of people including older adults. IGL as a pedagogical strategy is just one of many possible ways in which the role of the ECEC setting can be extended to generate linkages between children, their families and other settings in the broader community and become an interactive relational space which can activate and support links between people, places and resources. It may be that there is a need to move away from viewing ECEC centres as places that are exclusively concerned with the provision of education and care for young children. As Duncan (2012, cited in Hamer & Loveridge, 2020) states, services could "position themselves as the *heart of each community* and build their practices around discourses that support social capital, family reliance, community cohesion, and society wellness" (p. 84, original emphasis).

## New technologies and an expanding world

When Bronfenbrenner introduced the idea of a bioecological model of human development, the microsystems he described were located in a world where there were clearly defined public/private systems with recognisable boundaries. In considering the world in which young children were developing he identified the home, the preschool and the school as the primary microsystems of relevance and, within these microsystems the adults, children and learning opportunities were fairly obvious. Access into the microsystems was straightforward, with adults in different roles acting as guardians and protectors. At this time, the most obvious external technologies that influenced the home or the early childhood setting from the wider environment were the TV and video, which Bronfenbrenner located within the exosystem. These technologies were visible and wide spread, and one could control them within the home or educational setting. They were influential in that they contributed to children's learning and development by bringing aspects of the outside world into their microsystems. However, in his early writings Bronfenbrenner did note some concern that these technologies would impact on the patterns and processes of family life and expressed curiosity about how this might influence children's behaviour and development (Bronfenbrenner, 1977).

Within the world where TV and video became a visible part of the home there was a reasonably clear relationship between the dynamic world of the specific microsystem and the context and content of the outside world. This was mediated through a definable process of communication through unambiguous mesosystemic relationships between the microsystems and the exosystem. However, this is no longer the case. Since the turn of the twenty-first century, the expansion of the media landscape has been extraordinary and the 'new technologies' are everywhere and have entered directly into the lives of children, even very young children (Palaiologou, 2016). With the rapid growth and spread of the more invisible

Relational spaces linking people, places and resources **153**

technology of the internet into all aspects of our world, the sense of system control is less strong and the straightforward power dynamic between the person and the technology no longer exists. Consider the two developments outlined in the following and how they change the relationship between parents or carers and children at sleep time. Reflect on the issues raised and how they might influence future setting planning, procedures and early childhood practices.

> Many homes and early childhood settings use baby monitors. They provide a comfortable way to check in on sleeping infants as we go about other activities, and the built-in microphone systems of monitors allow adults to calm and relax unsettled infants through voice without actually interacting physically with them. This changes the style of interactions in ways that distance the adult from children and disrupt a previously dependable type of proximal process. As the name suggests baby monitors allow adults to monitor children's behaviour. While this is useful for checking in on sleeping infants it becomes ethically challenging when used, for instance, to observe older children in their private worlds of wakeful play without their knowledge.
>
> Another sleep-time/rest-time activity in which the new technologies have entered the world of adult–child relationships is storytelling. Recognised as an important factor in the socialisation and development of children, through which customs and culture are passed on, story time is also important in educating young children in the skills of reading and writing. Screen-based technologies and storytelling robots have been added to traditional story-telling methods and are now available to augment or replace the role of the adult in varying degrees (Lin et al., 2021). While adults often participate in such storytelling, the context of the story-time event itself is altered and the social interactions which surround person-to-person storytelling change.

Such situations and the opportunities and dilemmas they present were not available to, and thus not considered by, Bronfenbrenner when reviewing and refining his model of development. Clearly, this new interconnected world of porous systems, flimsy boundaries and vast quantities of information must be considered when theorising child development within a bioecological model for the twenty-first century. As noted in Chapter 7, questions and debates tend to be framed around competing public narratives: the relative value of or the danger of the internet to the future of humankind (Buckingham, 2008; Kewalramani, Palaiologou, Arnott, & Dardanou, 2020; Palaiologou, 2016; Warger and Dobbin, 2009). Is it dehumanising or life-enhancing? How can we as educators balance enabling children to develop the skills and knowledge they will need in the future with the suspicion that the media presents insurmountable risks for children? How can the inequities of access be overcome to counteract any social and educational disadvantage? In viewing the world of the internet from a Bronfenbrenner perspective we can see that, as

**154** Relational spaces linking people, places and resources

in the case of the baby monitor and technology-mediated storytelling, technology necessarily becomes part of children's lived experiences and affects the relationships children encounter across their microsystems, influencing the pace and pattern of the way they engage, and are engaged with, by the adults and objects in their world.

New technologies introduce a new and powerful influence on us all, one that acts both on and across systems and needs careful consideration in any study of the bioecological model (Johnson, 2010; O'Neill, 2015; Plowman, 2016). The impact of the Internet can be considered both within a child's own microsystem or across a network of microsystems, while also presenting as an encompassing meta system, that is, a system external to but including the bioecological model, which has consequences for all systems. The reach and contextual extent of technology will require further careful research in terms of young children's development. The bioecological model provides a useful model from which to explore and expand our understanding in line with the changing world. In recognising the pervasive reach of media in contemporary life, O'Neill (2015) examined the bioecological model as a framework for theorising the interactions of young internet users. He highlights the value of an ecological approach to studying children's engagement with the media environment at the microsystem level of the individual, noting that in his research on risk, it has provided "a rich resource for examining the patterns of risk, the role of mediating factors and the vulnerabilities of particular populations defined by key demographic and psychological variables" (2015, p. 14). He argues that an ecological approach to studying children's engagement with the media environment offers a way to study internet use while recognising it "as a complex interplay between technology and society in which modes of communication and mediated interaction … shape human behaviour" (2015, p. 14).

Rather than fear or reject the arrival and use of technology it would be wise to acknowledge the reality that all the children attending early childhood settings will have had experiences of technology to differing degrees and it will be necessary for early childhood educators to consider this new 'media ecology' (Palaiologou, 2016). The bioecological model of human development can assist those working with young children to reflect on how best to respond to the changing climate in which children are now developing and learning. The traditional understandings of the experiences children bring into settings are no longer sufficient. The experiences of parents and their young children have expanded to include features outside their immediate environments through opportunities offered by the new media from the baby monitor and screen-based storytelling in their homes (microsystem) to the parent mobile phone check-in apps (mesosystem) to the wider internet impact on parents and early childhood educators through exo-, macro- and chronosystem influences.

During the COVID-19 pandemic, online teaching and learning became the norm for primary and secondary school children and raised our awareness of the powerful and helpful role that technology can play in children's lives, learning and development. For early childhood educators, access to technology has allowed for changes in practice in relation to areas such as administration and management and in relation to parent communication. The flourishing of technology in our

Relational spaces linking people, places and resources **155**

lives provides us in early childhood education with opportunities to rethink play by including technology in our thinking (Kewalramani et al., 2020). However, research on the topic of how new technologies influence the broader early childhood education system is limited. Edwards (2016) notes that research into technology in early childhood education, as in education in general, has tended to focus on the attitudes and confidence of educators rather than on considering the issue from the perspective of children and "the foundational concept used to drive curriculum provision in early childhood education … children's play" (p. 514).

According to Kewalramani et al. (2020), recent research has begun to highlight the potential benefits of incorporating technology into early childhood education curricula regarding creativity and imagination (Fleer, 2018), literacy and numeracy (Huber, Highfield, & Kaufman, 2018) and social interactions (Danby, Fleer, Davidson, & Hatzigianni, 2018). Equally, in her review of internet use and child development, Johnson (2010) notes that it can have negative developmental outcomes in which children are exposed to inappropriate content but reports other research suggesting that access to computers during the preschool years can assist school readiness, emergent literacy and concept development. Reflecting on this through a Bronfenbrenner lens, she proposes the concept of a 'techno-microsystem' to guide the way in which we can 'coordinate children's learning experiences across home, school, and childcare environments, protect children from harmful at-home online experiences by community-based web-awareness initiatives, and prioritise school-based hardware for children without home connectivity" (2010, p. 35).

In their position statement relating to technology and early childhood education the National Association for the Education of Young Children (NAEYC; 2012) recommend that early childhood educators strive to achieve a balance in their activities with young children. Through using professional judgement they suggest that educators evaluate the use of new technologies in comparison with the use of natural and traditional materials and objects. They provide guiding principles which are helpful in supporting educators consider the place of technology within early childhood settings including the following:

1. Select, use, integrate, and evaluate technology and interactive media tools in intentional and developmentally appropriate ways, giving careful attention to the appropriateness and the quality of the content, the child's experience, and the opportunities for co-engagement.
2. Provide a balance of activities in programmes for young children, recognizing that technology and interactive media can be valuable tools when used intentionally with children to extend and support active, hands-on, creative, and authentic engagement with those around them and with their world.
3. Provide leadership in ensuring equitable access to technology and interactive media experiences for the children in their care and for parents and families.

*(2012, p.11)*

**156** Relational spaces linking people, places and resources

Using technology to support children in their play and learning is not new. Many early childhood settings are well equipped with, for instance, microscopes and cameras which allow children to explore the world around them in minute detail. TV and video are occasionally used for special treats. However, more extensive use of technologies is becoming more common with researchers such as Fleer (2018, 2021) exploring the development of STEM skills in her work on the Conceptual Play Lab (see https://www.monash.edu/conceptual-playworld/home); Sullivan and Bers (2018) looking at the potential of robots in expanding the options in creative play; Kewalramani et al. (2020) investigating interactions in the ecology of the playroom to show how the 'Internet of Toys' can provide a platform for children's rich symbiotic explorations, creativity, collaboration and problem-solving; and Marsh et al. (2021) exploring the use of tablets by children under three. Such research helps broaden our understanding of the possibilities that new technologies open up to re-imagine children's play and their learning environments.

We can also see the impact of new technologies on early childhood settings in relation to documentation and assessment. Technology-based systems are now offered across a number of different platforms providing technological solutions to streamline documentation in, for instance, recording and sharing learning stories. Research into how these technologies function in practice and how early childhood educators respond raises some interesting points (Flewitt & Cowan, 2019; White et al., 2021b). In their study into the documentation of learning and the potential of digital documentation, Flewitt and Cowan (2019) argue that the absence of sufficient research or guidance on the use of the different technologies runs the risk of early childhood educators being guided by the structural features and limitations of the technology rather than by evidence-based theories of child development and learning. Their research with early childhood educators found that video was valuable in observing and documenting children's play, particularly highlighting aspects of play that might otherwise be overlooked. It was also useful in staff reflections and helping parents and children know that play is valued. However, they also noted the challenges that exist around the time needed to record and re-watch material which impacts on time available for interactions with children. This point was developed by White et al. (2021b), and their research found that the designs of different platforms may direct educators to see young children's learning in a particular way or from a particular perspective and could guide interpretation and assessment in particular directions that may be at odds with the ethos of underpinning curriculum and practices. They suggest that the use of digital platforms in their study raised many questions and "reveal inequities and relations of power that privilege some voices, while other remain silent" (2021, p. 16). In their research into digital learning and literacy development, Rice and Cun (2021) call for an informed use of technology that reflects the psychosocial realities of young children's lives with a cautious consideration of the various technological platforms and instructional materials that are being developed in this area.

The potential of the online and digital world in early childhood settings, as in other educational settings, has been amplified by the impact of the COVID-19

Relational spaces linking people, places and resources **157**

pandemic on practices across all dimensions of early educational provision. The arrival of this new material and contextual world, through the availability of service platforms and apps and in the different experiences that children have in their home microsystems, requires a level of understanding in educators about the functioning and usefulness of the online opportunities alongside an appreciation of the impact of the media ecology on children's development. It also invites us to consider how we can encourage digital literacy as part of the early childhood curriculum through our interactions with young children who may be more comfortable with screens, robots and voice-operated systems such as Alexa and Siri.

The dynamic relational interplay exposed by the expansion of technology within and across the systems of the bioecological model allows us to situate the various influences of the digital world in the microsystems young children experience and make connections through the mesosytems of communication across these and more distal environments. At the same time, it challenges us to consider the role and potential of technology on children's development and learning. For instance, it allows educators to introduce children to a wide variety of cultural worlds, customs and stories in an interactive and participatory way which can enhance inclusionary practices within settings. The new technology can also influence the chronosystem in that it disrupts the apparent linearity of time by bringing children's present lives into the world of the recent past (replaying events of yesterday or the day before) and the distant historical past with an immediacy heretofore impossible. While embracing the possibilities and recognising the challenges of this new interconnected ecology it is helpful to remind ourselves of the centrality of human relationships and interactions, the engines of development, elaborated in the bioecological model of development. Achieving a balance between the time spent on the inputs, outputs and distractions of technology and that spent directly with young children is important in guiding them as they learn about themselves and their place in this complex and expanding world.

## Key concepts for early years practice

1.  Greater focus on a *learning ecology* draws attention to a more complex network of people and places, beyond the ECEC setting, which young children engage with as part of their learning process.
2.  *Ensuring and promoting connections between and among the various settings and contexts* in which children are situated provides opportunities for encouraging and strengthening proximal processes.
3.  *Early childhood settings can act as a bridge between individual children or families and the world beyond.* Linkages across exosystems can be informal in terms of contacts children have with those in the community and can be more formal, as, for example, putting families in touch with other services like speech and language therapy, psychological support and the like.
4.  *There is a need to move away from viewing ECEC centres as places that are exclusively concerned with the provision of education and care for young children.* The ECEC

setting can be extended to generate linkages between children, their families and other settings in the broader community and become an interactive relational space which can activate and support links between people, places and resources. IGL as a pedagogical strategy is just one of many possible ways in which these linkages can be supported.

5. *With the rapid growth and spread of the more invisible technology of the internet into all aspects of our world*, the sense of system control is less strong and the straightforward power dynamic between the person and the technology no longer exists.

6. The impact of the Internet can be considered both within a child's own microsystem or across a network of microsystems *while also presenting as an encompassing meta system, that is, a system external to but including the bio-ecological model, which has consequences for all systems.*

7. *Early childhood educators can mediate an informed use of technology in early childhood education,* mindful of the psychosocial realities of young children's lives while, at the same time, cautiously considering instructional materials available in this area.

8. *Achieving a balance between the time spent on the inputs, outputs and distractions of technology and that spent directly with young children* is important in guiding children as they learn about themselves and their place in this complex and expanding world.

## Note

1 This section draws on a chapter written by the authors in the book *Ecologies for Learning and Practice: Emerging ideas, sightings and possibilities* (Jackson & Barnett, 2020).

# 11

# REFLECTING THE BIOECOLOGICAL IN EARLY YEARS PRACTICE

## Introduction

Bronfenbrenner developed his bioecological model to illustrate the complexity of human development within contemporary society. He was driven by a belief that we need to consider how society impacts children and families and how, through enhanced understanding of developmental processes, to present some solutions to improve the position of children in a world that he saw as increasingly challenging. Through his advocacy, the bioecological model of human development contributed to improved understandings of the factors that influence inequality and poverty and impact human development. In his writings and presentations, he provided possible mechanisms for enhancing life chances, including contributing to the early years initiative Head Start. Throughout his life, Bronfenbrenner had a profound influence, nationally and internationally, on policy, practice and research across many disciplines.

In Chapter 2, we explored how the bioecological model of development provides a focus on the nested layers of influence which impact children's learning and development. We outlined how the model evolved over time to provide a greater emphasis on proximal processes, the close interactions which take place on a regular basis and over extended periods. We also reflected on the integrated nature of dynamic development, influenced by process, person, context and time (PPCT), and the implications for early years learning and development.

## Ecological systems as nested and networked

One of the key strengths of the model is that it helps us understand the complexity of a child's development. Specifically, the model reflects the interdependence of influencing factors and the multi-layered levels at which these influences may

DOI: 10.4324/9781003247760-11

**160** Reflecting the bioecological in early years practice

operate, from the direct, proximal and immediate influences within the microsystem, such as family and school interactions, to more distant and less immediate influences of the exosystem and macrosystem, in which the child may not participate directly. However, theorists have suggested recently that this 'nested' image may not adequately capture the precise relationship of the systems to one another and may, in fact, serve to obscure the relationship between these systems. One of the key arguments put forward by Neal and Neal (2013), for instance, is that in conceptualising systems as being nested within each other, we are placing emphasis on the importance of context or setting rather than focusing on the importance of interactions and relationships. They suggest that ecological systems or influences would be more accurately conceptualised as being 'networked', a term they suggest better reflects the way systems at different levels relate to one another in an overlapping rather than a nested manner.

Placing greater emphasis on networked systems of influence foregrounds the actual patterns of social interactions within the child's life rather than presupposing that these interactions will take place. In this way, we are foregrounding the processes of interaction that occur rather than the contexts in which they arise. As outlined in previous chapters, particularly in Chapter 8, early learning is a dynamic process. A greater emphasis on networks of interactions in Bronfenbrenner's bioecological model generates the sense of a model that is more dynamic in nature, where each system is defined in terms of the social relationships surrounding the child. The precise and quite distinct pathways to the quality of the relationship between a practitioner and each of these children is to some extent obscured if we see both relationships as 'nested' within the mesosytem. By placing more emphasis on the network of influences operating to build close and trusting interactions between children and adults working alongside them, we can identify more clearly the precise points of contact within these interactions, thus facilitating greater insight into the factors influencing children's development.

While considering the representation of the bioecological model as either a series of nested systems or a network of systems may seem somewhat disconnected from the day-to-day reality of early years practice, it is in fact quite an important consideration. In the decisions we make when working with children, individually or collectively, we are shaped by our awareness of the variety of interacting factors influencing those decisions. Being able to visualise, as well as articulate, the wide variety of influences and their various impacts on different elements of the systems within which we develop enriches the way we work with young children and their families.

## Transformation versus reproduction

In reading the work of Bronfenbrenner and the complex dynamic model he describes it is possible to become quite pessimistic about supporting young children in their learning and development. Educators may be overwhelmed by the idea of multiple influences on a child's development and wonder, with all that is out of their control,

Reflecting the bioecological in early years practice **161**

whether they can ever impact the course a child's life will take. In such situations, there is a danger that they will disengage from their responsibility to support children and avoid doing anything too novel or innovative because it is safer to just do what is always done. However, drawing on the emphasis on 'proximal processes' in the most recent versions of the bioecological model, we see that relationships matter in combatting the simple reproduction of the familiar. Chapter 3 showed how the bioecological model provides a framework within which to consider a variety of different theories, focusing on different aspects of development collectively. Within this framework, it is possible to draw linkages between, for instance, the concept of proximal processes and attachment theory and the humanist psychology of Carl Rogers, thus enhancing our understanding of the broad dynamic of human development. If children are living 'linked lives' (Bronfenbrenner), 'securely attached' (Bowlby/Ainsworth) through strong 'proximal processes' (Bronfenbrenner) with the adults that populate systems, then the 'capacity' of both adults and children for positive action should be activated (Rogers). To put it simply, if the adults in a child's life are involved in caring, mutually supportive relationships with her, then they are more likely to be empowered to act in the child's best interest, regardless of institutional norms. Equally, if children are on the receiving end of caring, mutually supportive relationships, they are more likely to be empowered to object when they experience unjust practices.

In the most up-to-date versions of the model (Bronfenbrenner and Morris, 1998, 2006), process is emphasised more than context. In this way, the adults who care most about children, including their parents and their early childhood educators, can work together through strong connections in the mesosystem to ensure that early care and educational experiences provide the foundation for children's future academic, social and emotional well-being. The educational philosopher Paulo Freire refers to the changes this can lead to as 'transformation'. This belief in the transformative potential of education for profound change can begin with the provision and support for high-quality early years practice, something early educators have to advocate for in societies where later education is privileged in terms of funding and status.

When we use the concept of proximal processes to make sense of other important psychological theories, it becomes obvious that relationships are vital for children's development emotionally, socially and cognitively, and building good relationships should be a central area of concern for early years practice. While the analysis in Chapter 3 focused largely on process, the bioecological model emphasises that such vital relationships are informed and shaped by the person characteristics of the children and adults involved, the context in which they take place and the time (both individual and historical time) in which those relationships are embedded. The bioecological model shows us that relationships do not happen in a vacuum and 'processes' are impacted by the 'person', 'context' and 'time' (PPCT) factors with which they interact.

Focusing on context, we saw in Chapter 4 and in Chapter 7 that Bronfenbrenner identified features of an optimally structured environment, or context, for child

**162** Reflecting the bioecological in early years practice

development, including the provision of "objects and environments that invite manipulation and exploration" (Bronfenbrenner and Morris, 2006, p. 815). As well as providing materials and planning learning environments, early childhood educators also have an important role in creating stability and consistency within settings, avoiding chaotic contexts while at the same time maintaining a measure of flexibility to respond to individual needs. Supporting strong contact and mutual support between microsystems through the concept of the mesosystem is also important.

According to the most up-to-date iteration of the model, strong proximal processes provide a buffer in less than ideal contexts. In fact, Bronfenbrenner draws on the work of Rutter (see Rutter, 1985; Rutter et al., 1998) to show that the impact of protective forces, such as strong, supportive proximal processes with an important adult, on the development of resilience in children is even greater in 'at-risk' contexts. As such, context factors are less emphasised than in earlier models, and now in Bronfenbrenner's work, the relationship (process) is foregrounded. This is consistent with the contemporary trends in developmental psychology generally and the move away from simple linear models of causality towards an understanding of the interaction of risk and protective factors (Downes, 2014).

As explored in Chapters 4, 5 and 10, the integrated nature of the PPCT approach helps illustrate why we must understand issues of diversity and inclusion if we are to understand individual behaviours, perceptions and outcomes. Experiences and behaviour are influenced by factors such as socio-economic class, gender, disability and personal circumstances. Thus, it becomes clear that individual choices around issues like how educators support children or how parents provide for their educational and developmental needs must be understood as stemming from a joint freedom–determinism base. What this means is that people make active choices, but only within the range of options they perceive to be available to them.

The bioecological model helps us look beyond the individual person to the context in which they are developing and the relationships (processes) through which they do so, in and across time. This may help to avoid the emergence of a deficit narrative, for instance, characterising children and their families as responsible for difficulties and 'blaming' them for any potential educational difficulties, or the identification of certain groups of parents as 'not interested' in their children's education. It allows us to draw together a comprehensive picture of how individual characteristics interact with, are influenced by and impact the educational system in which they are present. The bioecological model recognises that no one cog in a system moves in isolation; experiences of context are influenced by the relationships or process within them, the person experiencing them and the time periods involved.

This emphasises the imperative on all, including early childhood educators, to interrupt negative cycles of alienation in order to give all children and families a fair chance in education and in life, reminiscent of the idea of scholar-activism. While educational interventions cannot be presented as the total solution for every problem that confronts society as a whole or the more localised school community, a bioecological perspective shows us the huge role that early education has

Reflecting the bioecological in early years practice **163**

to play in potentially changing lives for the better. The model highlights that if the design of educational interventions is based on a flawed expectation that all children and families are the same as each other, we run the risk of inadvertently reproducing the very inequalities we aim to address. For example, if we disregard the interaction of person factors with context and expect all children and parents to be similarly 'motivated' regardless of aspects such as socio-economic status, gender, age, linguistic and cultural background and prior educational experiences, it is no surprise that deficit models result because we criticise those children and parents who, for whatever reason, do not appear to show the expected levels of motivation. Certain groups are then seen as being uninterested in education, devaluing them even further.

Since children's access to education is mediated through their parents and some parents are not in a position to actively promote their children's interests, we cannot argue that educational approaches that depend on all parents behaving similarly will provide equitable outcomes for all children. The reality of development and education for individual children, parents, educators and schools is complex and contextual, and as a result, educators must consider diversity and its potential impact on the kinds of pedagogical approaches required. On the other hand, educational interventions that look solely at individual person characteristics to explain why they succeed in education or not can run the risk that a deficit perspective will develop – one that sees the problem as located within the individual and, as a result, 'blames the victim' rather than considering the many other factors of influence. Education then inappropriately becomes about 'fixing' the child rather than recognising and embracing the child's funds of knowledge, and if the child cannot be 'fixed', education itself is inappropriately seen as having failed.

What is important to note here is that *contexts can be changed* to support more healthy learning and development, providing researchers and educators with a rationale and, in fact, a moral imperative to identify optimal environments for individual children and their families. Bronfenbrenner's bioecological model imposes a responsibility on early childhood educators to acknowledge and act on contextual knowledge, individual characteristics, environmental factors and processes in relationships while also taking account of the sociocultural time in which development takes place, thereby supporting the potential of all children and families to benefit from good-quality early childhood experiences. Through creating strong 'linkages' across early years settings, home, schools and communities, educators can take account of the needs of diverse children and families to ensure the creation of an early childhood context where everyone feels welcome. Drawing on the funds of knowledge that children and their families bring with them to an early years setting can enrich the context within which early learning occurs.

Understanding that our behaviour as early educators has so profound an impact on children's development, and at such a crucial and deep level, can be daunting and even paralysing! The thing is that even without our understanding the influence of our practice, it has an impact on the children we work with – knowledge helps us consider our practice a little more carefully; it challenges us to consider the

**164** Reflecting the bioecological in early years practice

implications such knowledge has for our practices, and it allows us to recognise that feedback and the form that such feedback takes has an influence on young children's confidence, mental flexibility and self-control.

In Chapter 5, we considered the research evidence showing how this can work in practice. Recognising the importance of positive proximal processes for children during transitions, these can be supported through promoting friendships; involving families and communities, particularly parents; avoiding jarring cultural shifts in educational approaches and behavioural expectations; and ensuring the availability of supports for children with specific vulnerabilities such as special educational needs or behavioural difficulties. Through the provision of opportunities, materials, times and space to explore, play, take risks and rise to social and physical challenges in a setting that is secure and comfortable, children develop a sense of belonging and they feel that they are trusted participants in the learning environment, and this, in turn, facilitates healthy development and learning.

The analysis presented in this book, and summarised in this chapter, opposes any interpretation of the bioecological model that presents the functioning of systems as static, immutable and deterministic. The most up-to-date version of the model certainly leaves much room for dynamic change within systems, given certain circumstances. In fact, the idea of human beings as potential change agents in their world is flagged from the start of Bronfenbrenner and Morris's seminal chapter:

> [W]e are the only species that …has developed the capacity to engage successfully in scientific inquiry, and thereby, in many respects, has been able to change the nature of the world in which we live. As a result, within certain limits, we humans have altered the nature and course of our own development as a species.
>
> …Our primary emphasis …is on the role of developmental processes and outcomes in producing large scale changes over time in the state and structure of the broader society over time, and the implications of those changes for the society's future.
>
> *(2006, pp. 793–794, 796)*

Bronfenbrenner and Morris (2006) provide an imperative for educators at all levels to identify and implement optimal conditions for human development, warning that otherwise children will not be free to reach their full potential, to their detriment and the detriment of society as a whole. While allowing for Downes's point that generally systems tend to develop inertia and resistance to change in those who are a part of them, the bioecological model highlights research, policy and practice "committed to transforming experiments" (2014, p. 37). As Bronfenbrenner tells us, "no society can long sustain itself unless its members have learned the sensitivities, motivations and skills involved in assisting and caring for other human beings" (1979, p. 53). Quite simply, relationships matter, and with careful attention, these relationships can be empowering, and enabling, and lead to transformation.

At the conclusion of each chapter, we have provided key concepts to consider for early years practice. In the following, we outline a series of points to remember in considering the bioecological model as a totality. These points provide the broad theoretical framework guiding the model within which early years practice can be considered, reviewed and transformed.

## 'Process' in the microsystem

The bioecological model yields the strong recommendation that educators must emphasise the creation of supportive contexts through which positive relationships can develop. Early years settings ought to focus strongly on relationship building between children, parents, educators, educational settings and beyond. While contextual supports for families are vital in early childhood, these supports should be aimed at facilitating strong proximal processes rather than tick box or politically motivated systems with false models of 'quality'. An ethos of respectful consideration and caring for children and families is important for all, but is vital for the protection of potentially vulnerable children and adults, as is support for individual child agency and capacity that fosters positive social, emotional and educational outcomes. Such an ethos can be hard to measure and requires proactive efforts and ongoing reflection to achieve and maintain. As predicted by the bioecological framework, this *can* be successful and can make all the difference to individual experiences.

The importance of engaging with children and families as individuals with their own needs and strengths cannot be overestimated. Brooker's recommendation of "a serious and respectful listening, and not …a home school dialogue that assumes the school is always right" (2005, p. 128) is relevant here. Settings must consider issues of diversity such as language, culture, religion, socio-economics, gender, disability and family structure in developing support systems for children and families. Unicultural approaches may be doomed to failure and may actually widen pre-existing gaps in experience and understanding, leading to damaging levels of disjuncture at the mesosystem level. We cannot assume that one 'truth' exists for all human beings.

## 'Process' in the mesosystem – the creation of 'linkages'

The emphasis on relationships in the bioecological framework highlights the importance of considering the nature and quality of interactions in the mesosystem. We saw in Chapter 5 that minimising the differences between educational levels can support positive experiences. This echoes Bronfenbrenner's ideas on linkages in the mesosystem so that children can 'drag' (Slesnick et al., 2007) their skills across settings. In terms of meso-level recommendations, one of the strongest outcomes of a bioecological approach relates to the importance of including and supporting parents and families. As explained by the bioecological model, outcomes such as 'behaviour' or 'motivation' are not solely a function of individual child factors but also result from complex interactions with contexts and relationships experienced.

**166** Reflecting the bioecological in early years practice

Parents can act as the interpretive bridge between home and the early years setting for children. It is important that early childhood educators realise that expecting all parents and families to behave in the same way or to hold the same values, beliefs and capacities regardless of background or personal circumstances may be futile and, in fact, unfair. The onus is on the settings to be proactive on these issues because previous experiences of education can leave some children and adults vulnerable to marginalisation and intimidation.

## 'Process' in the exosystem and the macrosystem

When considering exosystem impacts on child development, Bronfenbrenner was reflecting on the world he knew. He saw technologies such as the TV and video as located within the exosystem and as exerting an influence on families which, in turn, might affect children's development and learning. Were he writing today, he may have been exploring the impact of our more complex and interactive technologies across all systems, and he may have been questioning how they might influence the behaviour of children, parents and others. It is important, therefore, that early childhood educators be alert to the extensive reach of technology into the lives of families and children and reflect on how early childhood practice should respond positively and proactively to such changes.

Those involved in early education at every level, from research to policymaking to practice, must recognise the impact of diversity and the need to be vigilant in supporting and maintaining inclusive practice, incorporating this recognition into all initiatives. The development of a 'one-size-fits-all' approach can feed into the very problems we aim to address through the development of deficit models and alienation of traditionally marginalised groups.

In spite of financial pressures, significant direct investment and support are required for the early years sector in many countries; too often there is investment in regulation and monitoring without sufficient support or improvement for those working directly with children and families 'on the ground'. Systems of measuring quality in the early years tend, in some countries, to depend on crude indicators of quality of provision. Systems sometimes emphasise structural, contextual ratings using a tick box – for instance, whether there is a fridge and bottled water in an early years setting – rather than asking more difficult questions regarding relationships and interactions (process) between children and those who care for and educate them. There is an urgent need for research into the quality of early years provision and practice through an examination of genuine nurturing, educative and caring practices and processes rather than simply examining contexts in isolation from the social nature of that context and the elements comprising it.

## Guiding practice bioecologically

Bronfenbrenner's bioecological model of human development provides a powerful argument for reflective and dynamic early educational practices. In Chapters

Reflecting the bioecological in early years practice **167**

6 through 10, we have provided detail on how we might use the learning by exploring the real potential of the bioecological model in early years practice. We have seen that the model necessitates a view of behaviours and learning within the dynamic social and historical contexts in which they occur. For instance, in Chapter 6, we saw how Bronfenbrenner's model positions the child at the centre of her learning and development in early years practice. The unique constellation of dispositions and characteristics that individual children bring to their early years settings influences and shapes the experiences they will have within these settings. As highlighted in Chapter 6, children's agency is not an innate characteristic but develops in nurturing contexts, typically facilitated and supported by adults. It is important to emphasise the essential role which early childhood educators play in facilitating and supporting children's agency and participation in their learning and development and in providing rich learning opportunities for children to explore and develop their interests and abilities. Working closely alongside children in the early years, we soon become familiar with and tune in to the particular and distinct characteristics of each individual child, and the extent to which we succeed in doing this is undoubtedly influenced by the characteristics of individual educators and their associated responses to individual children.

Consistent with Bronfenbrenner's bioecological model, we support children's autonomy by providing them with opportunities to explore and develop their own particular interests and competencies rather than prescribing learning aims and objectives which do not reflect their individual talents and interests. Those curricula which emphasise presumed and prescribed learning objectives for children tend typically to benefit a small number of children while serving to impede or restrict the potential for other children to thrive. Ideally, early childhood educators should aim to support children to become agents and co-constructors of their knowledge of the world around them. Knowledge of the social world occurs when an interaction is a shared vehicle for thought. Individuals who are teaching and individuals who are learning can both make meaning from their activities. Through such engagement, there is true participation in the learning process when learners and early childhood educators are mutually involved. While locating the child at the centre of practice, Bronfenbrenner's bioecological model also acknowledges children's vulnerability and their need for protection and their dependence on adults as well as their need for space for self-development, greater autonomy and independence.

The model also provides a valuable conceptual space within which to consider other important theoretical insights into education and learning, including those provided by Lev Vygotsky, who proposed a cultural-historical theory of human development. It is a model that also incorporates more contemporary thinking such as the work of Fleer, Wood and others on the complex role of play in early learning and development. The important unifying feature of Bronfenbrenner's model is the priority placed on the central role of process and context as integrated and integrating mechanisms in the development of the young child across time and setting.

**168** Reflecting the bioecological in early years practice

In Chapter 7, we focused on the importance of creating a welcoming learning environment where children encounter invitations to learn in a space that not only provides them with a sense of security and belonging but also offers them a space with dynamic and stimulating opportunities to explore and discover new experiences and concepts. A rich learning environment in the early years provides opportunities for children to explore and discover meanings in a manner that is characterised as emergent rather than prescribed. Learning is informed and guided by the child's interest, and consistent with the bioecological model of human development, the emphasis is on the processes that are generated through careful observation and documentation of children's interests and skills in order to provide meaningful and rich learning experiences.

Guided by the PPCT structure, we explored the concept of 'rich learning environments' through a focus on the process, person, context and time factors that may influence and shape their development. Consistent with the concept of a learning environment that evokes the sense of emergent rather than prescribed learning opportunities, the importance of providing opportunities for children to change and transform their environments is highlighted in Chapter 7 and throughout this book with an emphasis on flexibility – opportunities for children to transform their environments and to experience a sense of autonomy and control within these environments. In considering key features of a rich learning environment, we emphasised the value and significance of creating invitations for children to learn. We highlighted the importance of designing and developing environments rich in affordances for children to engage in joint activities and tasks, providing opportunities to work together and negotiate shared meanings with other children and adults in early years settings. Rich learning environments do not require sophisticated tools or equipment but will be enhanced through innovative and creative inputs from both children and adults working together, consistent with the bioecological model's emphasis on the interaction between process, person and context. Rich learning environments also ensure that time is available to allow for reciprocal, meaningful interactions between those who share early learning spaces. An emphasis on rich learning environments beyond the immediate ECEC setting was also outlined, with a focus on children's engagement and interactions within the wider community.

In Chapter 8, we saw that viewing development as a dynamic and discontinuous process, or as a 'to-ing and fro-ing' process, allows us to see behaviour and development in early childhood as being adaptive to the immediate demands of the child in context. Such an approach to early education is not tied to the age and stage of development of the child but, rather, is linked to the sociocultural context of development for the child in the present. It is exemplified by the internationally recognised practices at Reggio Emilia in Italy and in the *Te Whāriki* early years curriculum of New Zealand, where pedagogy is directed by the connections, interactions and relationships between children and the wider world and by social, physical and emotional elements rather than by any prescribed expectations of

Reflecting the bioecological in early years practice **169**

developmental outcome. There is increasing evidence from psychological research and neuroscience to support Bronfenbrenner in his contention that the proximal processes of daily life are crucial engines of development. Evidence suggests that these interactive processes are particularly important in early childhood given the role that interactions (their quality, bidirectionality and content) play in facilitating the development of thinking skills (cognitive and metacognitive) and affective skills (dispositions).

Reflecting on the central role of relationships in children's early learning and development, Chapter 9 considered how best to provide a nurturing learning experience for young children and introduced the critical importance of pedagogical leadership. Despite recognising the powerful framework for early practice provided by Bronfenbrenner's bioecological model, working ecologically in day-to-day practice is not simple. In fact, there are many cases where, despite an expressed commitment to a rich, dynamic and relational pedagogy, more traditional practices dominate. Implicit in early years practices consistent with the bioecological approach to human development, which we have characterised as a 'nurturing pedagogy', is a commitment to democratic principles that recognise the need to respect and engage meaningfully with children. This approach is reflective of an understanding of early years settings as sites of democratic practice where children are respected for who they are and what they bring and where both children and adults can participate collectively in interpreting experiences and shaping decisions affecting children's development and the nature of the context within which development occurs.

In Chapter 10 we explored the position of the early childhood setting as a nexus for communication and learning. We introduced the concept of learning ecologies as spaces which encompass opportunities for learning through engaging with people and resources across a number of contexts, both immediate and more remote (Jackson, 2014). The concept of parental involvement was explored in some depth and the crucial issue of power dynamics and communication was addressed. We also explored the potential of learning beyond the physical space of the ECEC setting and engaging with the wider community as a site for learning. To enhance setting, home and community connectivity we illustrated that a healthy mesosystem requires a reciprocal flow of communication and regard, not a one-way directive in which power is held only by one party. To this end educators are encouraged to use multiple means of communication, tailored to the individual needs, with strategies for creating links with parents and others rooted in relationship building. This brought us to the presence and potential of technologies across the various microsystems in children's early lives. The chapter examined the reality of technology in the lives of even very young children and considered the possibilities and challenges posed for early childhood educators.

Bronfenbrenner's model of human development provides an impetus for responding to contemporary understandings of child development. Changing early years practice to incorporate this new knowledge, based on scientific understandings of

## 170 Reflecting the bioecological in early years practice

development, is not an easy task. Such transformation rests with all those concerned with good-quality early years practice and requires ongoing reflection and a commitment to learning and change. As Bronfenbrenner puts it:

> Human beings create the environments that shape the course of human development. Their actions influence the multiple physical and cultural tiers of the ecology that shapes them, and this agency makes humans – for better or for worse – active producers of their own development.
>
> *(2005, p. xxvii)*

# GLOSSARY

**ACTIVE LEARNING** The idea of the child as curious, meaning-making and doing everything possible to understand the world.

**AGENCY** A quality allowing the child to engage in intentional action to achieve particular valued goals.

**ATTACHMENT** Bond formed by an infant with the primary caregiver, thought by attachment theorists to form the basis of all future relationships and of psychological well-being for the rest of the individual's life.

**BIOECOLOGICAL MODEL** Model of human development conceptualised by Urie Bronfenbrenner and colleagues. Central features include an emphasis on relationships and interactions with other human beings and objects/symbols and the importance of context in understanding development.

**CHRONOSYSTEM** A level of context within Bronfenbrenner's bioecological model. The patterning of environmental events and transitions over time.

**CULTURAL CAPITAL** Bourdieu's idea that the taken-for-granted behaviours and ways of being of certain groups are valued by the dominant culture, whereas other groups may be devalued.

**DEMAND CHARACTERISTICS** Characteristics of the child inviting or discouraging reactions from the social environment that can foster or disrupt the operation of proximal processes.

**DIRECTIVE BELIEF SYSTEMS** Beliefs developed through internalisation of experience whereby children begin to conceptualise a sense of agency within the world. Such belief systems may direct behaviour, thereby impacting future experiences and, in turn, reinforcing directive belief systems in a two-way process. This concept is evident in many theories, such as social cognitive theory and bioecological theory.

**DISPOSITIONS** Characteristics of the child that may be 'generative', inviting positive responses from others, or 'disruptive', inviting negative responses from others.

**172** Glossary

**EDUCATIONAL TRANSITION** May refer to multiple transitions. In the current work, educational transition refers to the move from preschool to primary school.

**EXOSYSTEM** The level of context within the bioecological model that the child may never enter but which may, nevertheless, affect what happens to them.

**HEAD START** American programme initiated by Bronfenbrenner and others, incorporating a range of early interventions for disadvantaged young children and their families.

**INTERNAL WORKING MODEL** A concept from attachment theory. Internalisation of the quality of attachment with the primary caregiver, which forms the basis of a child's concept of self and directs future relationships.

**INTERNALISATION** Interweaving of cultural, relational and biological influences to determine the characteristics and behaviour of the child.

**INTERSUBJECTIVITY** Interactions in which there is dynamic and engaged input from both adults and children.

**LINKAGES** Experiences, structures and processes that tie various systems together and encourage individuals to apply learning from one setting to events in another.

**MACROSYSTEM** The level of context within the bioecological model reflecting the wider pattern of ideology and organisation of social institutions common to a particular social class or culture.

**MEDIATED LEARNING** A sociocultural concept. Acknowledges biological inheritance as the basis for subsequent development but maintains that higher-order functioning develops through social activity that is embedded in the cultural values of particular communities.

**MESOSYSTEM** The level of context within the bioecological model accounting for interconnections between two or more settings, such as school, peer group and family. The mesosystem is a system of two or more microsystems.

**MICROSYSTEM** The level of context within the bioecological model of which the individual has direct experience on a regular basis.

**NURTURING PEDAGOGY** An approach to early educational practice. Emphasises the educative value of care and the caring nature of education.

**PROXIMAL PROCESSES** Progressively more complex reciprocal interaction between an active, evolving, biopsychological human organism and the persons, objects and symbols in its immediate environment.

**RESILIENCE** Complex interaction of protective and risk factors with the personal characteristics of the child, leading to positive or normative outcomes in spite of challenging circumstances.

**RESOURCE CHARACTERISTICS** Experience, knowledge and skills required for effective functioning of proximal processes at a given stage of development.

**TECHNO-MICROSYSTEM** The ecological *techno-microsystem* situates the developing child in the context of internet use in the home, early childhood, school and community environments.

Glossary **173**

**SCAFFOLDING** A sociocultural concept capturing the gradual removal of adult support as a child becomes more competent.

**SELF-EFFICACY** A concept from social cognitive theory. A person's self-efficacy beliefs reflect the level of competence they believe themselves to have in a given domain.

**SYNAPTIC PRUNING** The process by which the brain adapts to experience. Synapses are brain connections. Those that have been reinforced through repeated experience in early life tend to become permanent. Synapses that are not used in the early years are eliminated. In this way, experiences (positive or negative) that children have in their early lives influence the ways their brains will be wired into adulthood.

**SYSTEM BLOCKAGE** The tendency for systems to instil inertia in those within them.

**TEMPERAMENT** The child's tendency to respond to the environment in characteristic ways, reflecting energy levels, persistence and tolerance of frustration.

**ZONE OF PROXIMAL DEVELOPMENT** A sociocultural concept. The gap between what a child can achieve alone and with support from a 'more expert other'.

# ABBREVIATIONS

| | |
|---|---|
| **DAP** | developmentally appropriate practice |
| **EPPE** | Effective Provision of Pre-school and Primary Education |
| **PPCT** | process–person–context–time |
| **UNCRC** | United Nations Convention on the Rights of the Child |
| **USSR** | Union of Socialist Soviet Republics |
| **ZPD** | zone of proximal development |

# REFERENCES

Aguiar, A., & Baillargeon, R. (1999). 2.5 month old infants' reasoning about when objects should and should not be occluded. *Cognitive Psychology, 39*(2), 116–157.

Aguiar, A., & Baillargeon, R. (2002). Developments in young infants' reasoning about occluded objects. *Cognitive Psychology, 45*(2), 267–336.

Ahn, J. (2011). I'm not scared of anything: Emotion as social power in children's worlds. *Childhood, 17*(1), 94–112.

Ahnert, L., Pinquart, M., & Lamb, M. E. (2006). Security of children's relationships with nonparental care providers: A meta-analysis. *Child Development, 77*(3), 664–679.

Ainsworth, M. D. S., Blehar, M., Waters, E., & Wall, S. (1978). *Patterns of attachment.* Hillsdale NJ: Erlbaum.

Alexander, R. (2004). Still no pedagogy: Principles, pragmatism and compliance in primary education. *Cambridge Journal of Education, 34*(1), 7–33.

Alverson, R., Ginn, L., & Gilbert, J. (2019). Sustained collaborative preschool partnerships and the challenges of educating the whole child. *International Journal of Child Care and Education Policy, 13*(9), 1–15.

Anastasi, A. (1958). Heredity, environment, and the question "how?" *Psychological Review, 65*(4), 197–208.

Armitage, M. (2011). Risky play is not a category – It's what children do. *ChildLinks: Children's Risky Play, 3*, 11–14.

Association for Cognitive Analytic Therapy (ACAT). (n.d.). *What is CAT understanding? How cognitive analytic therapy can help teams and groups.* Dorchester: ACAT Ltd.

Bae, B. (2009). Children's right to participation: Challenges in everyday interactions. *European Early Childhood Research Journal, 17*(3), 391–406.

Bandura, A. (2001). Social cognitive theory: An agentic perspective. *Annual Review of Psychology, 52*(1), 1–26.

Banica, I., Sandre, A., & Weinberg, A. (2019). Overprotective/authoritarian maternal parenting is associated with an enhanced error-related negativity (ERN) in emerging adult females. *International Journal of Psychophysiology, 137*, 12–20.

Baumrind, D. (1978). Parental disciplinary patterns and social competence in children. *Youth and Society, 9*(3), 239–276.

**176** References

Baumrind, D. (1996). The discipline controversy revisited. *Family Relations: An Interdisciplinary Journal of Applied Family Studies, 45*(4), 405–414.

Baumrind, D. (2005). Patterns of parental authority and adolescent autonomy. *New Directions in Child and Adolescent Development, 108,* 61–69.

Belsky, J. (1984). The determinants of parenting: A process model. *Child Development, 55*(1), 83–96.

Bergen, D. (2002). The role of pretend play in children's cognitive development. *Early Childhood: Research and Practice, 4*(1) [online]. Available at: http://ecrp.uiuc.edu/v4n1/bergen.html

Berghs, M., Atkin, K., Hatton, C., & Thomas, C. (2019). Do disabled people need a stronger social model: A social model of human rights? *Disability & Society, 34*(7–8), 1034–1039.

Berk, L. E. (2009). *Child development.* Hoboken, NJ: Pearson

Berk, L. E. (2018). *Development through the lifespan.* Hoboken, NJ: Pearson.

Bertram, T., & Pascal, C. (2002). *Early years education: An international perspective.* London: Qualifications and Curriculum Authority. www.inca.org.uk/pdf/early_years.pdf

Blair, C. (2002). School readiness: Integrating cognition and emotion in a neurobiological conceptualization of children's functioning at school entry. *American Psychologist, 57*(2), 111–127.

Blakemore, S. J., & Frith, U. (2005). The learning brain: Lessons for education: A précis. *Developmental Science, 8*(6), 459–471.

Bourdieu, P. (1990). *The logic of practice.* Cambridge: Polity Press.

Bourdieu, P., & Passeron, J. C. (1977). *Reproduction in education, society and culture.* London: Sage.

Bowlby, J. (1973). *Attachment and loss: Vol 2. Separation, anxiety and anger.* New York: Basic Books.

Bowlby, J. (1988). *Attachment and loss: Vol 4. A secure base: Clinical applications of attachment theory.* London: Routledge.

Bowlby, R. (2007). Babies and toddlers in non-parental daycare can avoid stress and anxiety if they develop a lasting secondary attachment bond with one carer who is consistently accessible to them. *Attachment and Human Development, 9*(4), 307–319.

Boylan, F., Barblett, L., & Knaus, M. (2018). Early childhood teachers' perspectives of growth mindset: Developing agency in children. *Australasian Journal of Early Childhood, 43*(3), 16–24.

Bradford, H. (2012). *The wellbeing of children under three.* Abingdon: Routledge.

Bredekamp, S., & Copple, C. (Eds.). (1997). *Developmentally appropriate practice in early childhood programmes.* Washington, DC: National Association for the Education of Young Children.

Brennan, M. A. (2005). *"They Just Want to Be with Us." Young Children Learning to Live the Culture: A Post-Vygotskian Analysis of Young Children's Enculturation into a Childcare Setting* [Unpublished doctoral dissertation]. Wellington, New Zealand: Victoria University of Wellington.

Brewster, S. (2004). Insights from a social model of literacy and disability. *Literacy, 38*(1), 46–51.

Broadhead, P. (2010). Cooperative play and learning from nursery to year one. In P. Broadhead, J. Howard, & E. Wood (Eds.), *Play and learning in early years: Research to practice* (pp. 43–60). London: Sage.

Bronfenbrenner, U. (1942/2005). Social status, structure, and development in the classroom group. In U. Bronfenbrenner (Ed.), *Making human beings human: Bioecological perspectives on human development* (pp. 22–26). London: Sage.

Bronfenbrenner, U. (1967/2005). The split-level American family. In U. Bronfenbrenner (Ed.), *Making human beings human: Bioecological perspectives on human development* (pp. 201–209). London: Sage.

## References  177

Bronfenbrenner, U. (1970a). *Two worlds of childhood: US and USSR*. New York: Russell Sage Foundation.

Bronfenbrenner, U. (1970b). Minority report of forum 15: 1970. White House conference on children. In U. Bronfenbrenner (Ed.), *Making human beings human: Bioecological perspectives on human development* (pp. 210–214). London: Sage.

Bronfenbrenner, U. (1971a). Day care USA: A statement of principles. *Peabody Journal of Education*, *48*, 86–95.

Bronfenbrenner, U. (1971b). Who cares for America's children? *Young Children*, *26*(3), 157–163.

Bronfenbrenner, U. (1973). Social ecology of human development. In F. Richardson (Ed.), *Brain and intelligence: The ecology of child development* (pp. 113–129). Hyattsville, MD: National Education Press.

Bronfenbrenner, U. (1975). Reality and research in the ecology of human development. *Proceedings of the American Philosophical Society*, *119*(6), 439–469.

Bronfenbrenner, U. (1977). The ecology of human development in retrospect and prospect. In H. McGurk (Ed.), *Ecological factors in human development* (pp. 275–286). Amsterdam: North Holland.

Bronfenbrenner, U. (1979). *The ecology of human development: Experiments by nature and design*. Cambridge, MA: Harvard University Press.

Bronfenbrenner, U. (1985). The future of childhood. In V. Greaney (Ed.), *Children: Needs and rights* (pp. 167–186). New York: Irvington Publishers, Inc.

Bronfenbrenner, U. (1986a). Ecology of the family as a context for human development: Research perspectives. *Developmental Psychology*, *22*, 723–742.

Bronfenbrenner, U. (1986b). Recent advances in research on the ecology of human development. In R. K. Silbereisen, K. Eyferth, & G. Rudinger (Eds.), *Development as action in context: Problem behavior and normal youth development* (pp. 287–309). New York: Springer-Verlag.

Bronfenbrenner, U. (1988/2005). Strengthening family systems. In U. Bronfenbrenner (Ed.), *Making human beings human: Bioecological perspectives on human development* (pp. 260–273). London: Sage.

Bronfenbrenner, U. (1989a). Ecological systems theory. In R. Vasta (Ed.), *Annals of child development*, Vol. 6 (pp. 187–249). Greenwich: JAI Press.

Bronfenbrenner, U. (1989b). *Who cares for children?* Paris: UNESCO.

Bronfenbrenner, U. (1992/2005). Ecological systems theory. In U. Bronfenbrenner (Ed.), *Making human beings human: Bioecological perspectives on human development* (pp. 106–173). London: Sage.

Bronfenbrenner, U. (1993). The ecology of cognitive development: Research models and fugitive findings. In R. Wonziak, & K. Fischer (Eds.), *Development in context: Acting and thinking in specific environments* (pp. 3–44). Hillsdale, NJ: Erlbaum.

Bronfenbrenner, U. (1995). Developmental ecology through space and time: A future perspective. In P. Moen, G. H. Elder Jr, & K. Lüscher (Eds.), *Examining lives in context: Perspectives on the ecology of human development* (pp. 619–647). Washington, DC: American Psychological Association.

Bronfenbrenner, U. (Ed.) (2005). *Making human beings human: Bioecological perspectives on human development*. London: Sage.

Bronfenbrenner, U., & Ceci, S. J. (1993). Heredity, environment and the question "how?": A first approximation. In R. Plomin, & G. E. McClearn (Eds.), *Nature, nurture and psychology* (pp. 313–323). Washington, DC: APA Books.

Bronfenbrenner, U., & Ceci, S. J. (1994). Nature–nurture reconceptualised in developmental perspective: A bioecological model. *Psychological Review*, *101*(4), 568–586.

**178** References

Bronfenbrenner, U., & Morris, P. (1998). The ecology of developmental processes. In W. Damon, & R. M. Lerner (Eds.), *Handbook of child psychology: Vol 1, Theoretical models of human development* (pp. 993–1028). New York: John Wiley & Sons.

Bronfenbrenner, U., & Morris, P. A. (2006). The bioecological model of human development. In R. M. Lerner, & W. E. Damon (Eds.), *Handbook of child psychology: Vol 1, Theoretical models of human development* (6th ed., pp. 793–828). Chichester: John Wiley & Sons.

Brooker, L. (2005). Learning to be a child: Cultural diversity and early years ideology. In N. Yelland (Ed.), *Critical issues in early childhood education* (pp. 115–130). Maidenhead: Open University Press.

Brooker, L. (2008). *Supporting transitions in the early years*. Maidenhead: McGraw-Hill.

Brooker, L. (2015). Cultural capital in the preschool years. In L. Alanen, L. Brooker, & B. Mayall (Eds.), *Childhood with bourdieu* (pp. 13–33). Basingstoke: Palgrave Macmillan.

Brooks, D. (2011). *The social animal: The hidden sources of love, character and achievement*. New York: Random House.

Bruce, T. (2001). *Learning through play: Babies, toddlers and the foundation years*. London: Hodder Stoughton.

Bruner, J. (1996). *The culture of education*. Cambridge, MA: Harvard University Press.

Buckingham, D. (2008). *Youth, identity and digital media*. Cambridge, MA: MIT Press.

Burchinal, M. R., Peisner-Feinberg, E., Pianta, R., & Howes, C. (2002). Development of academic skills from pre-school through second grade: Family and classroom predictors of developmental trajectories. *Journal of School Psychology, 40*(5), 415–436.

Burman, E. (2008). *Developments: Child, image, nation*. London: Routledge.

Capobianco, N. B., Bush, C. D., & Best, D. L. (2019). Emotional development: Cultural influences on young children's emotional competence. In T. Tulviste, D. Best, J. Gibbons (Eds.), *Children's social worlds in cultural context*. Cham: Springer. https://doi.org/10.1007/978-3-030-27033-9_5

Cárcamo, R. A., Vermeer, H. J., van der Veer, R., & van IJzendoorn, M. H. (2016). Early full-time day care, mother–child attachment, and quality of the home environment in Chile: Preliminary findings. *Early Education and Development, 27*(4), 457–477.

Carr, M. (2004). *The Marsden Learning Dispositions in Social Context (DISC) Project: Some Thoughts about the Framework*. Hamilton, New Zealand: Unpublished discussion for the Marsden DISC Project, Waikato University.

Carr, M., & Claxton, G. (2002). Tracking the development of learning dispositions. *Assessment in Education: Propositions, Policy and Practice, 9*(1), 9–37.

Carr, M., & Lee, W. (2019). *Learning stories in practice*. London: Sage Publications.

Carroll, N., Sadowski, A., Laila, A., Hruska, V., Nixon, M., Ma, D. W. L., & Haines, J. (2020). The impact of COVID-19 on health behavior, stress, financial and food security among middle to high income Canadian families with young children. *Nutrients, 12*(8), 2352. https://doi-org.tudublin.idm.oclc.org/10.3390/nu12082352

Castro, A., Ezquerra, P., & Argos, J. (2018). Profundizando en la transición entre educación infantil y educación primaria: la perspectiva de familias y profesorado [Deepening the transition between childhood education and primary education: The perspective of families and teachers]. *Educational Theory/Teoría de La Educación, 30*(1), 217–240.

Centre on the Developing Child at Harvard. (2016). *From best practices to breakthrough impacts*. Cambridge, MA: Harvard University.

Chess, S., & Thomas, A. (1991). Temperament and the concept of goodness of fit. In J. Strelau, & A. Angleitner (Eds.), *Explorations in temperament* (pp. 15–28). Boston, MA: Springer US.

Chirkov, V. (2020). The sociocultural movement in psychology, the role of theories in sociocultural inquiries, and the theory of sociocultural models. *Asian Journal of Social Psychology*, *23*(2), 119–134.

Cigala, A., Venturelli, E., & Bassetti, M. (2019). Reflective practice: A method to improve teachers' well-being. A longitudinal training in early childhood education and care centers. *Frontiers in Psychology*, *10*, Article 2574.

Clark, A., & Moss, P. (2001). *Listening to young children: The mosaic approach*. London: National Children's Bureau/Joseph Rowntree Foundation.

Coldsmith, H. H., Buss, A. H., Plomin, R., Rothbart, M. K., Thomas, A., Chess, S., Hinde, R. A., & McCall, R. B. (1987). Roundtable: What is temperament? Four approaches. *Child Development*, *58*(2), 505–529.

Commonwealth of Australia. (2009). *Belonging, being and becoming: The early years learning framework for Australia*. Canberra: Council of Australian Councils.

Corsaro, W. A. (2010). *The sociology of childhood*. London: Sage.

Covington, M. V., & Müeller, K. J. (2001). Intrinsic versus extrinsic motivation: An approach/avoidance reformulation. *Educational Psychology Review*, *13*(2), 157–176.

Curtis, D. (2001). Strategies for enhancing children's use of the environment. *Child Care Information Exchange*, *142*, 42–45.

Dahlberg, G., & Moss, P. (2005). *Ethics and politics in early childhood education*. Abingdon: Routledge Falmer.

Dahlberg, G., Moss, P., & Pence, A. (1999). *Beyond quality in early childhood education and care: Postmodern perspectives*. London: Falmer Press.

Dale Tunnicliffe, S., & Gkouskou, E. (2019): Science in action in spontaneous preschool play – An essential foundation for future understanding. *Early Child Development and Care*, *190*(2), 1–10.

Danby, S.J., Fleer, M., Davidson, C., & Hatzigianni, M. (Eds.). (2018). *Digital childhoods technologies and children's everyday lives*. London. Springer.

Department of Children and Youth Affairs (DCYA). (2016). *Diversity, equality and inclusion charter and guidelines for early childhood care and education*. Dublin: DCYA.

Department of Children and Youth Affairs (DCYA). (2019). *An end of year one review of the access and inclusion model [AIM]: Final Report*. Dublin: Department of Children and Youth Affairs.

Devlieghere, J., Li, Y., & Vandenbroek, M. (2020). Beyond the veil of parents: Deconstructing the concept of parental involvement in early childhood education and care. *Early Years: An International Research Journal*, 1–12. https://doi.org/10.1080/09575146.2020.1840526

Diamond, A. (2013). Executive functions. *Annual Review of Psychology*, *64*, 135–168.

Dockett, S., & Perry, B. (2013). Siblings and buddies: Providing expert advice about starting school. *International Journal of Early Years Education*, *21*(4), 348–361.

Dockett, S., Perry, B., & Kearney, E. (2012). Family transitions as children start school. *Family Matters*, *90*, 57–67.

Domitrovich, C., Durlak, K., Staley, R., & Weissberg, P. (2017). Social-emotional competence: An essential factor for promoting positive adjustment and reducing risk in school children. *Child Development*, *88*(2), 408–416.

Downes, P. (2014). *Access to education in Europe: A framework and agenda for system change*. London: Springer.

Duncan, J. (2012). Building communities: Begins in the early years. In J. Duncan, & S. Te One (Eds.), *Comparative early childhood services: International perspectives* (pp. 79–100). New York: Palgrave Macmillan.

## 180 References

Duncan, J., Jones, C., & Carr, M. (2008). Learning dispositions and the role of mutual engagement: Factors for consideration in educational settings. *Contemporary Issues in Early Childhood, 9*(2), 107–117. https://doi.org/10.2304/ciec.2008.9.2.107. https://cie.sagepub.com/content/9/2/107.full.pdf+html

Dunphy, E. (2008). *Supporting early learning and development through formative assessment, a research paper.* Dublin: National Council for Curriculum and Assessment.

Duschinsky, R., Van Ijzendoorn, M., Foster, S., Reijman, S., & Lionetti, F. (2018). Attachment histories and futures: Reply to Vicedo's 'Putting Attachment in its Place'. *European Journal of Developmental Psychology* (Online, Open Access), *17*(1) 138–146.

Dweck, C. S. (2007). *Mindset: The new psychology of success.* New York: Ballantine Books.

Early Childhood Ireland. (2016). *Just give me five minutes: Toddlers transitions within the daily routine,* Available at Toddlers Transitions within the Daily Routine | Early Childhood Ireland, (accessed 24 September 2021).

Early Childhood Matters. (2013). *Learning begins early.* The Hague: Bernard Van Leer Foundation.

Early-O'Brien, S. (2018). *Snack time at any time.* Available at Snack time at anytime-Scéalta Blog | Early Childhood Ireland, (accessed 24 September 2021).

Educational Transitions and Change Research Group. (2011). *Transition to school: Position statement.* Albury-Wodonga: Research Institute for Professional Practice, Learning and Education, Charles Sturt University.

Edwards, S. (2016). New concepts of play and the problem of technology, digital media and popular-culture integration with play-based learning in early childhood education, *Technology, Pedagogy and Education, 25*(4), 513–532.

Ellis, R. J. (2012). *The study of second language acquisition.* New York: Oxford University Press.

English, H. B., & English, A. C. (1958). *A comprehensive dictionary of psychological and psycho-analytical terms: A guide to usage.* New York: David McKay Company, Inc.

Epstein, A. S. (2007). *The intentional teacher: Choosing the best strategies for young children's learning.* Washington, DC: National Association for the Education of Young Children.

Epstein, J. L. (1995). School/family/community partnerships: Caring for the children we share. *Phi Delta Kappan, 76,* 701–712.

Epstein, J. L., & Sheldon, S. B. (2016). Necessary but not sufficient: The role of policy for advancing programs of school, family, and community partnerships. *Russell Sage Foundation Journal of the Social Sciences, 2*(5), 202–219.

Eun, B. (2019). The zone of proximal development as an overarching concept: A framework for synthesizing Vygotsky's theories. *Educational Philosophy and Theory, 51*(1), 18–30.

Fast, A., & Olsen, C. (2018). Gender development in transgender preschool children. *Child Development, 89*(2), 620–637.

Fawcett, C., & Liszkowski, U. (2015). Social referencing during infancy and early childhood across cultures. In James D. Wright (Ed.), *International encyclopedia of the social & behavioral sciences* (pp. 556–562). San Diego, CA: Elsevier Science.

Fitzpatrick, A. (2020). Towards a pedagogy of intergenerational learning. In M. Kernan, & G. Cortellesi (Eds.), *Intergenerational learning in practice. Together old and young* (pp. 23–39). London: Routledge.

Fitzpatrick, A. (2021). *Intergenerational learning: An exploratory study of the concept, role and potential of intergenerational learning (IGL) as a pedagogical strategy in Irish early childhood education (ECE) services* [Unpublished PhD thesis]. Dublin: TU Dublin.

Fitzpatrick, S. (2015). From sectoral to systemic solutions in educational policy. *Proceedings from Education Studies Association of Ireland annual conference, Educational Research and Practice in Times of Transition: Looking to the Future,* Maynooth University and Carton House, 9–11 April.

References **181**

Fjortoft, I. (2001). The natural environment as a playground for children: The impact of outdoor play on pre-primary school children. *Early Childhood Education Journal, 29*(2), 111–117.

Fleer, M. (2003). Early childhood education as an evolving "community of practice" or as lived "social reproduction": Researching the "taken-for-granted". *Contemporary Issues in Early Childhood, 4*(1), 64–79.

Fleer, M. (2010). *Early learning and development: Cultural-historical concepts in play.* New York: Cambridge University Press.

Fleer, M. (2018). Digital animation: New conditions for children's development in play-based setting. *British Journal of Educational Technology, 49*(5), 943–958.

Fleer, M. (2021). Re-imagining play spaces in early childhood education: Supporting girls' motive orientation to STEM in times of COVID-19. *Journal of Early Childhood Research, 19*(1), 3–20.

Fleer, M., Fragkiadaki, G., & Rai, P. (2020). Programmatic research in the conceptual PlayLab: STEM PlayWorld as an educational experiment and as a source of development. *Science Education Research and Praxis, 76,* 9–23.

Flewitt, R., & Cowan, K. (2019). *Valuing young children's signs of learning: Observation and digital documentation of play in early years classrooms: Final report.* London: The Froebel Trust.

Fonsén, E. (2013). Dimensions of pedagogical leadership in early childhood education. In E. Hujala, M. Waniganayake, & J. Rodd (Eds.), *Researching leadership in early childhood education* (pp. 181–192). Tampere: Tampere University Press.

French, G. (2007). *Children's early learning and development: Background paper to Aistear.* Dublin: NCCA.

French, G. (2013). *Early speech and language matters: Enriching the communication environment and language development in early childhood.* Dublin: Barnardos.

French, G. (2014). *Let Them Talk: Evaluation of the Language Enrichment Programme of the Ballyfermot Early Years Language and Learning Initiative.* Dublin: Ballyfermot/Chapelizod Partnership.

Frønes, I. (1993). Changing childhoods. *Childhood, 1*(1), 1–2.

Galinsky, E. (2010). *Mind in the making: The seven essential life skills every child needs.* New York: Harper Collins.

Gallagher, C., & Fitzpatrick, A. (2018). "It's a win–win situation" – Intergenerational learning in preschool and elder care settings: An Irish perspective. *Journal of Intergenerational Relationships, 16*(1–2), 26–44.

Gauvain, M. (2020). Vygotsky's sociocultural theory. *Encyclopedia of Infant and Early Childhood Development,* 446–465.

Gaylor, E., & Spiker, D. (2012). *Home visiting programs and their impact on young children's school readiness* [pdf file], Encyclopedia on Early Childhood Development. Available at: www.child-encyclopedia.com/sites/default/files/textes-experts/en/912/home-visiting-programs-and-their-impact-on-young-childrens-school-readiness.pdf (accessed 9 October 2016).

Gergen, K. J. (1997). Social psychology as social construction: The emerging vision. In C. E. McGarty, & S. Haslam (Eds.), *The message of social psychology: Perspectives on mind in society* (pp. 113–128). Oxford: Blackwell Publishing.

Gerhardt, S. (2004). *Why love matters: How affection shapes a baby.* Hove: Brunner-Routledge.

Glock, S. (2016). Does ethnicity matter? The impact of stereotypical expectations on in-service teachers' judgments of students. *Social Psychology of Education, 19*(3), 493–509.

Goldschmied, E., & Jackson, S. (1994). *People under three: Young children in day care.* London: Routledge.

**182** References

González-Moreira, A., Ferreira, C., & Vidal, J. (2021). Comparative analysis of the transition from early childhood education to primary education: Factors affecting continuity between stages. *European Journal of Educational Research, 10*(1), 441–454.

Goodall, J., & Montgomery, C. (2014). Parental involvement to parental engagement: A continuum. *Educational Review, 66*(4), 399–410.

Graham, I. (2012). *What's new?: Supporting children through transitions in their early years*. Dublin: Barnardo's Training and Resource Service.

Gray, J., Geraghty, R., & Ralph, D. (2016). *Family rhythms – The changing textures of family life in Ireland*. Manchester: Manchester University Press.

Greene, S., & Moane, G. (2000). Growing up Irish: Changing children in a changing society. *Irish Journal of Psychology, 21*(3–4), 122–137.

Greene, S., & Nixon, E. (2020). *Children as agents in their worlds: A psychological-relational perspective*. London: Routledge.

Greene, S., Williams, J., Layte, R., Doyle, E., Harris, E., McCrory, C., Murray, A., O'Dowd, T., Quail, A., Swords, L., Thornton, M., & Whelan, C. T. (2010). *Growing up in Ireland: National longitudinal study of children: Background and conceptual framework*. Dublin: Office of the Minister for Children and Youth Affairs.

Greeno, J. (1994). Gibson's affordances. *Psychological Review, 101*(2), 336–442.

Gregory, A., Cornell, D., Fan, X., Sheras, P., Shih, T.-H., & Huang, F. (2010). Authoritative school discipline: High school practices associated with lower bullying and victimization. *Journal of Educational Psychology, 102*(2), 483–496.

Grieshaber, S., & McArdle, F. (2014). Ethical dimensions and perspectives on play. In L. Brooker, M. Blaise, & S. Edwards (Eds.), *The Sage handbook of play and learning in early childhood* (pp. 103–114). London: Sage.

Guay, F., Stupnisky, R. H., Boivin, M., Japel, C., & Dionne, G. (2019). Teachers' relatedness with students as a predictor of students' intrinsic motivation, perceived competence and reading achievement. *Early Childhood Research Quarterly, 48*(3), 215–225.

Guerrettaz, A. M., & Johnston, B. (2013). Materials in the classroom ecology. *The Modern Language Journal, 97*(3), 779–796.

Hachfeld, A., Schroeder, S., Anders, Y., Hahn, A., & Kunter, M. (2012). Multikulturelle U ̈berzeugungen: Herkunft oder U ̈berzeugung? Welche Rollen spielen der Migrationshintergrund und multikulturelle U ̈berzeugungen fu ̈r das Unterrichten von Kindern mit Migrationshintergrund? (Cultural background or cultural beliefs? What role do immigration cackground and multicultural beliefs play for teaching children with immigrant backgrounds?). *Zeitschrift Fu ̈r Pa ̈dagogische Psychologie, 26,* 101–120.

Halpenny, A. M. (2021). *Capturing children's meanings in ECE research and practice: a practical guide*. Abingdon, Oxon: Routledge.

Halpenny, A. M., Greene, S. M., & Hogan, D. M. (2008). Children's perspectives on coping and support following parental separation. *Child Care in Practice, 14*(3), 311–325.

Halpenny, A. M., Nixon, E., & Watson, D. (2010). *Parents' perspectives on parenting styles and disciplining children*. Dublin: Office of the Minister for Children and Youth Affairs.

Halpenny, A. M., & Pettersen, J. (2014). *Introducing Piaget: A guide for practitioners and students in early years education*. Abingdon: Routledge.

Hamer, J., & Loveridge, J. (2020). Exploring notions of community in a privately owned early childhood education and care centre in New Zealand, *Early Years, 40*(2), 254–266.

Harper, N. (2017). Outdoor risky play and healthy child development in the shadow of the "risk society": A forest and nature school perspective. *Child & Youth Services, 38*(4), 318–334.

Hayes, N. (2004). Towards a nurturing pedagogy – Reconceptualising care and education in the early years. In N. Hayes, & M. Kernan (Eds.), Transformations: Theory and practice in early education. *Proceedings of the annual OMEP conference*, (pp. 140–152). OMEP, Ireland: University College Cork, 5 April 2003.

Hayes, N. (2007). *Perspectives on the relationship between education and care in early childhood – A background paper*. Dublin: National Council for Curriculum and Assessment.

Hayes, N. (2008). Teaching matters in early educational practice: The case for a nurturing pedagogy. *Early Education and Development, 19*(3), 430–440.

Hayes, N. (2013). *Early years practice: Getting it right from the start*. Dublin: Gill and Macmillan.

Hayes, N. (2015). Troubling outcomes: A challenge for early childhood education. *An Leanbh Óg. The OMEP Ireland Journal of Early Childhood Studies, 9*, 13–29.

Hayes, N. (2019). Animating Early Childhood Play Within Bronfenbrenner's Bioecological Model. In M. Peters, R. Heraud (Eds.). *Encyclopedia of Educational Innovation*. Springer, Singapore. https://doi.org/10.1007/978-981-13-2262-4_163-1

Hayes, N., & Filipovic, K (2018). Nurturing 'buds' of development: From outcomes to opportunities in early childhood practice. *International Journal of Early Years Education, 26*(3), 220–232.

Hedges, H. (2014). Children's content learning in play provision: Competing tensions and future possibilities. In L. Brooker, M. Blaise, & S. Edwards (Eds.), *The Sage handbook of play and learning in early childhood* (pp. 192–203). London: Sage.

Heft, H. (1988). Affordances of children's environments: A functional approach to environmental description. *Children's Environments Quarterly, 5*(3), 29–37.

Heikka, J., Pitkäniemi, H., Kettukangas, T., & Hyttinen, T. (2021). Distributed pedagogical leadership and teacher leadership in early childhood contexts. *International Journal of Leadership in Education, 24*(3), 333–348.

Holmes, C. L. (2009). An intergenerational program with benefits. *Early Childhood Education Journal, 37*(3), 113–119.

Hornby, G., & Lafaele, R. (2011). Barriers to parental involvement in education: An explanatory model. *Educational Review, 3*(1), 37–52.

Howard, S.J., & Vasseleu, E. (2020). Self-regulation and executive function longitudinally predict advanced learning in preschool. *Frontiers in Psychology*. https://doi.org/10.3389/fpsyg.2020.00049

Huber, B., Highfield, K., & Kaufman, J. (2018). Detailing the digital experience: Parent reports of children's media use in the home. *British Journal of Educational Technology, 49*(5), 821–833.

Huizinga, J. (1950). *Homo Ludens: A study of the play element in culture*. New York: Harper Row.

Irish National Teachers' Organisation (INTO). (2009). *INTO consultative conference on education, 2008: Transitions in the primary school*. Dublin: INTO.

Jackson, J. (2020). The couch. *Early Childhood Ireland Scéalta Blog*, The Couch – Scéalta BlogEarly Childhood Ireland.

Jackson, N., & Barnett, R. (2020). (Eds.). *Ecologies for learning and practice*. London. Routledge.

Jackson, N. J. (Ed.). (2011). *Learning for a complex world: A lifewide concept of learning, education and personal development*. Bloomington, IN: Authorhouse.

Jackson, N. J. (2014). Lifewide learning and education in universities & colleges: Concepts and conceptual aids. In N. Jackson, & J. Willis (Eds.), *Lifewide learning and education in universities and colleges*. Available at: http://www.learninglives.co.uk/e-book.html

James, A., Jenks, C., & Prout, A. (1998). *Theorising childhood*. Cambridge: Polity Press.

Johnson, G. M. (2010). Internet use and child development: The techno-microsystem. *Australian Journal of Educational and Developmental Psychology, 10*, 32–43.

## 184 References

Joseph, S., Murphy, D., & Holford, J. (2020). Positive education: A new look at freedom to learn. *Oxford Review of Education, 46,* 549–562.

Katz, L., & Chard, S. C. (1994). *Engaging children's minds: The project approach* (2nd ed.). Norwood, NJ: Ablex Publishing.

Katz, L. G. (1988). What should young children be doing? *American Educator, 12*(2), 28–33, 44–45.

Katz, L. G. (1993). *Dispositions: Definitions and Implications for Early Childhood Practices.* Perspectives from ERIC/EECE: A Monograph Series, No. 4. Urbana, IL: ERIC Clearinghouse on Elementary and Early Childhood Education.

Kavanagh, L., Weir, S., & Moran, E. (2017). *The evaluation of DEIS: Monitoring achievement and attitudes among urban primary school pupils from 2007 to 2016.* Dublin: ERC.

Kemple, K.M., Oh, J., Kenney, E., & Smith-Bonahue, T. (2016). The power of outdoor play and play in natural environments, *Childhood Education, 92*(6), 446–454. https://doi.org/10.1080/00094056.2016.1251793

Kernan, M. (2007). *Play as a context for learning and development: A research paper.* Dublin: National Council for Curriculum and Assessment.

Kernan, M. (2010). Space and place as a source of belonging and participation in urban environments: Considering the role of early childhood and care settings. *European Early Childhood Education Research Journal, 18*(2), 199–213.

Kernan, M. (2015). Learning environments that work: Softening the boundaries. A paper prepared for the symposium, *Early Educational Alignment: Reflecting on Context, Curriculum and Pedagogy,* Trinity College Dublin, 15 October.

Kernan, M., & Devine, D. (2010). Being confined within? Constructions of the good childhood and outdoor play in early childhood education and care settings in Ireland. *Children and Society, 24*(5), 371–385.

Kernan, M., & Singer, E. (Eds.) (2011). *Peer relationships in early childhood education and care.* Abingdon: Routledge.

Kewalramani, S. Palaiologou, I., Arnott, L., & Dardanou, M. (2020). The integration of the internet of toys in early childhood education: a platform for multi-layered interactions, *European Early Childhood Education Research Journal, 28*(2), 197–213.

Kiely, J., O'Toole, L. Haals-Brosnan, M., O'Brien, E. Z., O'Keeffe, C., & Dunne, C. (2021). *Parental involvement, engagement and partnership in children's education during the primary school years: Final report.* Dublin: Marino Institute of Education.

Kilderry, A. (2015). Intentional pedagogies: Insights from the past. *Australasian Journal of Early Childhood, 40*(3), 20–28.

Kim, Y., Calzada, E. J., Barajas-Gonzalez, R. G., Huang, K. Y., Brotman, L. M., Castro, A., & Pichardo, C. (2018). The role of authoritative and authoritarian parenting in the early academic achievement of Latino students. *Journal of Educational Psychology, 110*(1), 119.

Konstantoni, K. (2012). Children's peer relationships and social identities: Exploring a case of young children's agency and complex interdependencies from the Minority World. *Children's Geographies, 10,* 337–346.

Kraftsoff, S., & Quinn, S. (2009). Exploratory study investigating the opinions of Russian-speaking parents on maintaining their children's use of the Russian language. *Irish Journal of Applied Social Studies, 9*(1), 65–80.

Kuhl, P. K. (2010a). Brain mechanisms in early language acquisition. *Neuron, 67*(5), 713–727.

Kuhl, P. (2010b, October). *Patricia Kuhl: The linguistic genius of babies.* Available at: https://www.ted.com/talks/patricia_kuhl_the_linguistic_genius_of_babies?language=en (accessed 24 October 2016).

Lantolf, J., & Thorne, S. (2006). *Sociocultural theory and the genesis of second language development.* Oxford: Oxford University Press.

## References **185**

Lave, J., & Wenger, E. (1991). *Situated learning: Legitimate peripheral participation.* Cambridge: Cambridge University Press.

Lawrence, V. (2019). Quality interactions and brain development in young children. *Keynote address, keeping your child in mind conference,* Dublin, Ireland, 16 January, 2019.

Lester, S., & Russell, W. (2010). *Children's right to play: An examination of the importance of play in the lives of children worldwide.* Working Paper 57. The Hague: Bernard van Leer Foundation.

Lewis, R., Fleer, M., & Hammer, M. (2019). Intentional teaching: Can early-childhood educators create the conditions for children's conceptual development when following a child-centred programme? *Australasian Journal of Early Childhood, 44*(1), 6–18.

Lin, C., Sabanovic, S., Dombrowski, L,. Miller, A.D., Brady, E., & MacDorman. K.F. (2021). Parental acceptance of children's storytelling robots: A projection of the uncanny valley of AI. *Frontier Robot. AI, 8,* 579993. https://doi.org/10.3389/frobt.2021.579993

Lindsay, C. A., & Hart, C. M. (2017). Exposure to same-race teachers and student disciplinary outcomes for Black students in North Carolina. *Educational Evaluation and Policy Analysis, 39*(3), 485–510.

Lippman, P. C. (2010). *Evidence-based design of elementary and secondary schools: A responsive approach to creating learning environments.* New York: Wiley.

Little, H., & Sweller, N. (2015). Affordances for risk-taking and physical activity in Australian early childhood education settings. *Early Childhood Education Journal, 43*(4), 337–345.

Lockhart, S. (2010). Play: An important tool for cognitive development. *Extensions, 24*(3), 1–8.

Lund, E., & Seekins, T. (2014). Early exposure to people with physical and sensory disabilities and later attitudes toward social interactions and inclusion. *Physical Disabilities: Education and Related Services, 33*(1), 1–16.

Lynch, H., & Hayes, N. (2015). An affordance perspective on infant play in home settings: A "just-right environment". *Childlinks, 2,* 17–22.

Machowska-Kosciak, M. (2013). A language socialization perspective on knowledge and identity construction in Irish post-primary education. In F. Farr, & M. Moriarty (Eds.), *Language Learning, & Teaching: Irish Research Perspectives* (pp. 87–110). Bern: Peter Lang.

Machowska-Kosciak, M. (2019). Language and emotions: a follow-up study of 'moral allegiances'-the case of Wiktoria. *TEANGA, the Journal of the Irish Association for Applied Linguistics, 10,* 172–185.

MacNaughton, G., & Williams, G. (2009). *Techniques for teaching young children: Choices in theory and practice* (3rd ed.). French's Forest, NSW: Longman.

Maconochie, H. (2019). The brain and children's early development. In Fitzgerald, D., & Maconochie, H. (Eds.), *Early childhood studies: A student's guide.* London: Sage.

Malaguzzi, L. (1993). For an education based on relationships. *Young Children, 49*(1), 9–12.

Marbina, L., Church, A., Tayler, C., & Department of Education and Early Childhood Development. (2011). *Victoria early years learning and development framework.* Evidence Paper: Practice Principle 6: Integrated Teaching and Learning Approaches. Melbourne: University of Melbourne.

Margetts, K., & Kienig, A. (Eds.). (2013). *International perspectives on transition to school.* Abingdon: Routledge.

Markstrom, A. M., & Hallden, G. (2009). Children's strategies for agency in preschool. *Children and Society, 23*(2), 112–122.

Marsh, J., Lahmar, J., Plowman, L., Yamada-Rice, D., Bishop, J., & Scott, F. (2021) Under threes' play with tablets. *Journal of Early Childhood Research, 19*(3), 283–297.

Mashford-Scott, A., & Church, A. (2011). Promoting agency in early childhood education. *Novitas-Royal (Research on Youth and Language), 5*(1), 15–38.

**186** References

McClintic, S., & Petty, C. (2015). Exploring early childhood teachers' beliefs and practices about preschool outdoor play: A qualitative study. *Journal of Early Childhood Teacher Education*, *36*(1), 24–43. https://doi.org/10.1080/10901027.2014.997844

McDermott, M. (2016). *The key-person approach: Positive relationships with children in the early years*. Dublin: Barnardos.

McLachlan, C., Fleer, M., & Edwards, S. (2013). *Early childhood curriculum: Planning, assessment and implementation*. New York: Cambridge University Press.

McLowry, S., & Collins, A. (2012). Temperament-based intervention: Reconceptualized from a response to intervention framework. In R. Shiner, & M. Zentner (Eds.), *Handbook of childhood temperament* (pp. 607–627). New York: Guilford Press.

McMurray, A., & Clendon, J. (2011). *Community health and wellness: Primary health care in practice* (4th ed.). Sydney, Australia: Elsevier.

Melhuish, E. (2014). The impact of early childhood education on improved wellbeing. In British Academy (Ed.), *"If you could do one thing…": Nine local actions to reduce health inequalities* (pp. 32–43). London: British Academy.

Melhuish, E., Phan, M., Sylva, K., Sammons, P., & Siraj-Blatchford, I. (2008). Effects of the home learning environment and preschool center experience upon literacy and numeracy development in early primary school. *Journal of Social Issues*, *64*(1), 95–114.

Mentha, S., Church, A., & Page, J. (2015). Teachers as broker: Perceptions of "participation" and agency in early childhood education and care. *International Journal of Children's Rights*, *23*(3), 622–637.

Merçon-Vargas, E. A., Lima R., Rosa, E., & Tudge, J. R. H. (2020). Processing proximal processes: What Bronfenbrenner meant, what he didn't mean, and what he should have meant. *Journal of Family Theory and Review*, *12*(3), 321–334. https://doi.org/10.1111/jftr.12373

Mhic Mhathúna, M. (2011). *An Traein: Ag Aistriú ón Naíonra go dtí an Bhunscoil: Eolas agus Moltaí do Stiúrthóirí Naíonraí agus do Mhúinteoirí Gaeilscoileanna*. Baile Átha Cliath: Forbairt Naíonraí Teo.

Ministry of Education, New Zealand. (1996). *Te Whāriki: Early childhood curriculum*. Wellington, New Zealand: Learning Media Limited.

Mitchell, L. (2011). Enquiring teachers and democratic politics: Transformations in New Zealand's early childhood education landscape. *Early Years*, iFirst, 1–12. https://doi.org/10.1080/09575146.2011.588787

Mitchell, L., Wylie, C., & Carr, M. (2008). *Outcomes of early childhood education: Literature review*. Wellington, New Zealand: Ministry of Education.

Molapour, T., Hagan, C. C., Silston, B., Wu, H., Ramstead, M., Friston, K., & Mobbs, D. (2021). Seven computations of the social brain. *Special Issue: Computational Methods in Social Neuroscience*, *16*, 745–760.

Morss, J. R. (2013). *Growing critical: Alternatives to developmental psychology* (3rd ed.). London: Routledge.

Mosier, C. E., & Rogoff, B. (2003). Privileged treatment of toddlers: Cultural aspects of individual choice and responsibility. *Developmental Psychology*, *39*(6), 1047–1060.

Mullin, A. (2007). Children, autonomy, and care. *Journal of Social Philosophy*, *38*(4), 536–553.

Murphy, D., & Joseph, S. (2018). Contributions from the person-centred experiential approach to the field of social pedagogy. *Cambridge Journal of Education*, *49*(2), 181–196.

National Association for the Education of Young Children/ Fred Rogers Center. (2012). *Technology and interactive media as tools in early childhood programs serving children from birth through age 8. Position statement*. Washington, DC: NAEYC/Fred Rogers Center.

National Council for Curriculum Assessment (NCCA). (2009). *Aistear: The early childhood curriculum framework*. Dublin: National Council for Curriculum Assessment.

References **187**

National Scientific Council on the Developing Child. (2007). *The science of early childhood development: Closing the gap between what we know and what we do.* Cambridge, MA: Center on the Developing Child, Harvard University. Available at: https://developingchild.harvard. edu/resources/the-science-of-early-childhood-development-closing-the-gap-between-what-we-know-and-what-we-do/ (accessed 10 October, 2016)

National Scientific Council on the Developing Child. (2020). *Connecting the brain to the rest of the body: Early child- hood development and lifelong health are deeply intertwined*: Working Paper No. 15. Available at: www.developingchild.harvard.edu.

National Scientific Council on the Developing Child. (n.d.). *In Brief: The Science of Early Childhood Development.* Available at: https://46y5eh11fhgw3ve3ytpwxt9r-wpengine. netdna-ssl.com/wp-content/uploads/2007/03/InBrief-The-Science-of-Early-Childhood-Development2.pdf

Navarro, J., Doucet, F., & Tudge, J. (2020). Bioecological systems' influences on early childhood education. In D. F. Gullo, & M. E. Graue (Eds.), *Scientific influences on early childhood education* (pp.55–58). London: Routledge.

Neal, J. W., & Neal, Z. P. (2013). Nested or networked? Future directions for ecological systems theory. *Social Development, 22*(4), 722–737.

Neaum, S. (2020). Engaging with literacy provision in the early years: Language use and emergent literacy in child-initiated play. *Journal of Early Childhood Literacy, 20*(4), 680–705.

Neugebauer, R. (2010). The start of Head Start. *Exchange*, May/June, 20–21.

Newcombe, N. S., Uttal, D. H., & Sauter, M. (2013). Spatial development. In P. D. Zelazo (Ed.), *Oxford handbook of developmental psychology. Volume 1: Body and Mind* (pp. 564–590). Oxford: Oxford University Press.

Noser, A. E., Majidi, S., Finch, J., Clements, M. A., Youngkin, E. M., & Patton, S.R. (2018). Authoritarian parenting style predicts poorer glycemic control in children with new-onset type 1 diabetes. *Pediatric Diabetes, 19*, 1315–1321.

Nowak-Łojewska, A., O'Toole, L., Regan, C., & Ferreira, M. (2019). 'To learn with' in the view of the holistic, relational and inclusive education. *Kwatalnik Pedagogiczny/Issues in Early Education, 251*(1), 151–162.

Nutbrown, C., & Clough, P. (2009). Citizenship and inclusion in the early years: Understanding and responding to children's perspectives on "Belonging". *International Journal of Early Years Education, 17*(3), 191–205.

O'Connor, A. (2013). *Understanding transitions in the early years: Supporting change through attachment and resilience.* Abingdon: Routledge.

O'Donoghue Hynes, B., & Hayes, N. (2011). Who benefits from early childhood education and care policy tool design in Ireland? *Journal of Poverty and Social Justice, 19*(3), 277–288.

O'Kane, M. (2015). Multiple transitions. A Paper prepared for the symposium *Early Educational Alignment: Reflecting on Context, Curriculum and Pedagogy*, Trinity College Dublin, 15 October 2015.

O'Kane, M., & Hayes, N. (2006). The transition to school in Ireland: Views of pre-school and primary school teachers. *International Journal of Transitions in Childhood, 2*, 4–16.

O'Kane, M., & Hayes, N. (2013) "The child snapshot": A tool for the transfer of information from preschool to primary school. *International Journal of Transitions in Childhood, 6*, 28–36.

O'Malley, F. (2020). Promoting inclusion in early years care and education. *An Leanbh Óg/ Journal of Early Childhood Studies OMEP Ireland, 13*(1), 215–225.

O'Neill, B. (2015). Ecological perspectives and children's use of the Internet: Exploring micro to macro level analysis. *Eesti Haridusteaduste Ajakiri/Estonian Journal of Education, 3*(2), 32–53. https://doi.org/10.12697/eha.2015.3.2.02b

## 188 References

O'Toole, L. (2014). Cooperative learning in initial teacher education: Student experiences. *Problemy Wczesnej Edukacji/Issues in Early Education, 10*(2), 7–20.

O'Toole, L. (2015). Student-centred teaching in initial teacher education. *International Journal for Cross-Disciplinary Subjects in Education, 6*(1), 2111–2119.

O'Toole, L. (2016). *A bio-ecological perspective on educational transition: Experiences of children, parents and teachers* [Unpublished Doctoral Dissertation]. Dublin Institute of Technology, Dublin, Ireland.

O'Toole, L., & Hayes, N. (2020). *Supporting positive behaviour in early years settings and primary schools: Relationships, reciprocity and reflection.* London: Routledge.

O'Toole, L., Hayes, N., & Halpenny, A. (2020). Animating systems: The ecological value of considering Bronfenbrenner's bioecological model of development. In R. Barnett, & N. Jackson (Eds.), *Ecologies for learning and practice: Emerging ideas, sightings and possibilities* (pp. 19–31). London: Routledge.

O'Toole, L., Hayes, N., & Mhic Mhathúna, M. (2014). A bioecological perspective on educational transition. *Procedia – Social and Behavioural Sciences, 140,* 121–127.

O'Toole, L., Kiely, J., McGillicuddy, D., O'Brien, E., & O'Keeffe, C. (2019). *Parental involvement, engagement and partnership in their children's education during the primary school years.* Dublin: NCCA/NPC.

O'Toole, L., McClelland, D., Forde, D., O'Keeffe, S., Purdy, N., Säfström, C. A., & Walsh, T. (2021). Contested childhoods across borders and boundaries: Insights from curriculum provisions in Northern Ireland and the Irish Free State in the 1920s. *British Educational Research Journal, 47*(4), 1021–1038.

OECD (2006). *Starting strong II: Early childhood education and care.* Paris: Organisation for Economic Co-operation and Development.

Ofsted. (2014). *Research and analysis: Ensuring a smooth transition from nursery to school* [online]. GOV.UK. Available at: https://www.gov.uk/government/publications/ensuring-a-smooth-transition-from-nursery-to-school (accessed 10 October 2016).

Oliver, M. (1983). *Social work with disabled people.* Basingstoke: Macmillan.

O'Toole, L., Regan, C., & Nowak-Lojewska, A. (2019). 'To learn with' as an alternative voice for children's education. Introduction to a European project: Teaching for Holistic, Relational and Inclusive Early Childhood Education (THRIECE). *Problemy Wczesnej Edukacji/Issues in Early Education, 251*(1), 175–182.

Page, J. (2018). Characterising the principles of Professional Love in early childhood care and education. *International Journal of Early Years Education, 26*(2), 125–141. https://doi.org/10.1080/09669760.2018.1459508

Palaiologou, I. (2016). Children under five and digital technologies: Implications for early years pedagogy. *European Early Childhood Education Research Journal, 24*(1), 5–24. https://doi.org/10.1080/1350293X.2014.929876

Palaiologou, I. (2019). *Child observation: A guide for students of early childhood.* London: Sage.

Palaiologou I., & Male, T. (2019) Leadership in early childhood education: The case for pedagogical praxis. *Contemporary Issues in Early Childhood, 20*(1), 23–34.

Panken, J. (2005). *Behind the mirror image: Urie Bronfenbrenner in the Soviet Union* [Unpublished Doctoral Dissertation]. Cornell University, Ithaca, New York.

Parker-Rees, R. (2014). Playfulness and the co-construction of identity in the first years. In L. Brooker, M. Blaise, & S. Edwards (Eds.), *The Sage handbook of play and learning in early childhood* (pp. 366–377). London: Sage.

Parrish, M. (2014). *Social work perspective on human behaviour.* London: McGraw-Hill Education.

Pattnaik, J., & Jalongo, M. R. (2021). Early childhood education and care in the time of COVID-19: Introduction to a special issue of early childhood education journal. *Early Childhood Education, 49,* 757–762. https://doi-org.tudublin.idm.oclc.org/10.1007/s10643-021-01220-2

Pellegrini, A. D., & Bjorklund, D. F. (1998). *Applied child study: A developmental approach* (2nd ed.). Hillsdale, NJ: Lawrence Erlbaum Associates.

Penn, H. (1997). *Comparing nurseries*. London: Paul Chapman Publishing.

Perkins, D. (1995). *Smart schools: Better thinking and learning for every child.* New York: The Free Press.

Piaget, J. (1951). *The child's conception of the world.* Lanham, MD: Littlefield Adams Quality Paperbacks.

Piaget, J. (2001). *The psychology of intelligence.* Abingdon: Routledge.

Pinker, S. (1994). *The language instinct: The new science of language and mind.* London: Penguin UK.

Plowman, L. (2016). Rethinking context: Digital technologies and children's everyday lives. *Children's Geographies, 14*(2), 190–202. https://doi.org/10.1080/14733285.2015.1127326

Pramling-Samuelsson, I., & Asblond-Carlsson, M. (2008). The playing learning child: Towards a pedagogy of early childhood. *Scandinavian Journal of Educational Research, 52*(6), 623–641.

Punch, S. (2016). Exploring children's agency across majority and minority world contexts. In F. Esser, M. S. Baader, T. Betz, & B. Hungerland (Eds.), *Reconceptualising agency and childhood: New perspectives in childhood studies* (pp. 183–196). London: Routledge.

Regan, C. (2019). Relational approaches to early childhood education: CAT mapping and reflective practice. *Paper presented at the 8th International CAT Conference*, Ferrara, Italy, 27–29 June 2019.

Rice, M. F., & Cun, A. (2021) Personalising digital learning for young children: Leveraging psychosocial identities and *Techne* for literacy development. *British Journal of Educational Technology, 52*,1823–1838.

Rich, A. (1986). *Blood, bread, and poetry: Selected prose, 1979–1985.* New York: W. W. Norton.

Riley, P. (2011). *Attachment theory and the teacher–student relationship.* Abingdon: Routledge.

Ring, E., Mhic Mhathúna, M., Moloney, M., Hayes, N., Breatnach, D., Stafford, P., Carswell, D., Keegan, S., Kelleher, C., McCafferty, D., O'Keefe, A., Leavy, A., Madden, R., & Ozonyia, M. (2015). *An examination of concepts of school readiness among parents and educators in Ireland.* Dublin: Department of Children and Youth Affairs [DCYA]

Robinson, K., & Jones-Diaz, C. (2006). Diversity and difference in early childhood education: Issues for theory and practice. *British Journal of Educational Studies, 54*(4), 496–498.

Rogers, C. R. (1974). Questions I would ask myself if I were a teacher. *Education, 95*(2), 134–139.

Rogers, C. R. (1983). *Freedom to learn for the 80's* (No. 371.39 R724f). Ohio, US: Merrill Publishing.

Rogers, C. R. (1995). *Client-centered therapy: Its current practice, implications and theory.* London: Constable.

Rogers, C. R., & Freiberg, H. J. (1970). *Freedom to learn.* Columbus, OH: Charles Merrill.

Rogoff, B. (1998). Cognition as a collaborative process. In W. Damon, D. Kuhn, & R. S. Siegler (Eds.), *Handbook of child psychology, Vol. 2: Cognition, language and perceptual development* (pp. 679–744). New York: Wiley.

Rogoff, B. (2003). *The cultural nature of human development.* New York: Oxford University Press.

Rosa, E. M., & Tudge, J. R. H. (2013). Urie Bronfenbrenner' theory of human development: Its evolution from ecology to bioecology. *Journal of Family Theory and Review, 5*(6), 243–258.

Runions, K. C. (2014). Does gender moderate the association between children's behaviour and teacher-child relationship in the early years? *Australian Journal of Guidance and Counselling, 24*(2), 197–214.

**190** References

Rutter, M. (1985). Resilience in the face of adversity. *British Journal of Psychiatry, 147*(1), 598–611.

Rutter, M., & The English and Romanian Adoptees (ERA) Study Team. (1998). Developmental catch-up, and deficit, following adoption after severe global early privation. *Journal of Child Psychology and Psychiatry, 39*(4), 465–476.

Ryle, A. (1998). Transferences and countertransferences: The cognitive analytic therapy perspective. *British Journal of Psychotherapy, 14*(3), 303–309.

Ryle, A., & Kerr, I. B. (2002). *Introducing cognitive analytic therapy: Principles and practice,* Chichester: John Wiley & Sons.

Saffigna, M., Church, A., Tayler, C., & Department of Education and Early Childhood Development. (2011). *Victoria early years learning and development framework. Evidence paper: Practice principle 3: High expectations for every child.* Melbourne: University of Melbourne.

Sandseter, E. B. H. (2007). Categorizing risky play – How can we identify risk-taking in children's play? *European Early Child Education Research Journal, 15*(2), 237–252.

Santer, J., & Griffiths, C. with Goodall, D. (2007). *Free play in early childhood: A literature review.* London: Play England and the National Children's Bureau.

Santrock, J. W. (2007). *Child development* (11th ed.). New York: McGraw-Hill Companies, Inc.

Sayeed, Z., & Guerin, E. (2000). *Early years play: A happy medium for assessment and intervention.* London: David Fulton Publishers.

Singer, E. (2013). Play and playfulness, basic features of early childhood education. *European Early Childhood Education Research Journal, 21*(2), 172–184.

Singer, E. (2015). Play and playfulness in early childhood education. *Psychology in Russia: State of the Art, 8*(2), 27–35.

Siraj, I., & Mayo, A. (2014). *Social class and educational inequality: The impact of parents and school.* Cambridge: Cambridge University Press.

Siraj-Blatchford, I. (2009). Conceptualising progression in the pedagogy of play and sustained shared thinking in early childhood education: A Vygotskian perspective. *Educational and Child Psychology, 26*(2), 77–89.

Siraj-Blatchford, I., & Clarke, P. (2000). *Supporting identity, diversity and language in the early years.* Buckingham: Open University Press.

Siraj-Blatchford, I., & Mani, L. (2007) *Effective leadership in the early years sector: The ELEYS study.* London: Institute of Education.

Siraj-Blatchford, I., Sylva, K., Muttock. S., Gilden, R., & Bell, D. (2002). *Researching effective pedagogy in the early years.* Research Report RR365. London: Department for Education and Skills.

Siraj-Blatchford, I., Taggart, B., Sylva, K., Sammons, P., & Melhuish, E. (2008). Towards the transformation of practice in early childhood education: The effective provision of pre-school education (EPPE) project. *Cambridge Journal of Education, 38*(1), 23–36.

Skinner, R., & O'Toole, B. (Eds.) (2018). *Minority language pupils and the curriculum: Closing the achievement gap.* Dublin: Marino Institute of Education and University of Ulster. Ebook.

Slesnick, N., Prestopnik, J. L., Meyers, R. J., & Glassman, M. (2007). Treatment outcome for street-living, homeless youth. *Addictive Behaviors, 32*(6), 1237–1251.

Smidt, S. (2013). *Introducing Vygotsky: A guide for practitioners and students in early years education.* Abingdon: Routledge.

Smith, A. B. (2013). *Understanding children and childhood.* Wellington, New Zealand: Bridget Williams Books.

Sommer, D., Pramling-Samuelsson, I. P., & Hundeide, K. (2013). Early childhood education and care: A child-perspective paradigm. *European Early Childhood Education Research Journal, 21*(4), 459–475.

## References   191

Soule, N. (2020). Transitional high school parent-teacher home visits: Effects on parent engagement and student outcomes (Order No. 27993421). *Available from ProQuest Dissertations & Theses Global.* (2407343881). http://ezproxy.liberty.edu/login?qurl=https%3A%2F%2Fwww.proquest.com%2Fdissertations-theses%2Ftransitional-high-school-parent-teacher-home%2Fdocview%2F2407343881%2Fse-2.

Soule, N. E., & Curtis, H. L. (2021). High school home visits: Parent–Teacher relationships and student success. *School Community Journal, 31*(2), 131–153.

Strong-Wilson, T., & Ellis, J. (2007). Children and place: Reggio Emilia's environment as third teacher. *Theory into Practice, 46*(1), 40–47.

Sullivan, A., & Bers, M. U. (2018). Dancing robots: Integrating art, music, and robotics in Singapore's early childhood centres. *International Journal of Technology and Design Education,* 28, 325–346.

Swan, K., Chen, C. C., & Bockmier-Sommers, D. K. (2020). Relationships between Carl Rogers' Person-Centered education and the community of inquiry framework: A preliminary exploration. *Online Learning, 24*(3), 4–18.

Sylva, K., Melhuish, E., Sammon, P., Siraj-Blatchford, I., & Taggart, B. (2004). *The Effective Provision of Pre-School Education (EPPE) Project: Final report.* London: Institute of Education/SureStart.

Taft, J. (2015). Adults talk too much: Intergenerational dialogue and power in the Peruvian movement of working children. *Childhood, 22*(4), 460–473.

Tajik, M., & Singer, E. (2021). Collaborative research between academics and practitioners to enhance play engagement in the free play of two- and three-year olds. *Early Years, 41*(1), 64–78. https://doi.org/10.1080/09575146.2018.1478391

Tatalović Vorkapić, S., & LoCasale-Crouch, J. (Eds.) (2021). *Supporting children's well-being during early childhood transition to school.* Hershey, PA: IGI Global.

The TOY Project Consortium. (2013). *Reweaving the tapestry of the generations: A guide to community-based intergenerational initiatives in Europe.* Leiden: The TOY Project.

Thomas, A., & Chess, S. (1956). An approach to the study of sources of individual differences in child behavior. *Journal of Clinical and Experimental Psychopathology, 18*(4), 347–357.

Thomas, A., & Chess, S. (1977). *Temperament and development.* Oxford: Brunner/Mazel.

Thomas, F., & Harding, S. (2011). The role of play: Play outdoors as the medium and mechanism for wellbeing, learning and development. In J. White (Ed.), *Outdoor provision in the early years* (pp. 12–22). London: Sage.

Tovey, H. (2010). Playing on the edge: Perceptions of risk and danger in outdoor play. In P. Broadhead, J. Howard, & E. Wood (Eds.), *Play and learning in the early years* (pp. 79–94). London: Sage.

Townsend-Cross, M. (2004). Indigenous Australian perspectives in early childhood education. *International Journal of Equity and Innovation in Early Childhood, 2*(2), 2–11.

Trevarthen, C. (2011). What young children give to their learning: Making education work to sustain a community and its culture. *European Early Childhood Education Research Journal, 19*(2), 173–194.

Tudge, J. R., Navarro, J., Merçon-Vargas, E., & Payir, A. (2021). The promise and the practice of early childhood educare in the writings of Urie Bronfenbrenner. *Early Child Development and Care, 191*, 7–8, 1079–1088.

Tudge, J. R. H. (2008). *The everyday lives of young children: Culture, class, and child rearing in diverse societies.* New York: Cambridge University Press.

Tudge, J. R. H., Mokrova, I. L., Hatfield, B. E., & Karnik, R. B. (2009). Uses and misuses of Bronfenbrenner's bioecological theory of human development. *Journal of Family Theory and Review, 1*(4), 198–210.

Tzuo, P. W., Yang, C. H., & Wright, S. K. (2011). Child-centered education: Incorporating reconceptualism and poststructuralism. *Educational Research and Reviews, 6*(8), 554–559.

United Nations. (1989). *Convention on the Rights of the Child.* Geneva: United Nations. Available at: www.unhcr.org/uk/4aa76b319.pdf (accessed 10 October 2016).

Valentine, K. (2009). Accounting for agency. *Children and Society, 25*(5), 347–358.

Vygotsky, L. S. (1978). *Mind and society: The development of higher psychological processes.* Cambridge, MA: Harvard University Press.

Warger, T. and Dobbin, G. (2009) *Learning environments: where space, technology, and culture converge.* Boulder, CO: Educause Learning Initiative, available at: https://library.educause.edu/-/media/files/library/2009/10/eli3021-pdf.pdf

White, E. J., Rooney, T., Gunn, A. C., & Nuttall, J. (2021a). Understanding how early childhood educators 'see' learning through digitally cast eyes: Some preliminary concepts concerning the use of digital documentation platforms. *Australasian Journal of Early Childhood, 46*(1), 6–18.

White, R., Thibodeau-Nielsen, R., Palermo, F., & Mikulski, A. (2021b). Engagement in social pretend play predicts preschoolers' executive function gains across the school year, *Early Childhood Research Quarterly, 56,* 103–113.

Whitebread, D., Basilio, M., Kuvalja, M., & Verma, M. (2012). *The importance of play: A report on the value of play with a series of policy recommendations.* Brussels, Belgium: Toy Industries of Europe.

Wolf, S. (2020). "Me I don't really discuss anything with them": Parent and teacher perceptions of early childhood education and parent-teacher relationships in Ghana. *International Journal of Educational Research, 99,* 1–13.

Wood, D., Bruner, J. S., & Ross, G. (1976). The role of tutoring in problem solving. *Journal of Child Psychology and Psychiatry, 17*(2), 89–100.

Wood, E. (2013). *Play, learning and the early childhood curriculum.* London: Sage.

Wood, E. (2014). Free choice and free play in early childhood education: Troubling the discourse. *International Journal of Early Years Education, 22*(1), 4–18.

Woodhead, M. (1999). Reconstructing developmental psychology: Some first steps. *Children and Society, 13*(1), 3–19.

Woodhead, M. (2000). Towards a global paradigm for research into early childhood. In H. Penn (Ed.), *Early childhood services: Theory, policy and practice* (pp. 15–33). Buckingham: Open University Press.

Woodhead, M. (2006). Changing perspectives on early childhood: Theory, research and policy. *International Journal of Equity and Innovation in Early Childhood, 4*(2), 1–43.

Wyness, M. G. (2012). *Childhood and society: An introduction to the sociology of childhood.* Basingstoke: Palgrave Macmillan.

Xia, M., Li, X, & Tudge, J. R. H. (2020). Operationalizing Urie Bronfenbrenner's process-person-context-time model. *Human Development, 64*(1), 10–20.

Yamauchi, L. A., & Sousa, E. B. C. (2020). Early childhood educators' perspectives on early childhood settings and collaborations to promote kindergarten transition. *The Professional Educator, 43*(1), 100–113.

Zhao, H., Zhang, N., & Guo, K. (2020). A Chinese lens on children's learning dispositions. *Educational Studies, 48*(2), 233–252

Zigler, E., & Muenchow, S. (1992). *Head start: the inside story of America's most successful educational experiment.* New York: Basic Books.

Kuhl, P. (2010b, October). *Patricia Kuhl: The linguistic genius of babies.* Available at: https://www.ted.com/talks/patricia_kuhl_the_linguistic_genius_of_babies?language=en (accessed 24 October 2016).

# INDEX

Pages in *italics* refer figures.

Access and Inclusion Model (AIM) 149
active behavioural dispositions 18–19, 21
active role of child: active behavioural
  dispositions 18–19; biological influences
  16; demand characteristics 20–21; notion
  of agency 17; resource characteristics
  19–20; rich child 17
adulthood 36, 113, 119, 124
adults 112, 116, 119–120, 125,
  131–133, 138, 142
agency 77; children's 79, 81–83, 90;
  concept of 79; and proximal processes in
  early childhood 86–88
agentic child 85–86; in early years 79–81
Ahnert, L. 32
Ainsworth, M. D. S. 31–32
Anastasi, A. 8–9
anxiety 31, 33, 36, 61–63
Armitage, M. 96
Arnott, L. 155–156
Association of Cognitive Analytic Therapy
  (ACAT) 35
attachment theory 31; aspects of 32;
  CAT 35; Children 33; ideas of
  mother–infant attachment 32; internal
  working model 32; parent–child
  relationship 34; reciprocal roles 35–36;
  vignettes 34
The Australian Early Years Learning
  Framework 133
authoritative style 37–38, 64

Bae, B. 83
Barnett, R. 144
Baumrind, D. 29, 36–37
beliefs and practices 52
Bell, D. 26
Belsky, J. 37–38
Berk, L. E. 55
the bioecological model 46–47, 49, 55, 59,
  72, 95, 127, 144, 162, 169; and early
  education 9–11; of human development
  8–9; places the child at the centre 77,
  89–90
bioecological model of development
  8–9, *13*; active role of developing
  child, *see* active role of child; ecology
  between organism and environment
  12–13; guiding practice bioecologically
  166–177; systems of influence,
  development in context 14–16
bioecological theory 8, 17, 34, 41, 47–49,
  57, 60, 80–81, 86, 90–91, 96, 99, 101,
  103, 105, 107, 148–149
Bishop, J. 156
Black Vernacular English 51
Blehar, M. 31–32
Bourdieu, P. 50–51
Bowlby, J. 31–32, 63
brains 120–122
Bronfenbrenner, U. 49, 51–54, 57;
  ambition 2; bioecological theory 1, 8,
  17, 34, 41, 47–49, 57, 60, 80–81, 86,

**194** Index

90–91, 96, 99, 101, 103, 105; *see also* bioecological model of development; concept of process, *see* proximal processes; developmental psychology 1, 5; ecological model of human development 5–8; EPPE project 3; fluency in Russian language 3; ideas 44; importance of early childhood education 2; interested in Soviet Union 3; schooling 1; sociocultural ideas, *see* sociocultural theory and bioecological model; systems of contextual influences 12; theory 28, 46, 77, 87; work in the USSR 4; during World War II 2–3
Brooker, L. 50–51, 69, 165
Bruner, J. 115
Buckingham, D. 108

Cárcamo, R. A. 33
Carr, M. 50, 53–54, 100–103
Ceci, S. J. 8–9
The Center on the Developing Child 33
Chard, S. C. 113
Chess, S. 53
child development 41, 58; active role, *see* active role of child; characteristics of 17; chronosystem 7, 16, 25; context and family 55–57; across cultures 52; exosystem 14–15, 25; and learning 46; and learning by changing contexts 26; macrosystem 14–15, 25; mesosystem 14, 25; microsystem 14, 25; proximal processes 122; within series of systems 6
child-oriented paradigm 83–84
children(s): agency in early years 79, 81–83, 90; be active participants in learning, supporting to 83; behaviour of 114–115; biological maturity of 123; as a biological reality 112; capacity 116, 125; characteristics 48–49; concept of 77; dispositions influence 50–51, 58; in early years assessment, locating the 88–90; in early years practice, listening to 83–85; with good executive function 126; high expectations 131; immediate environment 46; in isolation 5; mindsets 131–132; parental involvement in education 146–148; personal characteristics 26–27; perspective approach in practice 84–85; play 139–140, 143; respecting 130–131; tendency 53
chronosystem 7, 16, 25, 112
Clark, A. 89

Claxton, G. 50, 53–54
Cognitive Analytic Therapy (CAT) 35
cognitive development 113, 118, 121, 141
Collins, A. 53
contextual knowledge 67, 75, 79, 163
conversational opportunities 135
Cornell University 1–2
Corsaro, W. A. 87–88
COVID-19 pandemic 95, 108, 146, 154, 156–157
Cowan, K. 156
cultural arbitrary 51
Cun, A. 156
curriculum frameworks 141
Curtis, D. 92

Dardanou, M. 155–156
Delivering Equality of Opportunity in Schools (DEIS) scheme 73
demand characteristics 20–21, 51–52
Developmentally Appropriate Practice (DAP) approach 113
developmental psychology 1, 5
development as dynamic process: brain development 120–122, 125; development and learning 113–115; and discontinuous process 124; executive functions 122–124, 126; interactions in development 115–122; knowledge and skills 125
Devine, D. 94
Devlieghere, J. 146
directive belief systems 10
dispositions 49–51; definition of 54; disruptive 50, 54; generative 10, 50; learning 53–54
disruptive/negative dispositions 19, 50, 54
The Diversity, Equality and Inclusion Charter and Guidelines for Early Childhood Care and Education (DCYA) 57
Dockett, S. 70
Downes, P. 21
Duncan, J. 101–103, 152
Dunne, C. 147
Dunphy, E. 99
Duschinsky, R. 32

Early Childhood Education and Care (ECEC) 35, 59, 61–62; centres 151–152, 157; programmes 88; setting *see* ECEC setting
early childhood educators 23, 39–40, 74, 132–133, 137–138, 158
Early-O'Brien, S. 62

ECEC setting 157–158; in the exosystem 148–150; as a key, linking meso-system 145–148; learning ecologies 150–152
ecological systems 159–160
Ecological systems theory 8
ecology of human development 5–8, 12–13
*The Ecology of Human Development: Experiments by Nature and Design* 6
ecology of learning 145, 152
educators acknowledge 67, 75
Edwards, S. 155
Effective Provision of Pre-school and Primary Education (EPPE) 3, 105
Ellis, R. J. 43
English 1, 50–51, 66, 78
Erikson 41
European Together Old and Young project 132
exosystem 6–7, 14–15, 25; 148–149; process in 166

failure of success 7
family context 55–57
Ferreira, C. 63
Fitzpatrick, A. 83, 150–152
Fjortoft, I. 106
Fleer, M. 134–135, 167
Flewitt, R. 156
Fonsén, E. 136
Foster, S. 32
freedom and determinism 55
Freire, Paulo 161
Freud 28
Frones, I. 47

Gallagher, C. 151
gender and sex identity 24
generative/positive disposition 10, 18, 50, 54
genetic inheritances 20
Gergen, K. J. 28
Gilden, R. 26
Goldschmied, E. 61
González-Moreira, A. 63
goodness of fit 53–54
good-quality practice 118, 122; democratic practice 142; sustaining learning environments 132–137
Graham, I. 59
Greene, S. 79
Guerrettaz, A. M. 93

Haals-Brosnan, M. 147
Hallden, G. 80–81
Halpenny, A. 73, 79

Hatfield, B. E. 51–52
Hayes, N. 36, 44, 63, 68, 73, 79, 93, 128
Head Start 4–5, 146, 159
Home–School–Community–Liaison system 73
Hundeide, K. 83, 85
hypervigilance 33

independence and interdependence 86
intergenerational learning and practice (IGL) 98, 151–152, 158
internalisation 48–49
internal working model (IWM) 31
intersubjectivity 43, 86, 116
Irish National Teachers Organisation (INTO) 64

Jackson, J. 148
Jackson, N. 144
Jackson, N. J. 70
Jackson, S. 61
Johnson, Lyndon B. 4
Johnston, B. 93
Jones, C. 101–103

Karnik, R. B. 51–52
Katz, L. 113
Katz, L. G. 50
Kearney, E. 70
Kennedy, J. F. 4
Kernan, M. 94
Kerr, I. B. 35
Kewalramani, S. 155–156
Kiely, J. 147
Kohlberg 28, 41
Kuhl, P. K. 120

Lahmar, J. 156
Lamb, M. E. 32
Lave, J. 50
Lawrence, V. 62, 64
learning and development 133; importance of play 137–142; sustain good-quality pedagogy 132–137
learning dispositions 53–54
learning ecology 144, 150–152
Lester, S. 139
Lima R. 22
*The Linguistic Genius of Babies* 120
Lionetti, F. 32
Li, Y. 146
Lynch, H. 93

macrosystem 6–7, 14–15, 25; process in 166
macrotime 107

Malaguzzi, L. 17
Markstrom, A. M. 80–81
Marsh, J. 156
Mayo, A. 6
McDermott, M. 33
McLowry, S. 53
mediated learning 47–48
mental flexibility 124
Merçon-Vargas, E. 26, 98, 151
Merçon-Vargas, E. A. 22
mesosystem 6–7, 14, 25, 57, 150; process in 165–166
mesotime 107
microsystem 6–7, 14, 25; early learning 132; process in 165
microtime 107
middle-class children 3
Mikulski, A. 156
minority cultures 52
Moane, G. 79
Mokrova, I. L. 51–52
Morris, P. 9–10, 19
Morris, P. A. 44, 49, 52, 57, 62, 128, 164
Moss, P. 89
motivation 78
Muttock. S. 26

National Association for the Education of Young Children (NAEYC) 155
National Scientific Council on the Developing Child (NSCDC) 118–119
nature and nurture 47
Navarro, J. 26, 98, 151
Neal, J. W. 160
Neal, Z. P. 160
network 73, 77, 149, 160
networked 21, 160
new technologies 154; early childhood settings 153, 155–157
New Zealand Ministry of Education 7
nurturing pedagogy 116–117, 128–129, 142

O'Brien, E. Z. 147
Office of Economic Opportunity 4
O'Keeffe, C. 147
O'Neill, B. 154
O'Toole, L. 63, 73, 79, 147

Palaiologou, I. 108, 155–156
Palermo, F. 156
Panken, J. 4
parental involvement 146–148

parenting styles: authoritarian parents 36; authoritative style 37–38; idea of styles 37; model of parenting 38; permissive parents 36–37
parents and children 56–57
Passeron, J. C. 50
Payir, A. 26, 98, 151
pedagogical leadership 127, 136, 143, 169
pedagogical process 92, 128
Perkins, D. 54
Perry, B. 70
personal characteristics 54; demand characteristics 51–52; dispositions 49–51; resources 51–52; temperament 53
person factors impacting of transitions 65–67, 76
Piaget, J. 28–29, 41, 43–44
Piaget's theory 43–44
Pinquart, M. 32
Plowman, L. 156
Pramling-Samuelsson, I. P. 83, 85
Process–Person–Context–Time (PPCT) model 8–9, 43, 92, 159, 161–162; construct of 111; context 25; framework 60; networked systems of influence 21; person 23–25; process 21–23, 22; structure 168; time 25–26
proximal processes 9–11, 47–48, 57, 93–94; adults and children 45; and attachment theory 30–36; bioecological framework 42; bioecological model 29; concept of 29, 36, 42, 44–45; concept of scaffolding 43; direction of 23; importance of 12; inverse 22; and parenting styles 36–38; Piaget's theory 43–44; potential of 128; PPCT model 22, 22; quality of 45, 125; quality of relationships 30; and Rogers's humanism 38–41; sociocultural contexts 41; and sociocultural theory 42–43

Reggio Emilia model 91
Reijman, S. 32
relationships in psychological theory, see proximal process
resource characteristics 19–21, 24
Rice, M. F. 156
Rich, A. 56
rich learning environments 109–110; context factors and 105–106; creating an invitation to learn 92; educators in 98–99; naturalness and risk-taking 95–98; outdoor 94–95; person factors and 100–104; and proximal processes

in early years 93–94; time factors and 106–108; transformation 99–100

Rogerian therapy and proximal processes 38–41

Rogers, C. R. 29, 38–40, 44, 134

Rogers's humanism: concept of person-centredness 40; proximal processes 40; techniques in therapy 39

Rogoff, B. 99, 137

Rosa, E. 22

Rosa, E. M. 7–8

Russell, W. 139

Rutter, M. 57

Ryle, A. 34–35

Ryle, Tony 29

Sandseter, E. B. H. 96

Scott, F. 156

self-control 88, 123–124, 164

self-esteem 36, 67, 116, 131

self-regulation 37, 47–49, 53, 56, 82, 87–88, 90, 116, 123–124, 126, 139

sensitivity 51, 74, 84–85, 89, 114, 125, 137

Siraj-Blatchford, I. 26

Siraj, I. 6

sociocultural theory and bioecological model: internalisation and self-regulation 48–49; mediated learning 47–48; nature and nurture 47; Vygotsky's concept of ZPD 47

Sommer, D. 83, 85

stress 57, 60–63

Sylva, K. 26

Teaching for Holistic Relational and Inclusive Early Child-hood Education (THRIECE) 35

temperament 53

*Te Whāriki* 7, 125, 141, 168

theories of personality 50

Thibodeau-Nielsen, R. 156

Thomas, A. 53

transformation *vs.* reproduction 160–165

transitions: children's experiences of 65–67; children's friendships 65; children's relationships with educators 65–65; crucial time in early childhood 60–62, 76; exosystems 74–76; macro-level

factors 67, 75–76; mesosystems 69–74; microsystems 67–69, *68*

Tudge, J. R. 98, 151

Tudge, J. R. H. 7–8, 21–22, 26, 51–52

TV and video 152

*Two Worlds of Childhood: US and USSR* 4

Tzuo, P. W. 41

Union of Socialist Soviet Republics (USSR): good behaviour of children in 4; and US relations 3–4

The United Nations Convention on the Rights of the Child (UNCRC) 81–82, 86

United States: establishment of Head Start 4–5; society 4

US/ USSR relations 3–4

Vandenbroek, M. 146

van der Veer, R. 33

Van Ijzendoorn, M. 32

van IJzendoorn, M. H. 33

Vermeer, H. J. 33

Vidal, J. 63

Vygotsky, L. S. 3, 42, 47–48, 55, 78, 167

Wall, S. 31–32

war on poverty 4

Waters, E. 31–32

Wenger, E. 50, 103

White, R. 156

Wood, E. 87–88, 138, 167

Woodhead, M. 41

Wright, S. K. 41

Wyness, M. G. 83

Yamada-Rice, D. 156

Yang, C. H. 41

young children 5, 15, 30, 39, 44, 46, 52, 55, 59–62, 64–65, 78–79, 82–85, 87, 90–95, 98–99, 103, 107, 109, 112–114, 116–117, 119–123, 125–126, 128, 131–132, 135, 138, 142–143, 150–158, 160, 164, 169; play 139; transitions, *see* transitions; in USSR 4

zone of proximal development (ZPD) 42, 47